Microeconomics and Human Behavior

Microeconomics and Human Behavior

Toward a New Synthesis of Economics and Psychology

DAVID A. ALHADEFF

UNIVERSITY OF CALIFORNIA PRESS

Berkeley / Los Angeles / London

University of California Press
Berkeley and Los Angeles, California
University of California Press, Ltd.
London, England
© 1982 by
The Regents of the University of California

1 2 3 4 5 6 7 8 9

Library of Congress Cataloging in Publication Data
Alhadeff, David A.
    Microeconomics and human behavior.

    Includes bibliographical references and index.
    1. Economics—Psychological aspects.   2. Micro-
economics—Psychological aspects.   3. Consumers.
I. Title
HB74.P8A53   338.5'01'9   81-3356
ISBN 0-520-04353-7   AACR2

To Charlotte

Contents

Preface

The economic problems of the real world are directly and inescapably involved with questions of human behavior, but the psychological variables that control behavior have no place in the strictly logical structure of traditional microeconomic analysis. In the present study, by contrast, psychology is the centerpiece around which I have tried to formulate a model of the microeconomic behavior of consumers. In this attempt to introduce psychological insights into the corpus of economic analysis, I am joining a growing list of contributors—two distinguished recent examples are Tibor Scitovsky, *The Joyless Economy* (Oxford, 1976) and Harvey Leibenstein, *Beyond Economic Man* (Harvard, 1976). Since psychology is a large and diverse field, I should explain that, as used in this study, *psychology* refers to the experimental analysis of behavior.

This study presents a detailed analysis of buy behavior, and I hope that it will be regarded as a contribution in that area; but the analysis of buy behavior is a secondary objective. My main objective in this study has been to show that microeconomic analysis can be based on an alternative foundation, one which sidesteps the traditional emphasis on utility and rationality in favor of an operational analysis that is based entirely on the well-established findings of experimental psychology. This is not a small undertaking, and it goes without saying that I have not presented a completed alternative structure; but I think that I have gone far enough to indicate the lines along which an alternative to utility and rationality can be developed and also far enough to demonstrate that it is a feasible and viable alternative. It should be emphasized, however, that the validity of this alternative approach is separable from my own degree of success in trying to implement it. I mention this because an interdisciplinary study is subject to the double jeopardy of falling into serious error or deficiency in two fields rather than one, and I would not want my own failings in either field to discredit a promising approach. This is perhaps also the point to mention that, although this study has cleared the prepublication filters of anonymous reviewers in both economics and psychology, I bear sole responsibility for any errors that may have slipped through those filters.

Since an interdisciplinary study in economics and psychology must incorporate the language and concepts of both disciplines, a potentially serious communication problem exists with respect to specialists in each of the fields. To accommodate economists who are not familiar with the literature on the experimental analysis of behavior, I have provided a handy reference in the form of a couple of carefully selected textbooks that do not presume a previous background in experimental psychology. At a number of points where I thought it would be helpful, I have referred the reader to one of those textbooks, often in lieu of more technical sources scattered widely over the psychology literature. Although this study is addressed primarily to my fellow economists, I hope that its interdisciplinary approach will also be interesting to many psychologists. For those who do not have a background in technical economics, Hirshleifer's excellent text in price theory (cited in this study) is recommended as a background reference.

This attempt to reformulate the traditional economic theory of consumer behavior along interdisciplinary lines began with my reading of B. F. Skinner's works, and my general intellectual indebtedness to his writings will be obvious to all who are familiar with them. In addition, I have benefited greatly from Neal Miller's writings on conflict. At a personal level, I have been fortunate to have the support and counsel of my wife, Charlotte Pechman Alhadeff, as I struggled to clarify my thinking in an unfamiliar area. It is also a pleasure to acknowledge the clerical support provided by the Institute of Business and Economic Research at the University of California, Berkeley. The typing of the manuscript was carried out with superb professionalism by Betty Kendall.

D. A. A.

Berkeley
October 1980

CHAPTER ONE

Introduction

In the contemporary version of neoclassical microeconomics, the theory of the household is not based on an analysis of the biological and psychological makeup of consumers but rather on the pure logic of choice. As in any purely deductive approach, this theory rests on a number of axioms and on certain primitive notions (i.e., which are to be understood intuitively rather than by means of definitions).[1] In this traditional view, it is assumed that individuals are choosing agents who have preferences among goods, which they can order according to those preferences, and who then make choices from an attainable set. This traditional approach in microeconomics is consistent with a traditional view in psychology that "a person perceives the world around him, selects features to be perceived, discriminates among them, judges them good or bad, changes them to make them better (or, if he is careless, worse)" (Skinner, 1971, p. 211). This traditional view can be contrasted with an alternative view in psychology, in which "a person is a member of a species shaped by evolutionary contingencies of survival, displaying behavioral processes which bring him under the control of the environment in which he lives, and largely under the control of a social environment which he and millions of others like

---

[1] For a discussion of primitives, see Walsh, 1970, pp. 78, 85.

1

him have constructed and maintained during the evolution of a culture. *The direction of the controlling relation is reversed: a person does not act upon the world, the world acts upon him"* (ibid., pp. 211–12; italics added).

It is the purpose of this study to suggest in rudimentary form the outlines of an alternative approach in microeconomics. Instead of deducing the behavior of consumers from the pure logic of choice, this study will attempt to explain microeconomic behavior in terms of a model that is based on experimental findings about the behavior of organisms. This alternative approach will incorporate a number of behavioral paradigms derived from the findings of experimental psychology (e.g., respondent conditioning, satiation, discrimination, extinction, etc.), but it relies particularly heavily on the operant conditioning paradigm. In the experimental analysis of behavior, the operant conditioning paradigm has proved to be an insightful approach, and this study seeks to demonstrate that it can also be an insightful way to examine economic behavior. In putting this emphasis on operant conditioning, I do not mean to suggest that operant analysis can provide a complete explanation of human behavior or even of that limited range of behavior that interests economists. Human behavior (including economic behavior) is highly complex and, as Wilson (1975) has emphasized, there is obvious danger in relying on an overly simplified hypothesis to explain complex behavior. On the other hand, it is precisely because the behavior in question is complex that it becomes necessary in proposing models of that behavior to simplify (as in any model building) by incorporating only a limited number of elements—those, it may be hoped, that will turn out to be key elements in the analysis of the behavior. The question is, therefore, a practical one: How far can we get in understanding (and predicting) microeconomic behavior on the basis of economic models that put primary emphasis on operant conditioning? I hope the reader will share my own conclusion that an operant analysis provides a remarkably "economical" basis for modeling microeconomic behavior.

This study of consumer (and investor) behavior will dispense with the traditional reliance on the twin notions of rationality and utility. According to the traditional view in economics, "Irrational behavior can't be predicted. You can't model it, just because it *is* irrational. But good models have to assume that people act rationally" (Robert E. Lucas, Jr., in Guzzardi, 1978, pp. 75–76).[2] In an operant approach, by

---

[2] In a similar vein, Tom Sargent (in Guzzardi, 1978) has observed that "the economist always has to hope that neurotic or irrational behavior won't dominate markets. If it does, there's nothing he can do about it. But remember that in competitive markets, irrational people go out of business." In this connection, cf. also Stigler's view (in Selden, 1975, p. 314) that "the reason we reject the numerous nonrational theories

contrast, the emphasis is on finding instances of lawful behavior, i.e., behavior that tends to be emitted on repeated occasions when it is under the same controlling variables. An example of such a lawful relation is the experimental finding that "intermittent reinforcement raises the probability of responding above the value generated when all responses are reinforced" (Skinner, 1969, p. 118). Although this behavior is "irrational" (in the usual sense), it is not a barrier to modeling behavior. The true barrier to modeling behavior is not irrationality but the absence of a lawful relation—and the latter is the sole concern of an operant approach.

An operant approach dispenses with the notion of utility for the same reason that it does not appeal to rationality—neither is an operational variable. An approach that relies on operational variables and avoids the use of nonoperational variables has a number of advantages in economic analysis. First, the use of nonoperational variables in theory construction is likely to be most effective in areas where the predictions based on those theories can be tested by direct experimentation. The availability of this option in the physical sciences and the serious limitations on its availability in economics probably explain why the use of nonoperational variables has been more obviously successful in the former than in economics. Second, a viable alternative approach that is expressed in terms of operational variables will overcome the present dichotomy in economics whereby our theoretical constructs can be useful in organizing our logical thinking about economic problems, but cannot always be applied directly to the empirical investigation of those problems because the theory employs nonoperational variables (Shone, 1975, p. 45; Wallis and Friedman, 1942, pp. 175–89). Third, an analysis that depends on nonoperational variables is less satisfying (and less useful) than one which does not have that dependence. Paul Samuelson (cited in Okun and Perry, 1973, p. 10) once criticized a conceptual framework that appealed to a "taste for discrimination" on the grounds that it "wasn't so much wrong as it was empty; 'tastes for discrimination' are not an explanation of behavior but merely a ghost that gets blamed for observed events."[3] Fourth, in a theory based on preferences, we are obliged to hold those preferences constant, but we can do so only by assumption—and a theory based on nonoperational variables leaves us

---

of economic behavior is that they are promiscuous and ad hoc in scope and empty of predictions." For a different view on the assumption of rationality, see Simon (1979).

[3] Cf. also the view of Phelps Brown (1972, p. 3) that the usefulness of current work in economics is "not equal to its distinction" because it is "built upon assumptions about human behavior that are plucked from the air."

stranded if preferences change. The notion that preferences can change in an arbitrary way is an embarrassment in a scientific approach, because the scientific method is only applicable if nature is lawful. This can be a nonnegligible embarrassment, because "many of the great and small social changes in history have stemmed from shifts in people's goals for living" (Hirshleifer, 1977, p. 17), i.e., their "preferences."[4] Finally, an economic analysis framed in operational terms holds the promise of a more effective formulation of economic policy problems. At this stage, the obvious caveat is that we need to learn a great deal more about the determinants of human behavior. As Skinner (1969, p. 97) has aptly noted, "Technical knowledge is needed. We cannot deal effectively with human behavior by applying a few general principles (say, of reward and punishment) any more than we can build a bridge simply by applying the principles of stress and strain." An important advantage of the approach in this study is that it makes a start at formally and explicitly incorporating the findings of an experimental analysis of behavior into the corpus of microeconomic theory. By contrast, traditional economics explicitly and deliberately ignores what psychologists have learned about human behavior, including economic behavior. As stated by Slutsky (1952, p. 27), "if we wish to place economic science upon a solid basis, we must make it completely independent of psychological assumptions and philosophical hypotheses."[5]

Another important caveat concerns the nature of the experimental evidence. Although operant analysis is firmly rooted in experimental psychology, the experiments have mostly been conducted with animals rather than with human subjects. It is accepted as a working hypothesis for this study that the principles of operant analysis which have been derived from animal experiments will also be generally

---

[4] It is also true, however, that what has sometimes been attributed to a change in tastes is, on closer examination, attributable to changes in relative prices and income. (See Koenker, 1977, p. 228; Stigler and Becker, 1977.)

[5] There is a certain ambivalence in Slutsky's view, because he also wrote (1952, p. 27) that:

> On the other hand, since the fundamental concept of modern economics is that of utility, it does not seem opportune to disregard all connections existing between the visible and measurable facts of human conduct and the psychic phenomena by which they seem to be regulated. Utility must therefore be defined in such a way as to make it logically independent of every disputable hypothesis or concept, without however excluding the possibility of further research regarding the relations between the individual's conduct and his psychic life.

However, he then proceeded to praise the Pareto formulation of utility, because "its purely formal character and its complete independence of all psychological and philosophical hypotheses recommend it as a solid basis for the construction of our own theory" (Slutsky, 1952, p. 28).

applicable in the study of human behavior (and, specifically, economic behavior). The assumption of interspecies continuity is widely used in science. In any given case, however, it is only an assumption until it has been validated by independent investigation with human subjects. Even if subsequent research with human subjects validates the assumption of interspecies continuity in the application of operant principles to economic behavior, the present evidence based on animal experiments is not likely to provide a complete basis for understanding economic behavior. As Skinner has noted: "When we examine different individuals . . . we find certain differences in behavior— in their repertoires, in the frequencies with which given responses are emitted, and in the extent to which the behavior responds to reinforcement, deprivation, and other operations. *Between species these differences may be very large*" (Skinner, 1953, pp. 156–57, italics added). As noted above, the test of the usefulness of applying principles derived from animal experiments to interpret the economic behavior of humans is how far we can get in understanding (and predicting) economic behavior.

Unfortunately for economists, the experimental work of psychologists in the area of operant conditioning was not designed (except in a few isolated experiments) to elicit information in the form that would be most useful for economic analysis. Under the circumstances, economists cannot find straightforward and direct answers in the literature on the experimental analysis of behavior about the nature and determinants of a given instance of economic behavior. The findings of the experimental analysis of behavior can, however, be highly suggestive to economists about how to analyze economic behavior in terms of an alternative to utility theory, viz., the operant conditioning approach. In order to show how the experimental findings on the operant behavior of nonhuman organisms can be used to interpret human buy behavior, I have employed the expository device of the hypothetical experiment; and I have assumed that the outcomes of these hypothetical experiments can be predicted on the basis of animal experiments in operant conditioning. At various points, however, I have gone beyond the experimental evidence and resorted to "working hypotheses." Those points are reminders that much more laboratory work will be required to further the mutually reinforcing interaction of psychology and economics.

Another complication in using the device of a hypothetical experiment concerns the comparability of the operant response in animal experiments and in the hypothetical experiments with human subjects. The instrumental action in the animal experiments is "work done" (e.g., press lever, peck disc, etc.), i.e., behavior whose topography involves effort. By contrast, the relevant instrumental variable for the buy behavior of human consumers is the "act of purchase,"[6] i.e., a behavior whose topography is essentially effortless. The relation of these topographically different behaviors is a matter that clearly requires further empirical investigation (cf. Castro and Weingarten, 1970, pp. 600–601). In this study, however, it will be assumed that none of the independent variables that have been identified as relevant on the basis of animal experiments, which use work done as the instrumental variable, would have to be dropped from our model of buy behavior if the act of purchase is used as the instrumental behavior in human experiments.

A final word concerns the writing style (or lack of it) in this study. The reader will quickly become aware of the circumlocutory expressions that have repeatedly been employed. For example, instead of using the word "choose," I will often refer to "behavior that is emitted by an individual." This is done in keeping with an approach that seeks to be as sparing as possible in making substantive assumptions—in this example, the implicit assumption that there exists a choosing agent— or in appealing to intervening variables in discussing a particular instance of economic behavior.[7] This means that, insofar as possible, the discussion will be limited to a careful description of the events involved in a particular instance of economic behavior. Unfortunately, an attempt to be economical about (especially implicit) assumptions begets a noneconomy of expression. However, in an approach that is committed to description, it seems better to avoid terms with overtones that go beyond "simple" description—and to pay the price of an awkward style.

An operant analysis can be applied across a broad spectrum of economic problems in which a central position is held by the behavior of the economic agents. The present study concentrates on one of those areas, viz., the behavior of consumers in their role as buyers of commodities. As in the traditional theory of households, the question we ask is how the income of an individual consumer is allocated among commodities. The development of this analysis will occupy most of the study. When this has been accomplished, it will become readily apparent how the operant analysis can be extended to other economic problems. To illustrate, the penultimate chapter applies the operant analysis to an examination of how an individual's wealth is allocated among financial assets.

[6]This term is defined in chapter 2 (p. 13).

[7]See Herrnstein's view (1970, p. 389) that "choice is nothing but behavior set into the context of other behavior."

The plan of the study is as follows: Chapter 2 presents the operant conditioning paradigm and shows its relation to buy behavior. Chapter 3 shows that buy behavior can be interpreted as the outcome of conflicting behaviors, and it sets forth the determinants of response strength for those conflicting behaviors. Chapter 4 presents a preliminary model of buy behavior based on the evidence from animal experiments in conflict behavior. Chapter 5 discusses reinforcer-effectiveness limits, an important constraint on the outcome of buy behavior. Chapter 6 presents the full model of buy behavior and develops the notion of a (short-run and long-run) equilibrium buy outcome. Chapter 7 shows how the equilibrium outcomes are affected by changes in prices or incomes. Chapter 8 illustrates the application of the operant analysis of buy behavior to the allocation of financial portfolios. Chapter 9 presents an overview of the model developed in this study.

CHAPTER TWO

Buy Behavior and the Operant Conditioning Paradigm

Reflex Behavior and Operant Behavior

The main focus of this study is on the analysis of a particular form of human behavior—buy behavior. When we describe any kind of behavior, we describe what an organism does. In order to apply the experimental methods of science to the analysis of behavior, psychologists have broken down the stream of behavior into units called behavior responses and the changes in an organism's environment into arbitrary units called environmental stimuli. The experimental analysis of behavior involves the attempt to discover lawful relations between environmental stimuli and behavioral responses.

Reflex behavior is a prime example of a lawful relation between environmental events and associated behavioral responses. Reflex behavior is part of the familiar "stimulus-response" paradigm—the pupillary contraction when a bright light shines on the eye, the jerking of the knee when the patellar tendon is tapped, the discharge of saliva when food is placed in the mouth, etc. The stimulus provided by the environment is called the "eliciting stimulus," and the organism's response to that stimulus is called a "respondent." These elicited responses (respondents) are part of the innate mechanism that an organism inherits as part of its structure. Such reflex mechanisms are profoundly important from an evolutionary point of view, because they enable an organism to respond effectively from its earliest contacts with the environment.

The relations between the eliciting stimulus (environmental event) and the respondent (behavioral response of the organism) have been carefully studied, and the findings have been summarized in laws of the reflex. For example, a respondent may not occur unless the eliciting stimulus attains a threshold intensity. Although the occurrence of the respondent is uncertain below the threshold, it occurs regularly above the threshold. Moreover, the magnitude of the respondent increases as the intensity of the eliciting stimulus increases. If the eliciting stimulus is repeated too often, however, the magnitude of the respondent will gradually decline at least temporarily.

In the language of an earlier period, reflex behavior was characterized as "involuntary" (or automatic), and it was contrasted with "voluntary" (or purposive) behavior, in which individuals contemplated alternatives, made choices, satisfied needs and desires, and maximized utilities (or at least behaved as if they did). Although terms like voluntary or involuntary are not required for an operant analysis, it is conventional to make a distinction between reflex behavior and operant behavior.[1] The distinction is especially relevant for this study, because the operant conditioning paradigm rather than the stimulus-response (reflex) analysis of classical psychology is the major psychological fulcrum of this study.

In the operant behavior paradigm, the unit of behavior is called an operant (or instrumental) response, or, more simply, an operant; and the relevant environmental stimulus is called a reinforcing stimulus, or, more simply, a reinforcer. In the operant strengthening paradigm, we begin with an organism that exhibits the operant behavior (R) at some base (operant) level. Whenever that behavior occurs, it is reinforced with a suitable reinforcer. As a result of this procedure, the operant response is strengthened, as evidenced by an increase in the rate of R to a new stable value. By contrast with reflex behavior, specific instances of operant behavior are not part of the organism's inherited structure; but the organism does inherit a capacity to be reinforced by operant behavior.[2] Operant behavior also differs from

---

[1] According to Schoenfeld (1966, p. 152), however, "The discovery of ever more variegated behavioral effects, stemming from ever more comprehensive manipulation of situational parameters, will make the distinction between operant and respondent conditioning increasingly unprofitable and confusing to maintain." See also Schoenfeld and Cole (1972b, p. 151).

[2] As explained by Skinner (1953, pp. 156–57):

At any given time in its life, an individual displays certain behavior in certain states of probability. This is the background against which we study selected operants and

reflex behavior because operant behavior is not elicited by an environmental stimulus that has preceded it. In the operant behavior paradigm, an organism emits behavior. As noted, this behavior is part of its innate structure, but the frequency with which a particular behavior will occur depends on the consequences of that behavior. Thus the sequence of events involved in operant behavior is exactly reversed from that in reflexive behavior. In the latter, the eliciting stimulus precedes the behavioral response (respondent), and this pattern will be maintained regardless of the environmental consequences of the response. By contrast, the response under operant behavior precedes (rather than follows) the occurrence of the environmental stimulus, and the frequency with which that response is emitted is functionally related to the nature of the environmental stimulus that follows it.[3] Operant (or instrumental) behavior is thus behavior that operates upon the environment and is instrumental in obtaining consequences.[4]

It follows from what has been said above that an experimental approach to behavior emphasizes the environmental control of behavior. In reflexive behavior, an environmental stimulus elicits a particular response. In operant behavior, the environment also controls the behavior, but in a quite different way. As already noted, certain responses from a repertoire of emitted responses will occur more frequently if the environmental consequences of those responses are reinforcing. Inevitably, however, the reinforcement will occur in the presence of whatever environmental stimuli happen to exist at the time of reinforcement. As a result of this association, the particular environmental configuration becomes a positive discriminative stimulus (S^D), and the reinforced behavior is more likely to be emitted on future occasions in its presence.[5] Indeed, in the first instance, the response will tend to be emitted only for repetitions of the exact configuration of the environment in which the organism's behavior was reinforced in the past. However, psychologists have discovered

---

explore the effects of independent variables. These variables are seldom relevant in accounting for the *existence* of the behavior chosen for study; they merely affect its *probability*. Its existence is taken for granted.

[3] "In the Pavlovian experiment . . . a reinforcer is paired with a *stimulus*; whereas in operant behavior it is contingent upon a *response*" (Skinner, 1953, p. 65).

[4] For a further definition of operant and operant behavior, see Catania, 1968, pp. 340–41.

[5] In an analysis that strives to economize on substantive assumptions or intervening variables, we do not assume that S^D is a prod to behavior, but content ourselves with the empirically demonstrable fact that operant behavior is more likely in the presence of S^D. In this connection, cf. Skinner's observation (1969, p. 175) that "Operant reinforcement not only strengthens a given response; it brings the response under the control of a

that the response will also tend to be emitted when the environmental stimuli are similar to previous configurations. This behavioral phenomenon, called "stimulus generalization," spreads environmental control over a wider range of stimuli than the particular set that may have existed in previous instances of operant strengthening.

Environmental control of operant behavior becomes more selective (rather than generalized) when the operant behavior of the organism is more likely to occur in the presence of a more restricted set of environmental stimuli, and perhaps not at all in their absence. For example, in experiments with laboratory animals, the experimenter may arrange for a clicking sound to occur (perhaps associated with the opening of the food-dispensing mechanism) and/or for a light to come on immediately before or during the presentation of the reinforcement. If the experimenter reinforces a given kind of emitted behavior only in the presence of the click-light but never reinforces that same behavior in the absence of the click-light, the reinforced behavior will eventually come under the control of (i.e., it is more likely to occur in the presence of) the click-light and may not be emitted at all in the absence of the click-light. This illustrates the behavioral phenomenon called "discrimination." Discrimination training, whether provided in a laboratory situation or by nature, brings behavior under closer environmental control. In our example, the click-light becomes a positive discriminative stimulus, and the operant behavior is more likely to occur thereafter in the presence of the S^D.

The mechanism of operant conditioning is a powerful aid to the survival of an organism that is structured to respond to its environment in this way.[6] It is apparent, however, that this mechanism could also work against the evolutionary survival of such an organism if operant behavior which was reinforced in one environmental state continued to be emitted at the same rate (same strength) when the environment changed and the behavior was no longer reinforced. This is the significance of the behavioral phenomenon called operant extinction. In the operant extinction paradigm, the behavioral result when a *previously reinforced response* ceases to be reinforced—by definition, a change in the environment—is to undo the effects of operant strengthening, i.e., a decline occurs in the frequency (or rate) of operant behavior.

---

stimulus. But the stimulus does not elicit the response; it merely sets the occasions upon which the response is more likely to occur."

[6] Skinner (1979, p. 319) has noted that "like other biological processes, operant conditioning presumably evolved because it had survival value. When the environment was not stable enough for the natural selection of innate behavior in a species, a rather similar 'selection by consequences' was needed to build an effective repertoire in the individual."

Buy Behavior as Operant Behavior

Contingency of reinforcement. One major area of economics is concerned with the process of exchange between buyers and sellers. In most of this study, we will concentrate on one part of that process, viz., the behavior emitted by a buyer in the role of consumer. We call this "consumer buy behavior." This section relates consumer buy behavior to operant conditioning by showing that the purchase strengthening paradigm is just a particular instance of the operant strengthening paradigm. We begin with a discussion of a contingency of reinforcement, a critical component of the operant conditioning paradigm. A contingency of reinforcement is the interrelation among the following: the occasion upon which a response occurs, the response itself, and the reinforcing consequences (see Skinner, 1969, p. 7). In other words, a contingency of reinforcement specifies how the environment would be changed (i.e., the environmental stimulus consequences) after a given behavioral response has occurred in the presence of a discriminative stimulus. The world of nature contains countless contingencies of reinforcement, and these environmental contingencies describe how the environment controls the behavior of organisms via the workings of operant conditioning. The cultural world of human societies also contains numerous contingencies of reinforcement that also shape the behavior of the inhabitants of those societies. From an economic viewpoint, one of the most important contingencies describes the behavioral-environmental interrelation that involves buy behavior. In its most general form, the contingency states that if a consumer emits an appropriate response, he will find himself in possession of a given (amount of an) economic good.

In some contingencies that exist in nature, a specified behavioral response is invariably followed by a particular environmental stimulus (reinforcement); in other cases, the contingencies do not exhibit this kind of fixed nexus between behavior and environmental consequence. The world of cultural contingencies also exhibits a spread between certain and uncertain outcomes. In operant buy behavior, however, the reinforcement typically does occur.[7] Psychologists use the term continuous reinforcement (abbreviated crf) to denote a schedule in which reinforcement occurs every time *after a given behavioral response has been emitted;*[8] and they have shown that operant responses attain a steady rate under crf scheduling.

[7] The system is not perfect, however—e.g., purchase orders that have been paid for, but have not been delivered or are defective; or the coin machine that takes the coin, but fails to deliver the product, etc.

[8] Despite its name, the term does not mean, for example, that laboratory animals are

Act of purchase. Let us now look more closely at the operant response that we call buy behavior. In discussing such a strongly established cultural pattern, it is helpful to begin by considering a primitive form of buy behavior, e.g., the behavior of a child who faces a coin-operated candy machine. Under appropriate (perhaps parental) guidance, the child learns that the behavior of depositing a circular metal object into a slot and pressing a button is followed by the appearance of a candy bar in the open dispenser compartment of the machine, where it can be readily picked up and consumed. From the perspective of the child (inexperienced buyer), the operant behavior that precedes the reinforcement is totally arbitrary. It just happens that the environment is structured in such a manner that this particular arbitrary bit of behavior is followed by this particular reinforcing consequence. In this respect, the situation of the child is analogous to that of the pigeon in a Skinner box. In the latter case, an equally arbitrary bit of behavior (e.g., pecking at a disc) is also followed by a reinforcing consequence (viz., a grain of food in a food dispenser). The behavioral result is identical in both instances—a particular arbitrary bit of behavior will thereafter be emitted with greater frequency in the presence of the discriminative stimulus. In the case of the child, the candy-dispensing machine will have become a positive discriminative stimulus (S^D). Whenever the child (under appropriate condition of deprivation) is in the presence of the S^D, the behavior of inserting circular metal objects into a slot and pressing a button is likely to be emitted.

Consider now the child who spots the machine on another occasion and approaches it with a pocketful of assorted coins. Based on his previous history of conditioning with candy machines, he is likely to deposit one of the coins from his pocket; but, since a child has a limited history of conditioning in such matters, he may not deposit the "right" coin. Even without parental guidance, the child could probably eventually discover that reinforcing consequences do not follow the insertion of all circular objects, but only of circular objects with particular stimulus characteristics, defined with respect to size, markings, and (perhaps) color. Thus the child's operant behavior comes under the control of a more precise (and discriminating) element in his environment—and, of course, one which is even more stunningly arbitrary than the operant class that the child discovered in its earlier experience with candy machines. Again, the child's situation is analogous to that of the pigeon in a laboratory experiment in which disc

---

(say) fed continuously. A situation in which food is freely available to an animal and is not made contingent upon an operant response is called "ad lib" feeding.

pecking is not reinforced unless the discs are (say) green-colored and of a particular size. No matter how arbitrary the contingencies of reinforcement may happen to be, the pigeon's behavior (and, of course, the child's as well) becomes conditioned by those contingencies.

In the example of a child who faces a candy-dispensing machine, the topographical dimensions of the operant (buy) behavior are narrowly, even uniquely, defined.[9] This is not a necessary feature of the class of behaviors that we call buy behavior. Indeed, as the child becomes older and gains more experience with buy behavior, he will discover that the operant response (i.e., the behavior that is then followed by the consequence of acquiring the product) is any behavior of entering into an explicit or implicit contract to acquire a particular object under particular terms. In some transactions, the operant response takes the form of signing a formal contract; in others, it may take the form of a simple verbal response; in still others, a gesture may suffice. Accordingly, for the theoretical purposes of this study, the buyer's behavior in entering into a purchase contract will be treated as the operant response—and will be designated as an "act of purchase"; and the acquiring of the product and the loss of dollars surrendered in payment will be treated as the two consequences of having entered into the contract. It is pertinent to note in this connection that many acts of purchase occur without an immediate loss of dollars surrendered in payment—e.g., the delayed payment in connection with a purchase by credit card. In a similar way, many acts of purchase occur without an immediate acquisition of the product—e.g., in the case of a delayed delivery. Thus, both in principle and often in fact, there is a clear distinction between the purchase act qua act and either of its consequences.

The Nature and Kinds of Reinforcers

Although the economist's notion of a "good" and the psychologist's notion of a "reinforcer" have much in common, the theoretical foundations of the two concepts are quite different. In the familiar language of a standard economics textbook: "Persons are born with certain basic desires. . . . Material objects and services which are capable of satisfying human wants are called *goods*; the property or capacity of

[9] The topographical dimensions include the position, angle, location, and orientation of the behavior. These are called topographical dimensions because "a listing of their values at any given time will specify the precise form of the behavior . . . [i.e.,] the kind of information provided by a photograph of the organism caught in action" (Millenson and Leslie, 1979, p. 75).

goods which enables them to satisfy wants is known as *utility*" (Due and Clower, 1966, pp. 4–5).[10] In an operant approach, the resort to intervening variables—tastes, utility, needs, wants, etc.—is avoided in favor of operational variables. The identification of reinforcers begins with the statement that all reinforcers are stimuli. Operant behavior psychologists find it useful to distinguish between positive and negative reinforcers. A positive reinforcer is any stimulus that strengthens the behavior upon which the presentation of that stimulus is made contingent; a negative reinforcer is any stimulus that strengthens the behavior upon which the withdrawal (either partial or complete) of that stimulus is made contingent (see Skinner, 1953, p. 185). In laboratory experiments, food is a commonly used positive reinforcer; electric shock is a commonly used negative reinforcer. In keeping with the spirit of the experimental approach, a stimulus is identified as either a positive or negative reinforcer by means of appropriate experiments and not by appeal to intervening variables. If experimentation shows that a given stimulus strengthens a formerly unconditioned response (behavior) when the presentation of that stimulus is made contingent upon the response, that stimulus stands revealed as a positive reinforcer. Similarly, if a given stimulus strengthens a formerly unconditioned response when the partial or complete termination of the stimulus is made contingent upon the response, that stimulus is revealed as a negative reinforcer. Each kind of reinforcer is examined below.

Positive reinforcers. In the contingency of reinforcement for economic exchange, a physical object or service (economic good) is made contingent upon the emission of the buy response by the consumer. Since the buy response can be powerfully conditioned under this contingency of reinforcement, economic goods qualify as reinforcers as that term is used in the operant conditioning paradigm. Indeed, since purchase conditioning is just a specific instance of operant conditioning, it will be useful to classify economic goods and services according to the ways in which they reinforce behavior.

Consumer goods and services that are positively reinforcing can be divided into two categories according to the source of their capacity to strengthen consumers' behavior—positive primary reinforcers and positive secondary reinforcers.[11] A positive primary reinforcer is an

[10] In the early history of economic analysis, the concept of utility carried strong hedonistic overtones which have since been dropped. In modern economics, utility is a name for the rank ordering of preferences.

[11] The case of negative primary reinforcers is discussed later in connection with escape/avoidance goods.

unconditioned reinforcer, i.e., the consumer does not require the experience of prior conditioning before he can be reinforced by a primary reinforcer. A capacity to be reinforced by a primary reinforcer is part of the consumer's inherited biological structure. Some primary reinforcers (e.g., food and water) are directly essential to maintain the individual's life; and others, which are not essential to maintain the individual's life, have evolutionary survival value—the obvious example is sex. Many primary reinforcers exist in nature independently of human intervention; other primary reinforcers are contrived by man as cultural artifacts. Some contrived reinforcers are closely related to natural reinforcers, but many others are not.

A positive conditioned reinforcer (also called a secondary reinforcer) has no inherent capacity to reinforce the behavior upon which it is (made) contingent, but it can acquire this capacity by (an appropriate kind of) association with other reinforcers. In operant conditioning, the reinforcement comes after the behavior; but, any stimulus that is paired with the reinforcement acquires reinforcing power by virtue of Pavlovian pairing with the primary reinforcer (or, for that matter, with other conditioned reinforcers).[12] The stimuli that become acquired or conditioned reinforcers for a particular consumer are determined by that individual's past history of conditioning. Primary reinforcers have a broad appeal (at least potentially) because they need only to be discovered to become effective. By contrast, the dependence of secondary reinforcers on each individual's prior history of conditioning means that some objects (or services) are powerful reinforcers for some consumers but not for other consumers. This is conventionally passed over on the grounds that "there is no accounting for people's tastes." In an experimental analysis of behavior, these differences would be related to the prior history of conditioning of the individuals. In a given culture, the prior histories of conditioning of many individuals are likely to have a lot in common. Certain "tastes" (in food, clothing, furnishings, etc.) will accordingly be shared by members of one culture, but might be quite "foreign" to members of other cultures. However, even within a given culture, there is bound to be much that is unique in each individual's prior history of conditioning. Hence, the list of stimuli (services and objects) that are conditioned reinforcers, as well as their potency as reinforcers, is likely to

---

[12] This is a common and important element in much consumer buying. In the buying syndrome known as "keeping up with the Joneses," certain consumer goods are reinforcing even in the absence of any direct association with a primary reinforcer by virtue of an association with social approval, a powerful acquired positive reinforcer. Under other circumstances (e.g., a different social environment and a different prior history of conditioning), those same goods can become aversive by association with social disapproval, a powerful acquired negative reinforcer.

be different for different individuals. It should be noted that all stimuli that have become operant reinforcers, whether primary or secondary, owe their status as reinforcers to a particular prior history of conditioning. Obviously if a particular stimulus has never been experienced by an individual, it cannot become incorporated into the operant conditioning paradigm. But primary and secondary reinforcers differ here, too. As noted, the former have (potentially) a universal appeal; the latter are highly culture dependent.

Any otherwise neutral stimulus can acquire the capacity to reinforce behavior as a by-product of the same process that can make it into a discriminative stimulus. Indeed, Notterman (1951) has shown by laboratory experiments that the reinforcing value of the discriminative stimulus will be low where discrimination training is also low. Like primary reinforcers, the conditioned stimuli that become secondary reinforcers may already exist in nature or they may be contrived by man within the context of a particular culture. The latter is especially relevant for economics because of the very large number of consumer goods that have no independent (or inherent) capacity to reinforce (buy) behavior and owe their status as positive reinforcers to their association with one or more primary reinforcers. In the simplest cases, the association with a primary reinforcer is direct and close; in more complex cases, the association can exist as part of a long chain of operant responses.[13] Regardless of whether the association is direct or via a chain of operant behavior, once a stimulus has acquired the power to reinforce behavior, "the effects of making it contingent on a response appear indistinguishable from the effects of making a primary reinforcer contingent on the response" (Millenson and Leslie, 1979, p. 152). This, too, has been demonstrated in laboratory experiments (Zimmerman, 1957 and 1959; Kelleher, 1961).

Unlike the primary reinforcer, the potency of the secondary reinforcer—its ability to maintain a rate of responding (Reynolds, 1975, p. 63)—can become weakened, and the secondary reinforcer will return to its original status as a neutral stimulus, unless it is renewed by association with the primary reinforcer. Extinction is avoided for secondary goods that are functionally related to primary goods, because their reinforcing capacity is maintained intact by repeated association with the primary reinforcer. This holds especially for generalized reinforcers, i.e., secondary reinforcers that have been conditioned by association with more than one primary reinforcer. Although repeated association is less likely and may not occur at all for

---

[13] A chain of operant behavior is succinctly described as "a sequence of operant responses and discriminative stimuli such that each R produces the S^D for the next R" (Millenson and Leslie, 1979, p. 160).

secondary goods that are nonfunctionally related to primary goods, their potency may remain intact if they are reinforced on an intermittent schedule.[14]

Laboratory experiments have shown not only that the potency of a secondary reinforcer can be maintained without continuous reinforcement (crf) but also that intermittent reinforcement is a more powerful schedule for preserving the potency of acquired reinforcers than continuous reinforcement. The potency of generalized reinforcers can be particularly long lasting, if they combine continuous reinforcement with one (or more) primary reinforcer with intermittent reinforcement with some other primary reinforcer(s). In addition, as noted later (in the section on deprivation), the potency of a generalized reinforcer will be maintained during periods of temporary satiation with one or more primary reinforcers if deprivation exists for any one of the primary reinforcers on which it is based. Money, a notable economic example of a generalized positive secondary reinforcer with remarkably long-lasting potency, is a good example of this last point. As Skinner (1953, p. 79) has noted, "behavior reinforced with money is relatively independent of the momentary deprivation of the organism, and the general usefulness of money as a reinforcer depends in part upon this fact."

Escape from negative reinforcers. As mentioned earlier, a negative reinforcer is an aversive stimulus that can strengthen behavior upon which its (partial or complete) withdrawal is made contingent. The aversive stimulus can be a primary negative reinforcer (i.e., innate) or it can be a conditioned aversive stimulus (i.e., a case of Pavlovian pairing). These stimuli can become the basis for operant behavior when the withdrawal or abatement of those aversive stimuli are made contingent upon a specified response. When the behavior is followed by the withdrawal of the aversive stimulus, it is called escape behavior. The distinction between escape behavior and avoidance has been explained by Cofer and Appley (1964, p. 578) as follows:

---

[14] Intermittent schedules of reinforcement can take a number of forms. Some which have been examined in the laboratory are interval schedules; others are ratio schedules. Under interval schedules, the reinforcement occurs only for an emission of operant behavior that occurs after some minimum time interval. This minimum time interval, in turn, may be fixed, variable, or randomly determined. Under ratio schedules, the reinforcement is related to the number of unreinforced responses that have occurred. Again the ratio schedules may be based on fixed or variable ratios. In other cases, differential reinforcement is provided according to the rate at which the operant behavior is emitted. Combinations that involve these and other schedules have also been examined. A pioneer study on reinforcement schedules is Ferster and Skinner (1957).

In escape training, the organism receives the aversive stimulus (e.g., shock) but may escape from it by making some response. . . . Escape training develops a response which removes shock but does not permit its avoidance. Avoidance training permits the organism to learn a response which entirely obviates the receipt of shock. Under suitable time arrangements of the neutral stimulus and the shock, the avoidance can emerge out of escape. Both of these procedures may be distinguished from classical conditioning employing aversive stimulation. In the latter, the shock is inevitable, that is, nothing the organism does can either avoid or escape the full duration of the aversive stimulus.

In sum, escape behavior is followed by withdrawal of an aversive stimulus. When the aversive stimulus is conditioned as such by its association with a primary (or another conditioned) aversive stimulus, escape from the conditioned aversive stimulus makes it possible as a by-product to avoid the primary (or other conditioned) negative reinforcer. Although it is important for theoretical reasons in psychology to distinguish between escape and avoidance,[15] the two terms can often be used interchangeably for the purposes of this study.

For economics, it is relevant that one can often escape (or avoid) aversive stimuli by emitting appropriate acts of buy behavior. In a laboratory experiment with animals, the contingency of reinforcement may provide for an electric shock to be terminated after the animal has pressed a lever. In human society, the contingency may provide for the aversive stimulus of (say) a headache to be terminated after the sufferer takes an aspirin, or for the aversive stimulus of becoming drenched in a rainstorm to be terminated after an umbrella has been opened and/or a raincoat has been worn. It should be mentioned in this connection that escape from an aversive stimulus is a primary positive reinforcer;[16] and numerous objects (e.g., aspirin, umbrella, raincoat) become conditioned as positive reinforcers by their association with this particular positive reinforcer. Such goods are additional examples of secondary reinforcers. However, it will be useful to distinguish between secondary reinforcers that are based (directly or in a chain of behaviors) on escape (termination or abatement) from (a primary or conditioned) aversive stimulus and those that are based on all other positive reinforcers. We will call the latter "secondary goods"; and the former, "escape goods" (or "avoidance

---

[15] The distinction is important in operant conditioning theory for two reasons. First, it makes possible an explanation of operant behavior in terms of a past history of conditioning even though the aversive condition that has been avoided has not occurred. Second, the individual's behavior can be explained without the use of non-operational variables (e.g., "purpose").

[16] This is more fully examined in chapter 3.

goods"). This terminological distinction can also serve as a reminder that escape/avoidance goods and other positive secondary reinforcers are controlled by different reinforcer-effectiveness operations— aversive stimuli in the former case and (say) deprivation in the latter.[17]

The category of escape goods, whether based on primary aversive stimuli or on conditioned aversive stimuli, is important in economics. Many economic goods that are deemed to be necessary for the "good life" owe their capacity to reinforce buy behavior to their role in terminating, abating, or avoiding aversive stimuli. The list of such goods is seemingly endless. Thus there is a basis for a consumer demand for insulation (to escape or avoid loud noises, extreme heat, extreme cold); for smoke-alarm devices, lifeboats, and life jackets (to avoid loss of life and property); for refrigerators (to avoid food spoilage); for air conditioners (to escape or avoid extreme temperatures and humidity); for drugs (to abate or terminate pain), etc. The concept of an escape good has a parallel concept in escape service, i.e., a service that terminates, abates, or avoids an aversive stimulus—e.g., the services of someone who repairs a leaky roof.

Summary: An operant classification of economic goods. In an operant analysis of buy behavior, an economic good or service—hereafter often called a commodity—fills the role of the reinforcer for the operant response of buy behavior. For purposes of an operant classification of economic commodities, the universe of commodity reinforcers can be grouped according to the nature and kind of reinforcement that they represent. This is the basis for the following table, which provides a (somewhat expanded) summary of the kinds of commodity reinforcers that have been discussed in this chapter.

---

[17] The rationale for the category of escape goods is discussed in more detail in chapter 3.

An Operant Classification of Commodities

I. PRIMARY COMMODITIES: positive primary reinforcers (i.e., unconditioned or innate reinforcers)

II. SECONDARY COMMODITIES: positive conditioned reinforcers (i.e., based directly or indirectly on positive primary reinforcers)

A. Specialized: based on only one positive reinforcer

1. Functional: based on a functional pairing of stimuli, i.e., a secondary commodity that has a functional association to the reinforcer on which it is based (often through a chain of behaviors)

a. direct: based on a primary reinforcer (at end of chain)

b. indirect: based on a secondary reinforcer (at end of chain)

2. Nonfunctional: based on a nonfunctional pairing of stimuli, i.e., adventitious or spurious

B. Generalized: based on more than one positive reinforcer

1. Functional: based on a functional pairing of stimuli

a. direct: based on a primary reinforcer

b. indirect: based on a secondary reinforcer

2. Nonfunctional: based on a nonfunctional pairing of stimuli

III. ESCAPE/AVOIDANCE COMMODITIES: a special form of positive conditioned reinforcer that is based (directly or indirectly) on escape or avoidance of a negative reinforcer

A. Specialized: based on escape from only one negative reinforcer

1. Functional: based on a functional pairing of stimuli (i.e., functionally related to the escape)

a. direct: based on escape (or avoidance) from a negative primary reinforcer

b. indirect: based on escape (or avoidance) from a negative conditioned reinforcer

2. Nonfunctional: based on a nonfunctional pairing of stimuli

B. Generalized: based on escape from more than one negative reinforcer

1. Functional: based on a functional pairing of stimuli

a. direct: based on escape (or avoidance) from a negative primary reinforcer

b. indirect: based on escape (or avoidance) from a negative conditioned reinforcer

2. Nonfunctional: based on a nonfunctional pairing of stimuli

---

CHAPTER THREE

Buy Behavior: A Conflict Between Approach and Escape

Buy Behavior as the Outcome Between Two Incompatible Behaviors

The operant conditioning paradigm, the basic model on which this entire study is based, cannot be applied directly to explain buy behavior, because buy behavior is itself the resultant of conflicting behaviors. These conflicting behaviors will be designated *approach* and *escape* (including avoidance); and each is controlled by a different reinforcer. In the preceding chapter, we examined only the positively reinforcing consequences of buy behavior, viz., the acquisition of the positive reinforcers that we have called primary commodities, secondary commodities, and escape/avoidance commodities. These positively reinforcing consequences strengthen approach and, ceteris paribus, make the emission of the operant buy response more likely. As shown below, however, the operant response (buy behavior) is also punished behavior, i.e., it has its own aversive consequences. These aversive consequences strengthen escape behavior[1] and, ceteris paribus, make the emission of the operant buy response less likely. The outcome of this

---

[1] As noted earlier, the term "escape behavior" will (for convenience) include "avoidance behavior"—although technically the behavior is escape, and avoidance is a consequence of escape behavior.

conflict of behaviors[2]—in economic terms, "buy" or "not buy"[3]—is determined by the relative strengths of approach behavior and escape behavior. In this chapter, we examine the determinants of approach behavior and the determinants of escape behavior, i.e., the variables of which each behavior is a function. In the next chapter, we examine how the conflict of behaviors is resolved.

Determinants of Approach Behavior

As noted earlier, a major result of the operant strengthening paradigm is that the rate of emission of the operant response rises from its preconditioning level to a higher and stable value. In this section, we examine the determinants of approach behavior in terms of the purchase conditioning paradigm. The determinants of approach behavior will be examined for primary commodities, secondary commodities, and escape/avoidance commodities.

1. For Primary Commodities

Reinforcement-establishing operations and approach behavior. As noted earlier, each positive primary reinforcer is identified by its innate capacity to reinforce behavior upon which its presentation is made contingent. This innate capacity to reinforce does not become effective, however, until some reinforcement-establishing operation has occurred.[4] In experiments with laboratory animals, a large number of reinforcer-establishing (and reducing) operations have been employed. For example, some of the operations that make water a reinforcer are deprivation of all liquids, force excretion, inject atropine, feed salt, tie off salivary ducts, stimulate brain in certain regions (see Millenson, 1967, p. 367). In the case of many (and perhaps most) primary reinforcers, one of the most powerful and pervasive reinforcer-establishing operations consists of withholding the rein-

---

[2] Skinner (1953, p. 221) notes that "a conflict will arise if the behavior has its own aversive consequences."

[3] As shown below (p. 38), "not buy" is not an appropriate characterization of behavior in terms of the operant conditioning paradigm. It is used in this context as a loose description of behaviors that are incompatible with buy behavior.

[4] I have avoided the term "drive" in this discussion because the term has a meaning in operant analysis that is quite different from ordinary usage. In a nontechnical sense, a drive is often synonymous with a goad, i.e., something that motivates behavior. In an operant analysis, a drive is a relation between a reinforcer-establishing operation and the reinforcing value of a class of stimuli. Since a drive is a *relation*, it is perforce an abstraction and, as such, cannot be a "goad" to behavior; it cannot be "satisfied," or "located" somewhere, etc. (see Millenson, 1967, p. 383).

forcing stimulus for some period of time, i.e., deprivation.[5] This is, of course, also an important reinforcement-establishing operation for human consumers—but "deprivation" does not have quite the same meaning in the experimental analysis of behavior and in economics. In the former, the term does not carry any overtones about a consumer's "needs," whether physiological or "mental." In the operant conditioning paradigm, deprivation requires an effect upon behavior in order to be confirmed as such. It follows that the only way to determine whether a change in deprivation has occurred when a primary positive reinforcer has been withheld is to note the effect upon the organism's operant behavior. As Skinner (1953, p. 148) has noted, "We might deprive an organism of an essential food substance and still observe no change in its behavior, even though it might become ill or even die. . . . We do not list what we have done as an instance of deprivation." On the basis of this kind of experimental approach, a number of deprivations (and, therefore, also of primary reinforcers) have been discovered. Millenson (1967, p. 368) lists the primary reinforcers that are relevant for human subjects as follows: activity, air, food, love and affection, maternal activities, novelty,[6] sex, sleep, warmth, and water.[7] These are, therefore, also the primary reinforcers that are involved in the analysis of any given instance of economic behavior, such as buy behavior.

What, then, are the effects of (say) raising the level of deprivation of a primary positive reinforcer? The answer is that the reinforcing value[8] of a primary good whose presentation is made contingent on a particular operant behavior increases as the level of deprivation increases. There are, however, limits on the reinforcing value of a primary reinforcer. In experiments with rats in which food deprivation was maintained until the death of the animals, Heron and Skinner (1937) found that the reinforcing value of food increased with de-

---

[5] "The net result of reinforcement is not simply to strengthen behavior but to strengthen it *in a given state of deprivation*. Reinforcement thus brings behavior under the control of an appropriate deprivation. After we have conditioned a pigeon to stretch its neck by reinforcing with food, the variable which controls neck-stretching is food deprivation. The response of stretching the neck has merely joined that group of responses which vary with this operation. We can describe the effect of reinforcement in no simpler way" (Skinner, 1953, p. 149).

[6] This reinforcer, sometimes also described as exploratory activity or curiosity, plays a prominent role in Scitovsky's *The Joyless Economy* (1976).

[7] Manipulation of objects, such as involved in arts, crafts, or sports, is also a primary reinforcer, and it appears to be effective apart from any particular deprivation (Skinner, 1953, p. 77; 1969, pp. 67–68). In the laboratory, the operant behavior of monkeys, for example, has been conditioned by reinforcing them with the opportunity to solve puzzles.

[8] In laboratory experiments with animals, the reinforcement value of a particular set of stimuli denotes the covariance of a set of behaviors in relation to a particular

privation up to a maximum and then declined rapidly. However, in analyzing most consumer behavior, especially in countries like the United States, these limits can probably be ignored. A change in the level of deprivation can affect the reinforcing value not only of the particular reinforcer that has been withheld, but also the reinforcing value of related reinforcers.[9] The reason, as noted by Skinner (1953, p. 218) is that "by increasing the deprivation, we increase the range of effective stimuli or, to put it another way, reduce the importance of differences in stimuli." In other words, deprivation weakens the operant behavior based on discrimination training and instead strengthens generalization. As the primary reinforcer is presented to a deprived organism, the organism will eventually reach a point of satiation with respect to that reinforcer,[10] and its reinforcing value will accordingly decline. Thus the reinforcing value of the reinforcer—and, therefore, also the response strength of the operant behavior upon which the reinforcer is contingent—will vary from great strength to great weakness (including perhaps zero) as the individual moves between extreme deprivation and extreme satiation.[11]

Other variables that affect approach behavior. In addition to the reinforcer-effectiveness operation, the factors that comprise the contingency of reinforcement (i.e., the other conditioning parameters) can also have an important effect on response strength. On the basis of experiments with animals, one of the most important conditioning parameters is the schedule of reinforcement. An appropriate schedule can produce impressive response strength even with a minor reinforcer. This is particularly striking in gambling behavior, but "the same schedule explains the dedication of the hunter, fisherman, or collector, where what is caught or collected is not of any great significance" (Skinner, 1971, p. 179). In the chain of behaviors leading to, say, the catching of fish, a number of responses are emitted, and each outcome becomes both a reinforcer for the operant that preceded it and a positive discriminative stimulus for the next operant in the chain. The effects of schedules can become complex, because

---

reinforcement-establishing operation. Deprivation is one example of such an operation. Examples of behavior included in the "set of behaviors" are rate of responding under variable-interval reinforcement schedule, resistance to extinction, resistance to satiation, efficiency of acquisition, number of obstructions surmounted, amount of work done, and tolerance for poorer-quality (adulterated) reinforcer (see Millenson and Leslie, 1979, pp. 394–403).

[9] The implications of this relation are examined further in chapter 6.

[10] The satiation paradigm is discussed in chapter 5.

[11] When, as in this section, the conditioning parameters (contingencies of reinforcement) are held constant and the operant behavior is related to the reinforcer-

different schedules of reinforcement may be applicable to the different behaviors in the chain. For example, the behavior of using fishing gear is reinforced (with fish caught) on an intermittent schedule; but buy behavior is reinforced (by the acquisition of fishing gear) on a crf schedule. For our purposes, it is pertinent that the strength of the approach behavior which is applicable to buy behavior is affected not only by the schedule which reinforces that particular member of the chain, but also by the schedules which are in effect for the operant responses at later points along the chain that culminates in the reinforcement of fish caught.

A second factor that could affect approach behavior response strength is a delay between the response and the reinforcement. In laboratory studies with animals, the introduction of an interval of time between response and reinforcer in operant conditioning reduces the effectiveness of the reinforcement. Specifically, when response strength is measured by rate of reponse, experiments have shown that "the rate varies with the immediacy of the reinforcement; a slight delay between response and the receipt of the reinforcer means a lower over-all rate" (Skinner, 1953, pp. 100, 126). As might be expected from the principles of operant conditioning and chaining, the effectiveness of delayed reinforcement is enhanced when intervening stimuli which can bridge the time delay are available and become conditioned reinforcers in a chaining process. Again it is instructive to compare the responses of children and adults. Children exhibit a characteristic impatience about delayed reinforcement—as inexperienced consumers, their behavior has not yet been strongly conditioned by chaining. When we say that adults are more patient, we describe the fact that adult behavior has been affected by the chaining of conditioned reinforcers that serve to bridge the delay between response and reinforcement.

Since these findings about the effects of delay would not be surprising in a traditional economic view, it is important to emphasize that an operant approach does not ascribe the effect of delay to a "preference for present over future consumption." The reason is rather that a delay allows time for some other behavior to occur, and then the behavior that is reinforced is the (buy) response followed by the intervening behavior, rather than just the (buy) response alone (Reynolds, 1975, p. 31). Alternatively (or in addition), a delay allows time for other consequences to occur and to condition the operant

establishing operation (e.g., deprivation), the rate of behavior (i.e., the response strength) is usually taken to represent the strength of the reinforcer. When, as in the next section, the reinforcer-establishing operation is held constant, and the contingencies of reinforcement are varied, response strength is usually taken to be a measure of the strength of behavior (see Millenson and Leslie, 1979, p. 394).

response. In the example of the previous chapter, the approach behavior of a child who deposits a coin in a candy machine will probably be stronger if the candy is dispensed promptly than if there is a significant delay during which a possibly irate parent can scold the child.

Although delay is one of the independent variables of approach behavior strength, it can probably be ignored in most cases of consumer buy behavior. Delays do occur in some cases of consumer buying—e.g., when a new car which has been purchased (ordered) is not delivered for a few weeks; but most consumer buying is conducted without significant delays. Hence, delays are probably not an important variable in approach behavior strength for most cases of buy behavior, especially for commodities that are purchased repeatedly.

A third factor that can affect the strength of approach behavior is the quantity of the reinforcer available to the organism upon each presentation of the reinforcer. In laboratory experiments with animals, quantity can be varied by changing the number and/or size of food pellets which are provided on a given schedule of reinforcement. These tests must be carefully designed because the validity of the results can be undermined if the level of deprivation (reinforcer-effectiveness operation) is significantly changed while increasing the quantity of the reinforcement on each presentation. Another problem is to vary the amount of reinforcement without also varying the nature of the consumption of the reinforcement (Walker, 1967, pp. 44–45). This problem was avoided by Tombaugh and Marx (1965) who reinforced the lever-pressing responses of experimental animals by presenting the animals with the same amount of liquid while varying its sucrose concentration. They found that the sucrose concentration, and thus the amount of reward, did affect response strength. In other experiments, quantity has been varied by strictly regulating the time access to the reinforcer.[12]

The important finding which emerges from numerous laboratory investigations about the effect of amount of reinforcement is that operant response strength is positively related to the quantity of the reinforcer available to the organism upon each presentation of the reinforcer. There is substantial experimental literature on this point. Thus, Cofer and Appley (1964, p. 555) noted that "the influence of changes in the amount of reward is to alter the rate or speed of performance rapidly." In his review of the literature, Pubols (1960, p. 111) concluded that "asymptotic performance is an increasing func-

[12] See Millenson's statement (1967, p. 390) that "pigeons peck faster if allowed more access time to the contingent grain-reinforcer." Economists also have recognized the importance of time as a variable in consumption. Among others, see Linder (1970) and Schelling (1973).

tion of incentive magnitude." Similarly, Hutt (1954, pp. 235, 239) listed a dozen studies which support the idea that quantity of reinforcement is an important variable influencing the performance of learned and unlearned responses. Seward (1951, p. 136) also has stated that "a number of studies have shown that animals will approach a large reward more readily than a small one." Young (1952, p. 254) has reported (based on the work of Crespi and others) that "level of performance varies with the amount of food presented as a reward." Finally, Skinner (1953, p. 100) has observed that "the size or amount of each reinforcement affects the rate—more responses appearing in return for a larger reinforcement."

As in the case of delay, these findings about the effects of amount of reinforcement are based on experimentation. In fact, experimental psychologists have gone further and also attempted to discover in terms of operational variables exactly what it is about larger amounts of reinforcement that strengthens operant responses. Although the experimental findings have not yet been conclusive about the mechanism involved (Cofer and Appley, 1964, p. 557), the finding about the impact of amount of reinforcement is firmly established.

A fourth important determinant of operant response strength for primary goods is the quality of the reinforcer. In experiments with animals, this variation in quality sometimes takes the form of adulterating the food—e.g., by adding quinine, by mixing the food with nonmetabolized bulk cellulose, or by increasing the sucrose content, etc. The finding of such experiments is that a deterioration in the quality of the reinforcer is associated with a fall in the reinforcing value of the reinforcer, i.e., reinforcing value is closely positively related to reinforcer quality (Millenson, 1967, p. 390). Casual empiricism confirms that quality is also an important determinant of operant response strength among human consumers—an example of human response which resembles that of nonhuman subjects is the consumer response to "hamburgers" that have been "adulterated" with nonmeat fillers. In an experimental approach, quality is also an operational variable and not just something that is perceived in the minds of consumers. Quality (like quantity) has an effect on response strength by virtue of its effect on the stimulus properties of the reinforcer. The effect of quality upon strength of operant response is thus a report about the experimental findings with respect to one set of stimulus characteristics as compared with some different set.

2. *For Secondary Commodities*

The earlier discussion of deprivation (reinforcer-establishing operation) described the effects of withholding a primary reinforcer on the reinforcing value of (and, therefore, also on the response strength of behavior which is reinforced by) that primary reinforcer. Deprivation is also an important determinant of response strength for (behavior which is reinforced by) secondary commodities. Unlike the case of a primary reinforcer, it is not possible to isolate an independent deprivation which is applicable solely to the secondary reinforcer. The reason, of course, is that secondary reinforcers do not have an innate capacity to reinforce behavior. To paraphrase Skinner (1953, p. 150), no one "needs" (say) a taxi in the sense of having been deprived of a taxi for a lengthy period. But if a taxi has become a secondary reinforcer by its association in a chain of behavior leading, say, to a favorite restaurant, the response strength of the behavior of hailing a taxi is also strengthened whenever the level of food deprivation increases, i.e., the reinforcing value of taxis (for this individual at this moment of time) will also increase. In short, since secondary goods are based on primary reinforcers, the response strength of behavior that is reinforced by secondary commodities is controlled by the deprivation appropriate to the primary reinforcer. Accordingly, the behavior of hailing taxis is not strengthened by "withholding taxis," but rather by strengthening any behavior that requires a taxi.

The particular past history of conditioning of this individual could bring about a situation in which the reinforcing value of a particular primary reinforcer (say, food) might be increased (without any change in food deprivation) by an increase in the deprivation of some other primary reinforcer. This could happen if, say, food, in addition to being a primary reinforcer, also became an acquired (secondary) reinforcer by association with other primary reinforcers in this individual's prior history of conditioning (e.g., affection and warmth). When a particular primary product is also an acquired reinforcer, its reinforcement value will vary not only with the level of deprivation to which it is directly responsive, but also to the level of deprivation with respect to the primary reinforcer on which the acquired reinforcing strength is based.[13] In a similar way, the reinforcing value of a primary good can also be enhanced by association with secondary reinforcers, such as approval (e.g., consumption based on peer approval) or competitiveness (e.g., in the keeping-up-with-the-Joneses syndrome).

In addition to the effect from deprivation of the appropriate primary reinforcer, the potency of a conditioned reinforcer is also affected by other important factors (Reynolds, 1975, pp. 63–64). One is the frequency of pairing with the primary (or conditioned) reinforcer on which it is based. Specifically, potency increases with higher frequen-

---

[13] This is the theoretical basis for the view that people who are not in a state of food deprivation (as measured by normal food intake requirements) may nevertheless continue to consume food when they are in a state of deprivation with respect to other powerful reinforcers.

cies of pairing. The experimental evidence suggests that the potency curve is concave downwards and becomes asymptotic. In addition, when the conditioned reinforcer is part of a chain, its potency declines with greater distance from the primary reinforcement. Finally, the potency of secondary commodities is affected by the schedule of reinforcement with the primary (or conditioned) reinforcer on which it is based. Intermittent schedules are particularly effective. As Millenson and Leslie (1979, p. 150) have noted, intermittency plays a critical role in amplifying the effects of conditioned reinforcers.

> Used in testing the reinforcing value of the S^D, an intermittency imposed between the new R to be conditioned and the contingent S^D conserves the power of the secondary reinforcer. . . . A well-chosen intermittency here will not only conserve the power of S^D but will maintain a high rate of R_2 as well. . . . If S^D appears infrequently, R_1 has only infrequent opportunities to weaken.

It should also be mentioned that a stimulus becomes a conditioned reinforcer only when it is correlated nonredundantly with a reinforcement contingency (ibid., p. 159).

3. For Escape Commodities

Stimulus intensity and response strength. In an experimental approach, an important reinforcement-establishing operation that makes a positive primary reinforcer effective is to increase the level of deprivation. The reinforcer-establishment operation that makes a primary aversive stimulus effective is to increase the intensity of the aversive stimulus. In terms of making a reinforcer effective, therefore, the presentation of an aversive stimulus resembles a sudden increase in deprivation (Skinner, 1953, p. 172).[14] Both in logic and in terms of empirical results, there is a "close parallel . . . in the way that hours of deprivation and S^- intensity control behavior" (Millenson, 1967, p. 415).[15] Specifically, operant behavior cannot be strengthened by presenting a positive reinforcer when the level of deprivation is low or by terminating an aversive stimulus when the intensity of aversive stimulation is low; but it can be strengthened when the levels of deprivation or of aversive stimulation are high. In experiments to explore the effects of varying the intensities of aversive stimulus on rats, Dinsmoor and Winograd (1958) found that rate of response rose with

---

[14] Deprivation also resembles aversive stimulation because of the similar implications for evolutionary survival. Cf. Skinner's observation (1953, p. 173) about the advantage in natural selection when an organism is reinforced by the withdrawal of certain conditions. This also parallels the positive reinforcement case.

[15] Millenson (1967, p. 415) further states that "such considerations imply an interesting conceptual status for aversive stimuli. Their presentation is simultaneously drive arousing and negatively reinforcing."

the level of aversive stimulus intensity. They also found, however—and this, too, has its parallel in the earlier reported findings about the effects of deprivation—that the rate of escape responding reached a maximum at very great levels of aversive-stimulus intensity. Millenson and Leslie (1979, pp. 269–70) state that "the decline in responding associated with very intense aversive events is not well understood; it is thought to be due to a general suppressive (emotional) effect of strong aversive stimuli." Finally, an increase in deprivation raises the reinforcing value of secondary positive reinforcers that are based on that deprivation; and an increase in aversive-stimulus intensity will increase the reinforcing value of conditioned aversive stimuli (secondary negative reinforcers) that are based on given primary aversive stimuli.[16]

This discussion of the similarities between the reinforcer-effectiveness operations of deprivation and aversive stimulation is pertinent in analyzing the effect of an increase in the intensity of aversive stimulation upon the reinforcing value of escape goods, a particular class of secondary positive reinforcers. This (seemingly contradictory) relation between an increase in aversive stimulation and the reinforcing value of a positive reinforcer can be explained in theoretically consistent terms after a closer look at the nature and role of escape goods in an operant conditioning paradigm. We begin by noting that "in respondent conditioning, if a previously neutral stimulus, such as a bell, is frequently followed after an interval by a noxious stimulus, such as an electric shock, the bell becomes a conditioned *aversive* stimulus" (Skinner, 1974, p. 61, italics added). Similarly, if a previously neutral stimulus, such as a bell, is frequently followed after an interval by escape from a noxious stimulus, such as an electric shock, the bell becomes a conditioned *positive* stimulus. The explanation (as mentioned earlier—see p. 19) is that escape from a noxious stimulus is itself a positive reinforcer;[17] and, by association with that positive reinforcer, escape goods also acquire their power to provide positive reinforcement.

The above also suggests how a particular class of positive reinforcers (viz., escape goods) can be controlled by the intensity of an aversive

---

[16] The secondary negative reinforcers are (to mix the language of psychology and economics) conditioned "bads"—e.g., the sight of smoke rising from a factory smokestack (but before it has produced respiratory symptoms or eye irritation); and the primary aversive stimuli are primary "bads"—e.g., breathing difficulties and eye-smarting caused by severe air pollution.

[17] Walker (1967, p. 77) has noted that "most reinforcement theorists assume that positive and negative reinforcers are inextricably associated. A drive state, such as hunger, is regarded as a negative reinforcer and the food reward that relieves the state is a positive reinforcer; *escape from the noxious stimulus is a positive reinforcer*" (italics added).

stimulus. The basic explanation is in terms of the operant conditioning paradigm based on the presentation of an aversive stimulus. Thus, the individual escapes from the aversive stimulus by emitting the operant behavior that is successful in that context. Since escape from aversive stimulation is a positively reinforcing stimulus,[18] the presentation of the aversive stimulus necessarily also raises the level of deprivation with respect to the positive reinforcer, escape from aversive stimulation. Thus the increase in the reinforcement value of the escape good can be straightforwardly explained as a case of a positive (conditioned) reinforcer that is controlled by an increase in deprivation. In fact, of course, the increase in deprivation is directly paralleled by the simultaneous increase in the intensity of aversive stimulation. Indeed, since escape goods can only come into being in the context of aversive contingencies, it is convenient to treat escape goods as positive reinforcers that are controlled by aversive stimulation (rather than the theoretically accurate statement that they are positive reinforcers that are controlled by deprivation), because the way to control such "deprivation" (i.e., of escape from aversive stimulus) is to change the intensity of aversive stimulation.

Other variables that affect response strength. Escape goods are based on a special kind of positive reinforcer (viz., termination or reduction of aversive stimuli). Accordingly, if we hold constant the intensity of the relevant aversive stimuli, we find that the other variables that control the response strength of operant buy behavior which is reinforced with escape goods are strikingly similar to those discussed for the general case of positive reinforcers. As noted earlier, one of the independent variables is the schedule of reinforcement. As with other positive reinforcers, the strength of approach behavior is affected not only by the schedule that reinforces the operant buy response, but also by the schedules that are in effect for the operant responses at other points along the chain that culminates in reduction or termination of an aversive stimulus.

A second independent variable is the length of any delay between

---

[18] The fact that escape from an aversive condition is positively reinforcing can be demonstrated by experiments on operant conditioning in which the aversive stimulus precedes the positive reinforcements. Skinner (1953, p. 221) cites the example of swimming in cold water for the effect of the invigorating glow that follows. See, also, his explanation (1953, p. 73):

> Events which are found to be reinforcing are of two sorts. Some reinforcements consist of *presenting* stimuli . . . *positive* reinforcers; others consist of removing something . . . *negative* reinforcers. In both cases the effect of reinforcement is the same—the probability of response is increased. We cannot avoid this distinction by arguing that what is reinforcing in the negative case is the *absence* of the bright light, loud noise, and so on; for it is absence after presence which is effective, and this is only another way of saying that the stimulus is removed.

the emission of the operant response and the subsequent reduction or termination of the aversive stimuli. Among the numerous economic examples in everyday life, one of the most common, as the ads repeatedly remind us, is that the reinforcing value is greater when pain-relieving drugs are fast-acting rather than when they are slow-acting.

A third variable is the duration of stimulus-off time. If the aversive stimulus is, say, electric shock, the stimulus-off time refers to how long the electric shock remains turned off after the organism emits the operant response. Stimulus-off time in the case of escape goods corresponds to amount of reinforcement in the case of other positive reinforcers. Among human consumers, a common example of stimulus-off time is the duration of pain relief from a given medication (escape good). In experiments with animals, Dinsmoor and Hughes (1956) have found that long stimulus-off times have greater reinforcement value then brief shock-off times. The problem of varying the magnitude of the negative reinforcement without also varying the nature of the reinforcement is like the similar problem in cases of positive reinforcement. In one ingenious attempt to solve this problem, Bower, Fowler, and Trapold (1959) tested the responses of three groups of animals who were placed in a runway with a common level of voltage but in which the voltage was dropped by different amounts for the three groups. The response strength of the operant behavior that reduced the voltage (running to the goal box) was higher the greater the drop in voltage.

A fourth variable that affects approach behavior strength is the quality of the escape good. In the case of aversive stimulation, the quality of a reinforcer is reflected in its capacity to reduce the intensity of the aversive stimulus. Quality thus has a clear-cut operational interpretation in this context, viz., a particular bundle of stimulus characteristics that can provide a greater reduction in the intensity of an aversive stimulus. Although consumers will demand escape goods even when they are not completely effective, operant response strength is predictably higher for reinforcers that come closer to terminating the aversive stimulus than for those that do not. As with other positive reinforcers, quantity and quality affect reinforcing value by changing the stimulus properties of the escape good.

Determinants of Escape Behavior

As explained in chapter 2 (p. 14), for the theoretical purposes of this study, the operant response (act of purchase) is the behavior of entering into a purchase contract; and the two consequences of having entered into a contract are the acquisition of the product and the loss of dollars surrendered in payment. In the preceding section, we examined the determinants of approach behavior, i.e., of the positively reinforcing consequence of the act of purchase (viz., acquiring the product); in this section, we examine the determinants of escape behavior, i.e., of the aversive consequence of the act of purchase (viz., loss of dollars surrendered in payment). The loss of dollars becomes a conditioned aversive stimulus in at least three distinct ways, as shown below.

Disapproval. One way in which the loss of dollars surrendered in payment becomes a conditioned aversive stimulus is that it is paired with disapproval in the past history of conditioning of most individuals. Since approval is a powerful (conditioned) reinforcer, the withdrawal of approval (i.e., withdrawal of a positive reinforcer) or the expression of disapproval (i.e., the presentation of a negative reinforcer) are aversive consequences that can have important conditioning effects upon the loss of dollars surrendered in payment. The association between the aversive stimulus of disapproval and the loss of dollars surrendered in payment often begins during childhood training in money management. Since money has no innate capacity to reinforce behavior, the stimuli involved in its possession and manipulation (including its surrender) are neutral until a child has had the experiences that gradually convert money into a conditioned reinforcer. As part of the training in money management, children will sometimes be criticized or punished for "throwing their money away" (i.e., spending it in ways that their parents disapprove of). As a result of such experiences, the loss of money surrendered in payment can become a conditioned aversive stimulus (S⁻) based on the powerful conditioned reinforcer of parental disapproval. The loss of money surrendered in payment ceases to be a neutral stimulus and the act of purchase is no longer followed by exclusively positively reinforcing consequences. In the process by which the child "learns the value of a dollar,"[19] the stimuli accompanying the loss of money surrendered in payment may acquire aversive properties from which escape is reinforcing.

The disapproval which may (i.e., intermittently) follow the loss of money surrendered in payment is not, of course, limited to parental disapproval. At all ages, money surrendered in payment is subject to control by peers or by society—e.g., the disapproval of "extravagant" or "showy" money outlays. In a similar way, the disapproval of other

[19] Advice to parents on how to train their children in money management is a staple feature of many mass-circulation magazines aimed at middle-income families. For example, see Daly (1976).

family members can influence the loss of money surrendered in payment by any one member of the family.[20] In short, although the aversive consequences of the loss of dollars surrendered in payment will differ in strength and importance for different individuals, depending upon their past histories of conditioning, the disapproval that sometimes follows the loss of money surrendered in payment is a pervasive form of conditioning in money-using cultures. Insofar as discrimination training is effective, the conditioned aversive stimuli from the loss of money surrendered in payment will tend to be confined to socially disapproved outlays, instead of becoming generalized across all outlays.

Impeded or blocked access to other positive reinforcers. Another possible aversive consequence of the loss of money surrendered in payment takes the form of blocked or impeded access to other positive reinforcers. To the extent that the supply of dollars available to a consumer is limited, a loss of dollars surrendered in payment on one product may lead to (become associated with) blocked or impeded access to other reinforcers during the same or a later income period.[21] For any given level of deprivation, blocked or impeded access to reinforcers is an aversive consequence (S⁻), and the stimuli accompanying the loss of dollars surrendered in payment become conditioned aversive stimuli by association with this aversive consequence.

The blocked or impeded access to other reinforcers can occur at the same time as the loss of dollars surrendered in payment or it can occur at a later time. Notwithstanding a delay between operant response and aversive consequence, the contingency of reinforcement remains effective. In the event of a delay, escape behavior is strengthened by means of a chain of behaviors that lead ultimately to the aversive consequence of blocked or impeded access to other reinforcers. For some individuals, the chain is conditioned entirely by direct market experience. However, the chain of behaviors is also commonly strengthened during childhood as part of a child's training in money management.[22] Personal or family budgets are a common outcome of these experiences. Budgeting provides escape from the aversive stim-

---

[20] The importance of family input in spending decisions has traditionally been ignored in economics, but not by Leibenstein (1976 and 1979).

[21] For simplicity, we exclude the possibility of drawing on savings or of borrowing.

[22] In an article on "How to Teach Your Youngsters the Value of Money," one mass-circulation journal advised its readers to teach their children that "money involves choice: When you spend it on one thing, you don't have it to spend on another" (Daly,

uli associated with losing too much money in payments at any one time or on any one commodity and, as a by-product, avoids (or mitigates) the aversive consequences of impeded or blocked access to other reinforcers.

For any given level of income, the (objective) consequences in terms of blocked or impeded access to other reinforcers will be more pronounced as the loss of dollars surrendered in payment is increased. Conversely, for any given loss of dollars surrendered in payment, the (objective) consequences in terms of blocked or impeded access to other reinforcers will be more pronounced as the level of income is decreased. Under both circumstances, escape behavior is strengthened by the aversive consequences of the loss. The strength of escape behavior is related not only to the average level of income, but also to its stability. Moreover, the fact that the aversive consequences are experienced intermittently when income is a stochastic variable strengthens the durability of the effective escape behavior.

Loss of a positive reinforcer. A third reason why the loss of money surrendered in payment is aversive is an inescapable part of the experience of any individual in a money-using culture. Although money is not an innate reinforcer for anyone, it becomes a conditioned positive reinforcer for (almost) everyone. Hence, the loss of money surrendered in payment is the loss of a positive reinforcer—and that loss is per se aversive. As Skinner (1953, p. 391) has noted, "Since those who use economic control must give up the goods or money with which they reinforce behavior, economic reinforcement is by definition aversive to the controller." An exactly parallel statement could be made about a buyer who gives up one reinforcer and gets another. It follows that any behavior that avoids this aversive consequence will be reinforcing. As compared with the escape behavior for the loss of most other positive reinforcers, the strength of escape behavior for the loss of money is enhanced by the fact that money is also a generalized positive reinforcer.[23] Moreover, since money's reinforcing power is based on a number of deprivations (of innate reinforcers), its potency is not eliminated by momentary satiation with respect to any single reinforcer. These are the technical explanations

---

1976, p. 10). If a child buys a wind-up toy on the spur of the moment and ends up short of lunch money, the author's advice to parents is "don't bail him out automatically . . . let him figure out that . . . spending too much on impulse items won't leave enough over for other things" (p. 11).

[23] Millenson (1967, p. 455) describes the "sorrow" at losing a host of reinforcers at one fell swoop by losing a generalized reinforcer.

for the obvious facts that money is a powerful positive reinforcer for the overwhelming majority of people and that its loss is an aversive stimulus that can reinforce escape behavior of great strength.

It is interesting to note in passing that, at least for some people, the aversive intensity of a given loss of dollars surrendered in payment appears to be somewhat related to the form of payment. This difference is implicit in the statements of those who report that (and often behave as if) they "feel little or no pain" when their purchases are made by credit card. Part of the difference (if it truly exists) may be due to the fact that the loss of dollars is immediate in a cash purchase but occurs with a lag in a check or credit-card purchase, and that the difference is not fully bridged by chaining.[24] Another example concerns the behavior of some tourists, who accept a loss of foreign currency surrendered in payment more readily than an equivalent amount of their domestic currency. In such cases, the domestic currency has probably been more widely conditioned as a generalized reinforcer than the foreign currency, i.e., it's a matter of their past histories of conditioning.

Escape and avoidance. The aversive consequences of the loss of dollars surrendered in payment—disapproval, blocked or impeded access to other positive reinforcers, loss of a positive reinforcer—constitute a form of punishment. Punishment is related to negative reinforcement in the following way. Negative reinforcement precedes a response (i.e., the S⁻ is already in effect), and the negative reinforcement is terminated after the response is emitted. By contrast, punishers are not in effect prior to the response, but rather are made contingent upon the response.[25] Skinner (1953, p. 188) has explained the effects of punishment as follows:

---

[24] It will be interesting in this connection to compare the aversive intensity under EFTS when the loss of dollars will occur immediately, just as it now does with cash transactions. *Consumer Reports* (June 1978, p. 357) believes:

> The biggest problem of all may be one that can't be solved with legislation: How will people relate to the new money? Cash is something concrete. A check is something concrete. Electronic impulses whizzing through wires into computers cannot be seen or held in the hand. It will be hard to think of $10 as $10 when it is simply the push of a button on a machine in the middle of a shopping mall.
> "Money" will be so available it will be easy to overspend but hard to account for the spending. It will be easy for your financial plans to go astray. You'll have to learn new systems to keep track of your money. At the very least, financial institutions should tell consumers how to keep records and should provide documents for record-keeping.

[25] "We . . . define a positive reinforcer as any stimulus the *presentation* of which strengthens the behavior upon which it is made contingent. We define a negative reinforcer (an aversive stimulus) as any stimulus the *withdrawal* of which strengthens

> If a given response is followed by an aversive stimulus, any stimulation which accompanies the response, whether it arises from the behavior itself or from concurrent circumstances, will be conditioned. . . . [This] leads to the conditioning of aversive stimuli which serve as negative reinforcers. Any behavior which reduces this conditioned aversive stimulation will be reinforced. . . . Technically, we may say that further punishment is avoided.

This description is also applicable to buy behavior. After the formerly neutral stimuli (from the individual's behavior and from concurrent circumstances that are associated with the loss of dollars surrendered in payment) become conditioned aversive stimuli, any behavior that reduces these conditioned aversive stimuli will be reinforced.

It is tempting to say that escape can be achieved by not emitting the punished behavior. However, in an analysis that stresses the behavior of individuals (i.e., what they *do*), we must examine the positive probabilities of behavior instead of appealing to nonbehavior (e.g., not buying) as the way to escape (or avoid) the aversive condition. Accordingly, in examining escape behavior, we look for behavior that is emitted in lieu of buy behavior, i.e., behavior that is incompatible with the emission of the operant purchase behavior.[26] There are, of course, a large number of possible behaviors that could partially or completely avoid the aversive consequences of buy behavior. For example, an individual faced with a decision about a major purchase (house, car, etc.) can temporarily escape from the negative discriminative stimuli (and temporarily avoid the aversive consequences of loss of dollars) by "sleeping on it." A response that delays the full aversive consequence and reduces its intensity is to make the purchase on an installment basis. Another response that reduces the intensity of the aversive consequence is to buy a smaller quantity or a lesser quality of the reinforcer. The only way to avoid the aversive consequence completely is to emit behavior that is completely incompatible with the emission of buy behavior—e.g., an individual can avoid the aversive loss of dollars in, say, buying a car by placing the down-payment money into a long-term "compulsory" savings plan or nonnegotiable bond.

Three final comments are worth noting about the escape behavior that is reinforced by the aversive consequences of buy behavior. First, although the loss of dollars surrendered in payment can become a conditioned aversive stimulus in three independent ways, the intensity

---

behavior. . . . In solving the problem of punishment we simply ask: What is the effect of *withdrawing* a *positive* reinforcer or *presenting* a *negative?*" (Skinner, 1953, p. 185).

[26] Skinner (1953, p. 188) has noted that "the most important effect of punishment . . . is to establish aversive conditions which are avoided by any behavior of 'doing something else.'"

of the aversive stimulus (and, hence, the strength of escape behavior for any given loss of dollars) is probably enhanced by the conjunction of all three aversive consequences for an individual with a given past history of conditioning. Second, the intensity of the aversive consequences of the loss of dollars surrendered in the course of operant buy behavior varies positively with the number of dollars involved.[27] This was demonstrated for the case of impeded or blocked access to other reinforcers, but it is also a plausible hypothesis—and could undoubtedly be demonstrated experimentally—for both of the other aversive consequences associated with the loss of dollars surrendered in payment.[28] Third, most operant psychologists express doubts about the efficacy of punishment, especially its long-term effects. Some of the doubts about the efficacy of punishment as a means to control behavior reflect the view that "punishment effects only a suppression of responses, probably because it induces an emotional state, rather than eliminating responses, as does extinction" (Cofer and Appley, 1964, p. 514). In the case of buy behavior, however, punishment is often more effective. Unlike some other examples of punishment, the loss of monetary reinforcers in buy behavior is scheduled on a crf basis. When that loss is sufficiently intense, escape behavior becomes strongly conditioned—as it does in another well-known crf aversive contingency, viz., touching a hot stove and getting burned fingers. In addition, the other aversive consequences (disapproval, and blocked or impeded access to other positive reinforcers) are presented on an intermittent schedule that tends to produce strong and durable patterns of operant behavior. In sum, the punishment for loss of dollars surrendered in payment combines multiple aversive stimuli with a combination of crf and intermittent schedules that tend to build great strength and durability into escape behavior. The extent and duration of the reduction and suppression of the punished behavior are a function of the intensity of the punishment and the schedule on which it takes place (Glaser, 1978).[29]

[27] This important point will be shown later in diagrams of escape behavior response strength in relation to size of outlay.

[28] The aversive condition that follows the loss of dollars surrendered in payment is not inferred by any appeal to intervening variables. On the contrary, the existence of an aversive condition could (in principle) be verified by standard procedures that are employed in experiments with operant conditioning. Thus, "We can verify the aversive quality of any stimulus by making its removal contingent upon a hitherto unconditioned operant. If the strength of that operant subsequently increases, the stimulus is said to be aversive" (Millenson, 1967, p. 410).

[29] The outcomes of punishment are highly dependent on the characteristics of the aversive stimulus, and on the intensity, frequency, consistency, and timing of the punishment. For a review of some of this literature, see Cheyne and Walters (1970, pp. 283–96).

CHAPTER FOUR

A Preliminary Model
of Buy Behavior

The Evidence from Animal Experiments on Conflict

The conflict involved in buy behavior is a conflict between incompatible behaviors. As shown above, the act of purchase is strengthened by the presentation of a positive reinforcer (economic commodity), but its strength is undermined by the punishment that accompanies the loss of dollars surrendered in payment (viz., disapproval, blocked or impaired access to other positive reinforcers, and loss of positive reinforcers). The positive reinforcement strengthens approach behavior, but the punishment strengthens escape behavior. Thus, the inherent conflict in buy behavior is between two incompatible behaviors—approach and escape. This conflict has a parallel in those laboratory experiments with animals in which, after rats have been conditioned to press a lever by reinforcing that behavior with food, an electric shock is added every time the lever is pressed. In this case, too, there is a conflict between approach behavior (which is reinforced with food) and escape behavior (which is reinforced by elimination or reduction of electric shock). Clearly, both behaviors cannot be emitted simultaneously. The outcome of this conflict depends on the relative strength of the incompatible behaviors.

To develop a model for buy behavior, we will reply on the suggestive findings from some animal experiments on conflict.[1] In one important set of experiments, Brown (1948) made separate investigations of the strength of approach behavior and of escape behavior. To study the strength of approach behavior at different distances from a positive reinforcer (food), Brown trained a group of rats to run down an alley and to receive food at a particular point along the alley. The training occurred while each rat wore a light harness that did not interfere with its movement. After the rats had been trained to go down the alley for food, they were restrained by the harness at different distances from the goal, and the pull strength exerted on the harness was measured. The average pull strength was 56.5 grams when they were stopped at 30 cm from the food, and 40.9 grams at 170 cm. According to the evidence, therefore, the approach gradient varies positively with proximity to the (positive) reinforcer.

In a different and separate experiment, using different animals, Brown (1948) investigated the strength of escape behavior. He used a similar apparatus described above but administered an electric shock instead of food at the end of the alley. Thereafter the animals strongly tended to avoid that end of the alley when placed there without shock. Brown measured the strength of their escape behavior by using the harness apparatus to restrain one group of animals at a short distance from the shock point and another group at a greater distance from the shock point. Those that were stopped at 30 cm from the shock point pulled on the harness with a mean force of 198.4 gm. When the harness was arranged to restrain them at 170 cm, only four (out of twenty animals) reached the point of restraint and pulled with a mean force of 10 gm; the other animals did not run far enough away to be restrained by the harness. Again, the escape gradient varied positively with proximity to the (negative) reinforcer.

The results of these two separate experiments are plotted in figure 1, panel A, which is reproduced from Brown (1948, p. 457). The ordinate measures response strength in terms of grams of average pull strength; the abscissa measures the distance in centimeters of the test points from the point of reinforcement (POR). For convenience of exposition, the experimental outcomes of approach behavior (AB) and escape behavior (EB) have been joined by straight lines. It is important to stress that the relationship of the two curves is the outcome of separate experiments in which the reinforcer-establishing operations (food deprivation and electric shock intensity) were set at particular levels. By changing the relative strength of the reinforcer-establishing operations, it is possible to change the heights of the curves and to achieve different relationships—e.g., those depicted in

[1] For a survey of conflict literature, see Cofer and Appley (1964, pp. 429–41). Also see the seminal work on conflict reported by Miller (1971).

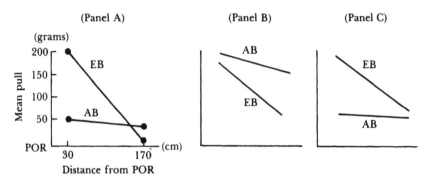

Figure 1. Approach and Escape—Experimental Outcomes

the hypothetical findings shown in panels B and C. These effects of different levels of the reinforcer-establishing operation have also been experimentally demonstrated by Brown.

On the bases of the actual experiments, we can conduct a hypothetical experiment in which an animal that has been conditioned to proceed along a runway to a point of positive reinforcement at the end of the runway also receives an electric shock at the point of reinforcement. We can plausibly interpret the animal's observed response in this contingency of reinforcement as the resultant of approach behavior and escape behavior, i.e., we infer that the outcome that we can observe is the resultant of the relative strength of conflicting responses (at different points along the chain of responses) that we normally do not have an opportunity to observe. For expository convenience, we will retain the AB curve and EB curve as derived from the separate experiments described above.

Psychologists analyze the predicted outcome in cases of conflict in terms of the net response strength, i.e., AB strength minus EB strength (Greeno, 1968, p. 59; Miller, 1971, p. 20). Accordingly, the kinds of cases depicted in figure 1 are shown in figure 2 by the use of Net AB curves. In the extreme cases (figure 2, panels B and C), the conflicting behaviors are overwhelmingly weighted either in favor of approach (panel B) or of escape (panel C). The subject moves towards both the food and the shock in one case (panel B) and away from both in the other case (panel C). In the intermediate case (panel A), approach behavior is stronger than escape behavior in the range of the net response curve that lies to the right of the intersection with the abscissa; hence, the subject approaches the point of reinforcement. As the intersection is crossed, escape behavior becomes stronger than approach behavior with increasing relative strength as the point of reinforcement is reached; hence, approach behavior ceases and es-

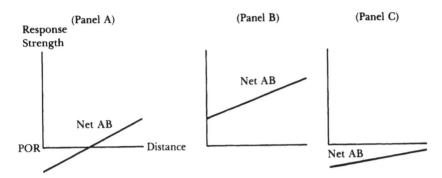

Figure 2. Net Response Strength

cape behavior is emitted. Although the intersection is an equilibrium position, the individual's behavior is likely to vacillate about that point (Miller, 1971, pp. 10–11).

The results described above depend on the relative levels of the approach and escape curves, the positive slopes of the curves, and the relative gradients. First, as for the levels of the AB and EB curves, it has been demonstrated experimentally that the levels can be controlled by changing the levels of the reinforcer-establishing operations. Second, as for the positive slopes of the two curves, this question has also been studied experimentally, as described above. However, at least part of the explanation can be inferred from the general principles involved in operant conditioning. As noted earlier, operant behavior (e.g., approach behavior) is generally reinforced by a process of chaining in which "stimuli with the dual role of discriminative cue and conditioned reinforcer . . . link each member (of the chain) to the next" (Millenson, 1967, p. 260). The stimuli that comprise the chain consist of external stimuli, but also of internal stimuli that arise from muscle and tendon movements that are emitted in the process by which operant responses are chained. Both the external stimuli and the proprioceptors become conditioned discriminative stimuli and conditioned reinforcers during operant chaining. However, the stimuli that are closest to the point of reinforcement become more strongly conditioned than those at a greater distance. The reason that cues nearer the goal elicit stronger responses than more distant cues is that they are "more immediately associated with the event of reinforcement and because they are more similar to those present during reinforcement" (Miller, 1971, p. 23). As a result, both the AB and EB curves exhibit positive slopes.

Third, as for the difference in the gradients, it appears to be explained by the differences in the levels of the reinforcement-effectiveness operation that is in force at different points along the alley. In the animal experiments described above, the reinforcement-effectiveness operation for approach behavior was deprivation of a primary reinforcer (food); and a given level of deprivation was in effect at the point of reinforcement and at all other points along the experimental alley. As a result, both the proprioceptors and the external cues at all points in the alley were conditioned under a constant level of the reinforcement-effectiveness operation in the case of approach behavior. Other things being equal, this tends to make for a flattish AB curve. The reinforcement-effectiveness operation for escape behavior was intensity of the primary reinforcer, electric shock. Although the intensity (or strength) of the reinforcement-effectiveness operation was held constant, it was in force only at the point of shock delivery. As a result, both the proprioceptors and the external cues were conditioned at the given level of the reinforcement-effectiveness operation at the point of reinforcement, but at a zero level at all other points in the alley. To summarize, in the case of both the AB and EB curves, the conditioning of distant cues is weaker than for cues close to the point of reinforcement; hence, both curves have positive slopes. However, the EB gradient is greater than the AB gradient, because a reinforcement-effectiveness operation of given strength is in effect at the point of reinforcement and at all other points along the alley in the case of approach behavior, whereas a reinforcement-effectiveness operation of given intensity is in effect only at the point of reinforcement in the case of escape behavior.

Application of Conflict Experiments to Consumer Buy Responses

In the animal experiments on conflict (and in the hypothetical experiments described below), the response strength was measured at different points along the chain of responses that collectively constitute the completed response. In a loose way of speaking, these measures of response strength may be considered to be measures of the strength of the tendency to emit the completed response. In the animal experiments on conflict, the strength of the operant responses (approach behavior and escape behavior) was measured in relation to spatial distance from a point of reinforcement, i.e., the chain of responses was distributed along a spatial dimension. It is the hypothesis of this study that the findings from the animal experiments about conflict behavior in a spatial context can be applied to human conflict behavior in a context that may be partly nonspatial.[2] It follows from

[2]This follows the position stated by Miller (1971, pp. 14, 303).

this hypothesis that there exists a measurable response strength at each point along the chain of responses that leads to a completed purchase transaction, just as there is a measurable response strength at each point along the alleyway in the animal experiments. The design of suitable experiments to measure response strength for human subjects is an important practical problem, but it is beyond the scope of this study. For our purposes, it is sufficient to point to the experimental evidence that objective measures of response strength (e.g., the grams of force exerted by the animals in Brown's experiments) can be obtained for nonhuman subjects. If the basic hypothesis of this paper is correct about the applicability of these experiments to human behavior, objective measures of response strength can, in principle, also be obtained for human subjects in suitably designed experiments. Accordingly, in the hypothetical experiments discussed below, we will not be concerned with the practical problems of developing an experimental measure of human response strength.[3]

In applying the principles from the animal experiments to human buy behavior contingencies,[4] the strength of approach behavior will depend on the level of the appropriate reinforcer-effectiveness operation for the particular economic good or service (positive reinforcer). The strength of escape behavior depends on the intensity of the aversive stimulation associated with the loss of dollars surrendered in payments for the goods or services, i.e., on the level of the reinforcer-establishing operation. For reasons explained earlier (in chapter 3), the stimulus of loss of dollars surrendered in payment (like the stimulus of electric shock) is both drive-arousing (i.e., a reinforcer-establishing operation) and negatively reinforcing; and the intensity of the aversive stimulus varies with the amount of the loss of dollars surrendered in payment.

We hypothesize that the slopes of the AB curves and the EB curves are negative for the same kinds of reasons that were adduced in the animal experiments, viz., the conditioned discriminative stimuli and the positive (or negative) reinforcers that constitute the chain of responses leading to the point of reinforcement become weaker with greater distance from that point. In extrapolating from the animal experiments to hypothesize about the relative gradients of approach and escape behavior, we note that there is nothing inherent in a

[3] In Brown's experiments, the measure of response strength is grams of pull-force. However, in laboratory experiments on operant conditioning, a common measure of the strength of behavior is the frequency of response.

[4] James Greeno (1968, pp. 60–61) has suggested that "the distance the rat has to run may be like a price that he has to pay to obtain the food."

conflict situation as such that necessarily makes for a steeper gradient on EB curves than on AB curves. This finding in the animal experiments was based on a particular kind of contingency and a particular combination of reinforcers and reinforcer-establishing operations— in particular, the contingencies that provided for shock to be administered at the end of the experimental alley. By shifting the point at which shock is administered, the pattern of escape behavior response strength in relation to distance from the point of food reinforcement could be altered (Miller, 1971, pp. 13–14). In experiments in which shock was administered throughout the length of the alleyway, the slope of the escape behavior gradient was much flatter.[5]

When these findings are applied to the loss of dollars surrendered in payment, it is apparent that, in the typical case, the response strength of escape behavior will tend to drop sharply with greater distance from the point of negative reinforcement. The reason, of course, is that the point of negative reinforcement typically coincides with the point of positive reinforcement—the loss of dollars surrendered in payment and acquisition of the good occur at the same time and place. Although this pattern makes for a steeper gradient for the EB curve, it is not inherent in a buy contingency. Indeed, in a common ploy to reduce buyer resistance, sellers sometimes separate the points of negative and positive reinforcement—e.g., in sales campaigns that offer "fly now, pay later" arrangements, or that offer immediate delivery on, say, a new car but with little or no down payment and twenty-four or thirty-six months to pay. This is analogous to those experiments with animals in which it has been shown (Miller, 1971, p. 14) that electric shock is less effective in keeping animals from proceeding to the point of positive reinforcement when the shock is administered after reaching the positive reinforcer.

The principles of operant conditioning also suggest that the slopes of AB curves will be different for different kinds of economic goods and services. For example, in the case of primary positive reinforcers that are controlled by deprivation (e.g., food), the external and internal stimuli in the chain of approach behavior are conditioned under a constant level of the reinforcer-establishing operation both at the point of reinforcement and at other points at a distance from the reinforcement point. Other things being equal, this tends to make for a flattish AB curve. This contrasts sharply with those cases of escape/avoidance goods in which the aversive stimulus on which the

[5] This was demonstrated by Miller and Brown in unpublished exploratory work (see Miller, 1971, p. 23).

escape good is based[6] occurs solely at a particular point (of time, place, etc.). Since an aversive stimulus is both drive-arousing and negatively reinforcing, the response strength of approach behavior to such escape goods will be strongest in close proximity to the point of negative reinforcement and fall off sharply at a greater distance. As in the similar cases already discussed, the strength of the conditioned stimuli (both external and internal) is weakened by distance and the associated change in the level of the reinforcer-establishing operation. Other things being equal, therefore, the gradient of approach behavior for such escape goods will be steeper than for the primary positive reinforcers mentioned above. To repeat, however, this will not hold for all escape/avoidance goods. If the aversive stimulus is experienced over a wide range of physical, temporal, and other kinds of distance, the AB curves for such escape/avoidance goods will be correspondingly flatter than in the previous cases.

Some Hypothetical Experiments in Buy Behavior

Case of a single commodity and fixed quantity. We can now illustrate the application of the findings of animal experiments on conflict to the conflicting behaviors involved in buy behavior contingencies. We begin with a simple case that closely parallels the experiments described earlier in this chapter.[7] In this first case (hypothetical experiment), the positive reinforcer is a fixed quantity of a given product and the punishment is the loss of a fixed number of dollars surrendered in payment. The individual's "choice" in such an experiment is to buy or escape from buying (not buy). This conflict can be described on the same kind of diagrams that were used for the animal experiments, i.e., with positively sloped approach and escape curves in which (as shown in the animal experiments) escape behavior typically has a steeper gradient than approach behavior. Except for the sizes of positive and negative reinforcement, all other aspects of the contingencies of reinforcement and the conditioning parameters are taken as given.

Two points are worth noting about this case. First, when purchase behavior does occur in this kind of all-or-nothing experiment, the inherent nature of the conflict in the buy behavior suggests that it must be because the AB curve is greater than, or equal to, the EB

---

[6] As explained earlier, escape goods are positively reinforcing because they provide escape from the aversive stimulus.

[7] The complete model of buy behavior cannot be presented until chapter 6, after the concept of reinforcer-effectiveness limits has been discussed in chapter 5.

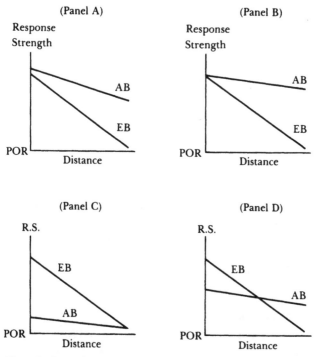

Figure 3. Case of a Single Commodity and a Fixed Quantity

curve at the point of reinforcement (figure 3, panels A and B). Similarly, if a purchase transaction does not take place, the AB curve must be below the EB curve at the point of reinforcement (panels C and D). Although the critical relationship that determines whether buy behavior is emitted (in this all-or-nothing experiment) is the relationship between the AB and EB curves at the point of reinforcement, the accompanying behavior may be quite different in two cases with the same outcome. For example, in the case where the EB curve lies above the AB curve at all points (panel C), the inherent conflict in buy behavior is easily and quickly resolved—just as it is also resolved in the two cases with a buy outcome (panels A and B). Although buy behavior is not emitted in panels C and D, the individual's behavior in one of these cases (viz., when the curves intersect, especially at a middle distance) will, as noted earlier, exhibit the typical symptoms of "indecision," viz., vacillation and oscillation about the point of intersection.

Case of two commodities with one quantity for each commodity. In this next case (hypothetical experiment), there are two possible positive reinforcers (a two-commodity model) with a fixed quantity for each commodity; and the punishment is the loss of a fixed number of dollars surrendered in payment. In the preceding case of a single commodity with a fixed quantity, a fixed level of income was included implicitly in order to derive the EB curve. It will be recalled that a fixed income is implicit in order for a loss of dollars surrendered in payment to have the aversive consequence of impaired or blocked access to other reinforcers in the present or some future period. In the present case, it behooves us to make the income limit explicit. Specifically, suppose that the consumer's fixed income is sufficient to purchase either X-product or Y-product but not both together—and suppose that combinations are excluded from the opportunity set in this contingency of reinforcement. In this case of two commodity reinforcers and a binding income constraint, buy behavior is the outcome of a double conflict. First, as in the case of a single commodity reinforcer, there is an inherent conflict between approach behavior and escape behavior, because buy behavior is followed by both positively reinforcing and punishing consequences. Second, there is a conflict between Net AB_x and Net AB_y, because the income limitation makes it impossible to acquire both commodities.

To keep this hypothetical experiment close to the animal experiments on conflict, the contingency of reinforcement provides for only a single quantity for each commodity. Similarly, to approximate the spatial distance feature of the animal experiments, the X-product is sold at one end of a store and the Y-product is sold at the opposite end. Finally, as background for this hypothetical experiment, we assume that we have already conducted separate and independent experiments to measure the strength of approach behavior for each product taken singly and to measure the strength of escape behavior from the loss of the fixed number of dollars (entire income) surrendered in payment, i.e., we have derived AB and EB curves for X-product when X was the only product in the experiment, and then repeated the procedure for Y-product when Y was the only product in the experiment. This conforms with the procedure in the animal experiments in which the strength of approach behavior—there was only one positive reinforcer in those experiments—and the strength of escape behavior were determined in separate experiments. In our case, the EB curve is the same whether the individual was initially conditoned on X-commodity or on Y-commodity, because the intensity of the reinforcement-establishing operation is the same—the outlay is the same for either commodity and the fixed level of income is also the same.

In order to show the outcome of the double conflict in this experiment, we draw diagrams for the AB and EB curves of each product separately (as in the single-commodity case). These diagrams are then combined by reversing the abscissa for one of the commodities and superimposing the two diagrams. For convenience in presenting the combined diagram, we plot only one curve for each product, viz., a Net AB curve (AB minus EB). Each Net AB curve implicitly reflects the inherent conflict of behaviors in the single-commodity case, and the relation of the two Net AB curves determines the outcome under the behavioral conflict in the two-commodity case. The reason that it is meaningful to compare the response strength of behavior for two different products (Net AB_x and Net AB_y) is the assumption noted earlier (p. 45) that, based on the experiments with nonhuman subjects, objective measures of human response strength exist and could be obtained, at least in principle, in suitably designed experiments.

In figure 4 (panel A), the Net AB_y curve lies above the Net AB_x curve at all distances from the points of reinforcement. If the individual enters the store at the end where X is displayed, approach behavior to Y will be stronger than to X, and he will move towards the end where Y is displayed. As he moves towards Y, the difference between the net response strength of the approach behavior to the two products is diminished; but it remains positive in favor of Y. Since Net AB_y is stronger than Net AB_x at all points, the stronger behavior will prevail,[8] and his entire income will be expended on Y-commodity. In panel B, Net AB_x is unchanged from panel A but Net AB_y is negative throughout its length. In this case, the consumer obviously spends his entire income on X-product. It is important to note that Y is a positive reinforcer ($AB_y > 0$); and the statement that Net AB_y is negative at all points simply means that $EB_y > AB_y$ at all points. Under different contingencies of reinforcement or different conditioning parameters, the Net AB_y curve could become positive—and Net AB_y might even become stronger than Net AB_x with the result that the consumer's income would be expended on Y rather than on X. Panel C illustrates a third possible relation, viz., when the Net AB curves intersect. As noted earlier, the point of intersection (if it exists) between AB and EB curves is an equilibrium outcome in the one-commodity case. In the two-commodity case, equilibrium occurs where Net AB_x = Net AB_y (if the curves intersect); but, at that point, $AB_x \neq EB_x$ and $AB_y \neq EB_y$. In other words, the outcomes in the two-commodity case may be unstable for each good taken separately, but that instability is overcome by the balancing pressures between Net AB_x and Net AB_y. In this example, the consumer buys neither product—he is stymied by the double conflict in which he is enmeshed and "can't make up his mind." As

---

[8] "In general, when two responses are strong at the same time, only one can be emitted. The appearance of one response is called 'prepotency'" (Skinner, 1953, p. 20).

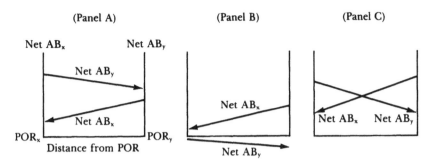

(Panel A)   (Panel B)   (Panel C)

Figure 4. Case of Two Commodities with One Quantity for Each Commodity

long as the contingencies of reinforcement and the conditioning parameters remain unchanged, the consumer will continue to solve his "choice" problem by buying neither product, i.e., buy behavior is not emitted.[9]

Case of one commodity with different possible quantities. In this final section, we apply the findings from the animal experiments on conflict to a case in which there is only one positive reinforcer (a single-commodity model), but with different possible quantities of the commodity, and the punishment is the loss of dollars surrendered in payment for different quantities of the reinforcer. This case does not have a direct parallel in the animal conflict experiments cited above, because the size of the positive or negative reinforcers was not a variable in those experiments. Accordingly, to relate this case to the animal conflict experiments, we must meet two requirements. First, as in the previous cases, the strength of approach behavior and of escape behavior must be determined in separate and independent experiments. Second, the strength of approach behavior for each amount of the positive reinforcer and the strength of escape behavior for the loss of different amounts of money surrendered in payment must also be determined in separate and independent experiments.

To accomplish the first requirement, we may design a preliminary set of hypothetical experiments, in which the contingencies of reinforcement provide that the act of buy behavior can be emitted without the complication introduced by opposed consequences (as in actual buy behavior). Diagrammatically, the actual contingency of reinforcement is as follows:

[9] This diagram and the analysis of outcomes is closely adapted from the presentation in Miller (1971, pp. 9, 20).

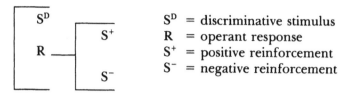

S^D = discriminative stimulus
R = operant response
S^+ = positive reinforcement
S^- = negative reinforcement

For analytical purposes (and in hypothetical experiments), we divide the actual contingency into two separate contingencies of reinforcement, as follows:

$$\begin{array}{|l} S^D \\ \\ R \;\rightarrow\; S^+ \end{array} \qquad \text{and} \qquad \begin{array}{|l} S^D \\ \\ R \;\rightarrow\; S^- \end{array}$$

In the hypothetical contingency on the left, the reinforcement is exclusively positive; and the positive consequences strengthen approach behavior. In the hypothetical contingency on the right, the reinforcement for the same operant response is exclusively aversive; and the aversive consequence strengthens escape behavior. To meet the second requirement, we repeat the above experiments for each possible size of S^+ and size of S^-.

This division for analytical purposes is, of course, artificial in terms of human buy contingencies, but it is nevertheless instructive to posit a set of hypothetical experiments structured along these lines. By such experiments, we could, in principle, determine the relation between the strength of approach (escape) behavior and the size of positive (aversive) reinforcement, and do so without the complication of simultaneously conflicting consequences.[10] Based on our earlier discussion of the determinants of response strength (pp. 27–28), we know that, for an individual with a given prior history of conditioning and under a given level of deprivation, the operant response strength would be positively related to the quantity of the reinforcer upon each presentation.[11] In the absence of sufficient experimental evidence on the

---

[10] Although the notion of buy behavior that has no aversive consequences is obviously strained, the situation is not unknown—e.g., the occasional vending machine or pay phone that malfunctions and returns the coin along with the reinforcer, or a business lunch that is reimbursed by an employer. Similarly, the notion of buy behavior that has no positively reinforcing consequences is also strained but not impossible—e.g., a malfunctioning vending machine that neither delivers the product nor returns the coin, or the mail-order item that has been paid for in advance but never arrives.

[11] In this connection, cf. the statement by Miller (1971, pp. 63–64) that "increases in amount of reward increase excitatory potential as measured either by the speed of

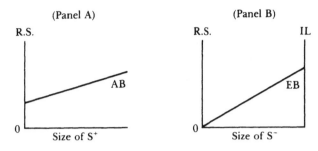

Figure 5. Response Strength with Different Quantities

matter, we will (for expository convenience) draw the AB curve as a straight line. In figure 5, panel A, the ordinate measures response strength, and the abscissa measures the size of positive reinforcement that is acquired upon each presentation of the reinforcer. Similarly, based on the earlier discussion of response strength (p. 36), we know that the strength of escape behavior would vary positively with the amount of the loss of dollar reinforcers. In the absence of sufficient experimental evidence on the matter, we will (again for expository convenience) draw the escape behavior curve as a straight line. In figure 5, panel B, the ordinate measures response strength, and the abscissa measures size of negative reinforcement upon each presentation. If borrowing is not possible, as we assume, the income limit (IL) sets a limit on the amount of the loss of dollars surrendered in payment; and this is reflected in the limit on the length of the EB curve—diagrammatically, the EB curve ends at the IL curve. Although the IL curve defines a limit for the length of the EB curve, it does not define the limit for the length of the AB curve. (This is discussed in chapter 5). Instead, it limits the point on the AB curve that can be reached (experienced) as a consequence of the operant response.

We can now proceed to determine the outcome for the case of a single commodity with different possible quantities, devising a hypothetical experiment in which an act of purchase has the usual positive and aversive consequences. For example, suppose that coffee is packaged in containers of different weight, ranging from one to five pounds, and displayed in a store on five adjoining display counters, each attended by a clerk. The contingency of reinforcement provides that the emission of the operant response in front of the clerk at the first counter is followed by the customer's receiving a single container of one-pound weight, and at the second counter, a single container of

running down a straight alley to reward or by the choice of that response receiving the larger of two rewards."

two-pound weight, etc. Only one transaction (operant response) is permitted during each trial period in this experiment. In addition, the only acceptable form of payment is by bank card rather than by currency. This is the equivalent of cash, because the card will make possible an immediate electronic transfer of funds from the buyer's to the seller's bank account. From the point of view of an operant analysis, the objects involved (currency or bank card) are alike in being inherently neutral stimuli; the topographies are essentially the same (viz., hand over a piece of "paper"); both are equally arbitrary bits of behavior; and both are virtually effortless to execute. Although the objects and topographies are almost identical, we are less likely to confuse the operant response (act of buy behavior) with its punishing consequence (loss of dollar reinforcers) if any loss of money surrendered in payment occurs after handing over a bank card rather than currency.[12]

In this hypothetical experiment, all counters are open for business, and an operant response in front of any one counter will produce both positively reinforcing and aversive consequences. We continue the earlier restriction that only one transaction is permitted during each trial period in which the experiment is run. As a result of the different consequences that follow the emission of the operant response at the different counters, a consumer could quickly learn to discriminate among the counters in this set. The critical question for an economist is: Given such an experimental situation, in front of which counter is the operant response most likely to occur? The model of buy behavior that we developed to analyze simpler cases suggests that, if all of the determinants of behavior (as described in chapter 3) are held fixed, except for the size of positive and aversive reinforcers, the outcome will depend on the relative strength of the approach behavior and escape behavior responses associated with the positively and negatively reinforcing consequences of emitting the operant response at the different counters.[13]

---

[12] The loss of dollars surrendered in payment can occur in a number of ways. In cash transactions, the loss of dollars is immediate. If payment is by check or credit card, the transfer of dollars does not occur until the check (paid to the seller or the credit-card company) is deposited in the bank and clears. In some forms of electronic funds transfers, the dollars are transferred immediately from buyer's bank account to seller's bank account. In sum, the loss of dollars surrendered in payment may or may not occur when the act of purchase is emitted, but the loss of dollar reinforcers is an inevitable consequence of the operant response.

[13] As a practical matter, it is not possible to be sure that all variables are held constant except for the size of positive and negative reinforcers. Accordingly, in this and all other hypothetical experiments described in this study, it is assumed that each experiment would be repeated a sufficient number of times (called "trials") so that the mean value of the outcome can be determined from the frequency distribution of outcomes.

In analyzing a consumer's actual buy behavior for the case of a single product with different possible quantities,[14] we simply combine the findings from the separate experiments on approach behavior and escape behavior. The relationships can be shown on a common diagram by measuring response strength along the ordinate and the consequences (size of S^+ and S^-) along the abscissa. In any given contingency of reinforcement with respect to buy behavior, a price is implicit in the relation between size of S^+ and size of S^-—diagrammatically, each point on the size-of-S^+ scale is paired with a given point on the size-of-S^- scale by the terms of the contingency of reinforcement. It follows that any "given act of purchase" refers to the behavior that is followed by an S^+ and S^- of given sizes, i.e., by some *particular* pair of size of S^+ and size of S^-. Accordingly, in order to plot on a common diagram the response strengths for approach behavior and escape behavior after any given act of purchase, we need to show only one scale explicitly and can allow the other to be implicit. In a study of contingencies of reinforcement involving commodity reinforcers, it is convenient for the explicit scale to be size of S^+ and for the implicit scale to be size of S^-.[15]

We are now in a position to interpret the buy outcome in a manner similar to that which was used in the earlier models. Thus, if the AB curve and EB curve do not intersect, the outcome is an all-or-nothing solution. If escape behavior is stronger than approach behavior at all quantity-outlay combinations, none of the product will be purchased. In the reverse case, the maximum amount would be purchased.[16] If the curves intersect, the outcome is determined by their relative gradients and (if the intersection yields an unstable outcome) by the point of entry. To illustrate, suppose that all combinations are arranged at counters that are placed along a line from the smallest to the largest quantity-outlay combinations. We can control the entry point onto the trading floor as part of the experiment or allow it to be determined by chance. In figure 6, panel A, the gradient of the AB curve is steeper than the gradient of the EB curve. Thus, the intersection at p is an

[14] The case of a product purchased in isolation is, of course, artificial, but it shows the mechanisms by which quantity and outlay are determined in a simplified buy contingency. The principles can then be utilized to explain the more realistic case of multiple products, discussed in chapter 6.

[15] This will become apparent when the effects of relative price changes are examined in chapter 7. For reasons to be explained later, however, an opposite procedure is followed in chapter 8 in connection with the analysis of contingencies of reinforcement that involve financial assets.

[16] The "maximum amount" is determined either by an income limit (as discussed in this chapter) or by a reinforcer-effectiveness limit (as discussed in the next chapter).

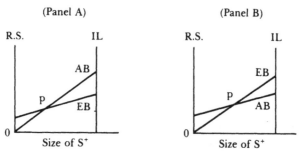

Figure 6. Case of One Commodity with Different Quantities

unstable outcome—at any outlay-quantity combination to the left of p, none of the product would be purchased; and, to the right of p, a maximum amount would be purchased. By contrast, the AB gradient is less than the EB gradient in panel B, and p is a stable quantity-outlay outcome.

It is clear from the foregoing that the relative gradients could be critical in predicting behavioral outcomes. When a similar question arose in the earlier hypothetical cases, I adopted the findings of the animal experiments with respect to relative gradients. However, those cases were much closer to the animal experiments, because (unlike the present case) they involved a fixed quantity of a positive reinforcer and the loss of a fixed number of dollars surrendered in payment. Although the general findings of the animal experiments are also applicable in this case, there does not exist (to my knowledge) any experimental evidence to guide us on the matter of relative gradients where such contingencies are involved. Under the circumstances, I have adopted as a working hypothesis the assumption that the EB curve typically has a steeper gradient than the AB curve (when both are plotted on a common quantity-outlay abscissa). In chapter 7, however, I have also examined some implications of the reverse assumption.

In the absence of experimental guidelines about relative gradients, I have for simplicity considered only linear AB and EB curves; and, to emphasize the difference in relative gradients, I have drawn the AB curve to intercept the Y-axis and the EB curve to go through the origin. Alternatively, I could have adopted the convention of showing both curves with a Y-axis intercept, while continuing to draw the EB curve with a steeper slope—e.g., as shown in figure 7, panels A, B, and C; but this would not affect the basic analysis of the buy behavior outcome. One interesting possibility is that the response strength of escape behavior may be close to, or equal to, zero up to some positive level of dollars surrendered, except perhaps at very low levels of

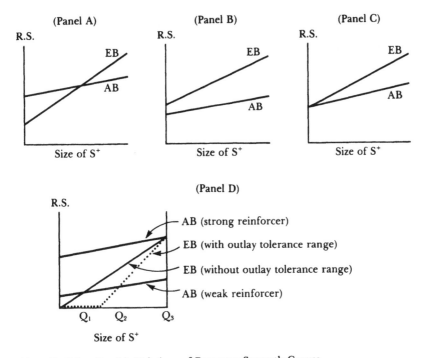

Figure 7. Other Possible Relations of Response Strength Curves

income.[17] If such an "outlay-tolerance level"[18] exists, as seems likely from casual observation, the point at which the EB curve deviates from the abscissa axis doubtless varies positively with the level of income.[19] The consumption of all goods would be greater with an outlay-tolerance level than without one, but the relatively greatest impact would be on the consumption of commodities with weak AB curves. In panel D, one EB curve is drawn with an outlay-tolerance level and another curve without it. In the latter curve, consumption of

[17] The flat part of the EB curve violates our working hypothesis that the slope of the EB curve is greater than the slope of the AB curve.

[18] The term "outlay-tolerance level" is borrowed by analogy with the concept of a shock-tolerance level. In experiments with laboratory animals in which the aversive stimulus is electric shock, experimenters have observed a response that holds the intensity of the aversive stimuli within a small range of (usually low) intensities (Millenson and Leslie, 1979, p. 272). This is known as the shock-tolerance level.

[19] In electric shock experiments with laboratory animals, the shock-tolerance level varies with the administration of certain analgesics and anesthetics. Consumer income plays an analogous role to the pharmacological agents in moderating the response strength of escape behavior and, therefore, also its intercept with the abscissa.

the weak reinforcer would come to a halt at Q_1, whereas it would not come to a halt until Q_2 when the EB curve has an outlay-tolerance range; the quantity of the strong reinforcer would remain unchanged at Q_3 under either EB curve.

Summary of major independent variables. In this chapter, the hypothetical experiments for the buy behavior models have been limited to simple (and, to that extent, also artificial) contingencies in order to relate them as closely as possible to the findings of the animal experiments on conflict cited earlier. As shown later (in chapter 6), however, the basic features that explain the buy behavior outcome in these simpler models can also explain the outcome in more realistic models. These models draw upon the findings from an experimental analysis of behavior to explain the buy outcome by the interplay of a rather restricted set of operational variables. The major independent variables appear to be: (1) the level of the reinforcer-effectiveness operation—the level of deprivation with respect to primary positive reinforcers and also for any secondary reinforcers that are based on these primary reinforcers, the intensity of aversive stimulation in case of escape goods, and the intensity of the aversive stimulus associated with the loss of dollars surrendered in payment (as measured by the size of the outlay); (2) the incentive functions (quantity and quality of the reinforcers); (3) the schedule of reinforcement; (4) the individual's past history of experience with the product, including the past history of association of secondary reinforcers with the primary reinforcers on which they are based; and (5) the level of income (and/or wealth), both as a constraint on the objective opportunity set and also in modifying the intensity of the aversive consequences of any given loss of dollars surrendered in payment. These variables jointly determine the strength of approach behavior and escape behavior and, therefore, of the resultant buy outcome.

A change in any of these independent variables will, of course, lead to changes in the pattern of consumer buy behavior. Hence, it is pertinent to note that at least some of these independent variables are likely to undergo change in the course of everyday living. This is particularly conspicuous in the case of food deprivation, which exhibits a lawful periodicity within a twenty-four hour period. Indeed, the primacy that has traditionally been accorded to food in the "hierarchy of human needs" is not unrelated to the fact that the reinforcement value of food deprivation fluctuates from extremely low strength to extremely high strength within an unusually short cycle period. If human beings (like certain tortoises) could survive for a year without food or water,[20] food and water would obviously continue to be essential for life; but they might have a different ranking in the hierarchy of human needs, based on the day-to-day activities of individuals. In an experimental analysis of human behavior, the concept of a need (and therefore also of a hierarchy of needs or preference ranking) is bypassed in favor of an analysis of the effects of changes in such operational variables as deprivation. Moreover, in such an approach, there is no point in trying to decide whether deprivation with respect to one particular reinforcer ranks higher in some presumed "internal index of deprivation rankings" than deprivation with respect to some other reinforcer. From the viewpoint of an experimental analysis of behavior, such a question is meaningless, because it is nonoperational. How can the need for, say, food be ranked with the need for, say, fresh air? At any moment of time, the ranking for an individual in a condition of deprivation with respect to both would obviously depend on, among other things, the relative levels of deprivation with respect to each reinforcer—and the hierarchy of needs must change as the relative levels of deprivation change.[21]

[20] In a story about the Galapagos islands, *Time* magazine (June 26, 1978) referred to tortoises "which often weigh more than 500 lbs. and live for a century or more, [and] can survive for a year without food or water."

[21] Cf. the criticism by Millenson and Leslie (1979, pp. 400–401) of the experiments by Warden (1931) that tried to compare objectively the *maximum* strengths of the various primary reinforcers.

CHAPTER FIVE

Reinforcer-Effectiveness Limits

There are two important constraints on the buy outcome—income limits and reinforcer-effectiveness limits. Chapter 4 discussed the implications of income limitations; the present chapter examines reinforcer-effectiveness limits, a term that will be used to describe the point at which any given commodity ceases to be a reinforcer. This limit depends on consumption rather than on buy behavior as such. Since we assume that buy behavior is part of a chain that leads to consumption of the purchased commodity, we will often refer to the reinforcer-effectiveness limit in relation to buy behavior.

In economic analysis, the allocation of a consumer's income is the outcome of a process in which the consumer maximizes utility subject to an income constraint. In the conventional view, an individual has needs and wants, and it is assumed that at least the latter extend beyond the income constraint for the overwhelming majority of individuals. For example, in indifference curve analysis it is customary (at least implicitly) to make the nonsatiety assumption that "the consumer is not oversupplied with either commodity, i.e., he prefers to have more of C and/or Z" (Baumol, 1977, p. 197). Accordingly, any limits on consumption due to satiation are typically ignored in analyzing the allocation of a consumer's income. By contrast, as shown below, an operant approach suggests that most consumers in countries like the

United States regularly reach the reinforcer-effectiveness limits of numerous commodities in the ordinary course of consuming a wide range of commodities.

The chapter will be divided into two main parts. The first will examine the reinforcer-effectiveness limits for individual goods considered separately. The second will examine those limits for two or more goods considered jointly. It should be noted in this connection that the reinforcer-effectiveness limit is based on a particular pattern of response (viz., the point at which the rate of response falls near to or reaches zero) under *given* conditions of all the relevant parameters. The parameters include (inter alia) the level of the reinforcer-effectiveness operation and the individual's prior history of conditioning. Under the former, the quantity of all other goods consumed by the individual is given as part of the experiment in which the reinforcer-effectiveness operation is deprivation with respect to some particular commodity. Thus the level of deprivation for any one good is measured in the context of the existing level of consumption of other goods. Under the latter, the composition and quality of all other goods consumed by the individual are also held constant. The products that are included under the stipulation of a given prior history of conditioning are those that have been experienced, proved to be reinforcing, and, as a consequence, have been incorporated as part of the individual's life style. These are the only commodities that are included in analyzing reinforcer-effectiveness limits for a particular individual. The reason for restricting the choice set in this way is that the reinforcer-effectiveness operation (e.g., deprivation) will not direct the consumer to a given reinforcer unless the behavior for getting to that reinforcer already exists, i.e., unless the reinforcer has already been incorporated into his life style. One consequence of incorporating this condition in the hypothetical experiments is that we do not ask what other products the individual might ("like" to) buy if he had experienced them. Our concern is solely with those goods that he has actually experienced, been reinforced by, and consumes regularly as part of his life style.

Reinforcer-effectiveness Limits for Goods Considered Separately

Reinforcer-effectiveness limits for primary goods. A number of different operations can affect the reinforcing value of particular primary goods (see chapter 2), but the most important, especially for human consumers, is deprivation. As noted earlier, primary commodities are biologically based reinforcers whose effectiveness depends upon deprivation. Deprivation and satiation are parts of the same reinforcer-altering operation. In deprivation, a reinforcer is withheld; in satiation, a reinforcer is presented. Both operations lead to a change in the strength of the operant response. In laboratory experiments to determine satiation limits in animals, the experimenter begins with (takes as given) a particular operant behavior that has been reinforced under appropriate conditions of deprivation of a particular reinforcer. The reinforcer is presented on a crf schedule, and the animal's behavior is recorded. In the typical case, the operant response is emitted at a fairly constant rate and then ceases rather abruptly. The point at which it drops to, or close to, the zero level is the point of satiation.[1] The sharp reduction or cessation of the rate of response thus identifies the fact that the satiation point has been reached; and, since the experiment is on a crf schedule, the total quantity consumed during the experiment is the amount required to reach satiation under a given level of deprivation.[2] Since the commodity (temporarily) loses its capacity to reinforce when satiation is reached, the satiation point is one example of a reinforcer-effectiveness limit.[3]

The satiation paradigm is, of course, also applicable to human consumers; and the satiation point is the reinforcer-effectiveness limit (REL) for a commodity that is controlled by deprivation. Diagrammatically, the REL curve sets a limit on the length of the AB curve (figure 8), i.e., on the maximum size of positive reinforcement that could be reinforcing in the operant conditioning paradigm. Although the REL curve does not set a limit on the length of the EB curve, it does limit the loss of dollar reinforcers that can be experienced, i.e., it limits the point on the EB curve that can be reached (experienced) as a consequence of the operant response.

In the buy behavior model that is being developed in this study, the reinforcer-effectiveness limit is an independent constraint on the emission of the operant (buy) response. In particular, it is important, especially from an economics point of view, that this limit should be

[1] In a condition of complete satiation (i.e., for all reinforcers), the animal may do nothing; it often goes to sleep (Millenson, 1967, pp. 370–72).

[2] "Satiation curves tend to differ principally in their point of termination rather than in their slopes" (Millenson and Leslie, 1979, p. 396)—and point of termination depends on level of deprivation.

[3] The operant view of satiation is different from the traditional economic view of satiation. In the latter, the existence of satiation implies that additional quantities of the commodity beyond the satiation point make it a "bad." From the operant view, however, this transformation is not possible. A "good" (i.e., positive reinforcer) can cease to be a reinforcer—in the language of economics, it can become a "neuter"; but it cannot become a "bad" (i.e., an aversive stimulus) unless we presume a malevolent force that could compel consumption beyond the point of satiation, a notion that clearly has no meaning in normal economic activity.

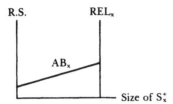

Figure 8. Reinforcer-effectiveness Limit

independent of price and income. However, it is apparent from the satiation experiments described above that price and income are *inescapably* implicit in the satiation paradigm. A price is involved because, as noted earlier (p. 55), price is a relationship between the positively reinforcing and the aversive consequences of an operant response. In the animal experiments on satiation, price is the relationship between the size (amount) of the positive reinforcer and the size of the loss of energy surrendered in payment.[4] In the hypothetical satiation experiments with human consumers, price is the relationship between the size of the positive reinforcer and the size of the loss of dollars surrendered in payment. An income level is also implicit in the satiation paradigm. In both the animal experiments and the hypothetical experiments with human subjects, size of income sets a limit on the intensity of the aversive consequences that can be experienced; and it indirectly limits the point on the AB curve that can be reached as a consequence of the operant response. In the animal experiments, the income level is measured by the animal's strength or energy reserve; and, in the case of human consumers, by the individual's supply of dollars. The importance of the price and income variables can be minimized, but (at least in principle) they cannot be eliminated.[5] It follows that, in principle, the satiation (or other reinforcer-effectiveness) limit for any commodity must be defined separately for each combination of prices (contingencies of reinforcement) and income. In practice, however, we can ignore this inherent relationship

[4] The intensity of the aversive consequence of the operant response is measured by the size of the loss of energy surrendered in payment. That the loss of energy is an aversive consequence can be inferred from the Law of Least Effort, which states that when there are two or more alternate chains to a given reinforcer, the one with the least work will show the greater strengthening. Alternatively, if there are two reinforced zones, the one with the lesser work requirement will show the greater strengthening (see Millenson, 1967, pp. 168, 428). Thus it can be inferred from this law that escape (or avoidance) behavior is reinforced by the aversive consequence of loss of energy after expending effort.

[5] In principle, it's not possible to eliminate these variables even by making the reinforcer free (e.g., ad lib feeding), because there is an inescapable level of effort (work)

for purposes of our hypothetical experiments by reducing the price to a nominal level, ie., the goods in our hypothetical experiments to determine reinforcer-effectiveness limits are essentially free in a monetary sense. In this way, we are able to derive reinforcer-effectiveness limits that, for all practical purposes, are independent of prices and incomes.

On the basis of the experiments with animal subjects (but also from casual observation of human consumers), it is clear that any primary good can temporarily cease to be a reinforcer under conditions of excessive satiation. The experimentally demonstrable fact of satiation means that there is an upper bound to the amount of a reinforcer that an individual will consume under given conditions of deprivation with respect to that particular primary positive reinforcer. This upper bound (satiation limit)[6] exists for all primary reinforcers.[7] For primary reinforcers like food and water, the reinforcer-effectiveness limits can be determined fairly easily under laboratory conditions using animal subjects; and they could also be determined for human subjects by appropriately designed experiments.[8] Moreover, it should also be possible in principle, even if very difficult in practice in some cases, to determine the satiation limits for *any* primary reinforcer, given the level of deprivation for that reinforcer. In this sense, and to this extent, the satiation limit of primary commodities (i.e., biologically based reinforcers) is determinate.

---

or time involved in consuming a reinforcer. That this effort may be nonnegligible is evident in the market place, where a consumer can buy foods in different degrees of preparation so that the effort (including time) involved in consumption can be significantly varied. In this connection, the "new theory of consumption" recognizes that "often, if not always, the market commodity does not generate its satisfying attributes unaided. Rather, the consumer generally elicits satisfaction from commodities by combining his own time and effort with the market goods themselves" (Hirshleifer, 1980, p. 171).

[6] The satiation limit in this study is different from the bliss point of traditional economics. The latter is a nonoperational notion of a most preferred combination of goods. By contrast, the satiation limit is an operational concept that can be controlled under experimental conditions.

[7] A capacity to be satiated has obvious evolutionary survival value. As Miller (1971, p. 332) puts it, "individuals that do not eventually become satiated on a given form of pleasure may starve to death while enjoying the thrill of tickling themselves."

[8] In this study, reinforcement and satiation are accepted as experimentally demonstrable facts, and we do not pursue the question of why commodities have these effects. For example, we do not suggest that, say, food satiation is related to needs or wants or that satiation is reached when a person is "full" or "satisfied," but rather that, for a given level of deprivation, an individual will in fact stop eating at some point. We do not know

Food items are a major example of primary positive reinforcers that are also economic commodities. The reinforcer-effectiveness limits for very expensive primary commodities (e.g., rare vintage wines) are reached presumably only by the affluent. By contrast, as casual observation can confirm, the satiation limits of many other food items lie well within the income boundaries of large numbers of nonwealthy people in affluent countries like the United States. For economic analysis, it is pertinent that satiation routinely constrains the purchase (and consumption) of numerous such primary goods by millions of consumers, including those who are not wealthy. It is also pertinent that, in such countries, satiation limits are routinely reached with respect to other primary reinforcers, including those that are economic commodities under some circumstances but not at other times (e.g., warmth).

As a final comment on this discussion of the reinforcer-effectiveness limits for primary commodities, satiation cannot occur unless the primary commodity is consumed (i.e., used). Ownership per se of a primary commodity cannot reduce the deprivation that makes the commodity a primary reinforcer. However, since there is normally no impediment to the consumption of owned commodities, the existence and size of inventories must be included in determining the given level of deprivation and, therefore, also in determining the individual's satiation limit for a commodity. Finally, the reinforcer-effectiveness limit for a given primary commodity may exceed the limit that would exist for the commodity in its role as a primary reinforcer if the commodity is also reinforcing as an acquired reinforcer.

Reinforcer-effectiveness limits for secondary commodities. An organism (consumer) is always located somewhere along the continuum between deprivation and satiation with respect to any of the primary reinforcers (food, liquid, sex, novelty, etc.).[9] To an economist, the concepts of deprivation and satiation are applicable to all consumer goods and services, i.e., to those commodities that, in this study, are called secondary goods as well as those that are called primary goods.

---

whether he is full or satisfied at that point—we know only that he has stopped eating. In an operational sense, the individual's presumed mental state when he stops eating is a redundant variable.

[9] Skinner (1953, p. 141) has noted that "the probability of drinking becomes very high under severe water deprivation and very low under excessive satiation. It is reasonable to assume that the probability always lies somewhere between these two extremes and that if the deprivation is changed, it simply moves toward one or the other."

However, in an operant approach, a secondary commodity is based (directly or indirectly) on a primary reinforcer; hence, it is not possible to have an independent operation of deprivation for a secondary commodity. By definition, deprivation is possible only with respect to the primary reinforcer upon which the secondary commodity is based. It also follows from our definition of a secondary good that consumption of a secondary reinforcer per se can not reduce the deprivation appropriate to the primary reinforcer on which it is ultimately based. A secondary good can reinforce the behavior of a hungry person, but it obviously cannot reduce his level of food deprivation, regardless of how much of the secondary good is made available to him. Does this mean that a reinforcer-effectiveness limit for secondary commodities does not exist?

We can find a clue to the answer to this question by looking again at what happens in the case of satiation for primary reinforcers. The existence of satiation is evidenced by the fact that the operant behavior upon which the reinforcer is contingent falls to zero or near-zero levels, i.e., the primary commodity ceases to be a reinforcer. We can use a similar criterion to determine the functional equivalent of a satiation limit for secondary commodities, viz., when the operant behavior upon which the secondary commodity is contingent falls to zero or near-zero levels, i.e., when it, too, ceases to be a reinforcer. This is, in turn, related to the durability and potency of a conditioned reinforcer. The durability of a conditioned reinforcer is measured by the "length of time or number of responses a conditioned reinforcer will continue to reinforce if the reinforcer on which it is based is discontinued"; the potency of a conditioned reinforcer is "measured in terms of the rate of responding which it's able to maintain" (Reynolds, 1975, p. 63). Since the factors that maintain the potency of a stimulus also prolong its durability, these two characteristics can be examined jointly for my purposes. As shown in earlier discussion (p. 29), the potency of an acquired reinforcer depends on a number of factors, but especially on the deprivation of the primary reinforcer on which it is based. If the consumer reaches a condition of satiation on the primary reinforcer, the rate of responding which is contingent on the secondary commodity (assuming it is not a generalized reinforcer) will of necessity fall towards the zero level. Thus the satiation limit on the primary reinforcer imposes a functional equivalent of a satiation limit on the secondary commodity as well. We will use the term "derived satiation limit"[10] to describe the maximum quantity of a secondary

---

[10] The word "derived" suggests that the limit does not inhere in the secondary commodity but is derived from the primary reinforcer.

commodity that can be consumed before it ceases to reinforce because satiation has been reached in respect to the primary reinforcer on which it is (directly or indirectly) based.

The potency (and also durability) of an acquired reinforcer is vulnerable by virtue of its dependence on the primary reinforcer in another important way, viz., it must be renewed by association with the primary reinforcer. If this renewal fails to occur, at least occasionally, a process of extinction will set in; and the end product of an extinction process is that the secondary commodity ceases to be a reinforcer.[11] We will use the term "extinction limit" to describe the maximum quantity of a secondary commodity that would be consumed under extinction conditions, i.e., until the response rate returns to the operant level (which, for all practical purposes, is the near-zero level at which the commodity ceases to be a reinforcer). The extinction limit, like the derived satiation limit, is defined for a given level of deprivation.

The reinforcer-effectiveness limits for secondary commodities will be different for different kinds of secondary reinforcers. In the case of specialized secondary commodities that are based on a functional pairing of stimuli and lead to a particular primary reinforcer, the derived satiation limit is determined by the functional relation that the secondary reinforcer bears to the primary reinforcer; and that determines the amount of the secondary commodity that is necessary for the individual to attain the satiation level with respect to the primary reinforcer. The derived satiation limit for specialized functional secondary commodities that lead to primary reinforcers (i.e., "direct" reinforcers) is determined by the "technological relation" between the secondary reinforcer and the primary reinforcer on which it is based, i.e., on the fact that the secondary reinforcer is incorporated into a chain that leads to the primary positive reinforcer.[12] When the individ-

[11] There is a difference between the rate of operant behavior under satiation and under extinction. In the former, the rate of operant behavior (that produces the reinforcer on crf contingencies) drops to a near-zero level; under the latter, the rate also declines but to the operant level (cf. Millenson, 1967, pp. 370–72). This distinction can be ignored for our purposes, because the critical result is the same in both cases, viz., the reinforcer ceases to reinforce.

[12] It will be recalled from chapter 2 that a functional secondary reinforcer that leads to a primary reinforcer is an acquired reinforcer that is related to the primary reinforcer by a chain of behavior in which the contingencies are permuted (either by nature or by artifical means) in such a manner that there is a primary reinforcer at the end of the chain of behavior. In some experiments with rats, the contingency of reinforcement requires the subject to pick up a marble, carry it a short distance, and drop it into a hole. Since the behavior with the marble is a necessary condition to get food, the marble becomes a functional secondary good—even though the behavior with the marble "causes" food to appear only in terms of the "artificial" conditions of the experiment.

ual reaches the satiation level of the primary reinforcer, the specialized functional secondary commodity as such also ceases to be a reinforcer, if only temporarily. Insofar as the satiation limit for the primary reinforcer is (at least in principle) determinate, the derived satiation quantity for a direct specialized functional secondary commodity can be determined from the satiation quantity of the primary reinforcer by taking account of the technological relation that relates them in the chain of behavior. In this sense, and to this extent, the derived satiation quantity for such commodities is determinate. Moreover, to the extent that large numbers of individuals regularly reach the satiation point for many primary reinforcers within their present income levels, it follows that they also reach the derived satiation limits for the secondary commodities that are functionally related to those primary reinforcers.

The case of secondary commodities that are generalized (conditioned) reinforcers is similar to the analysis of specialized secondary commodities. In principle, the derived satiation limit for a secondary commodity that is based on a functional pairing with more than one primary reinforcer could be calculated as the sum of the amounts required to reach satiation with respect to each primary reinforcer on which it is based. Thus, a derived satiation limit for direct functional generalized reinforcers is determinate in principle. Moreover, since satiation is regularly attained with respect to many primary reinforcers by numerous individuals at their present income levels (as explained earlier), the derived satiation limits for direct functional generalized secondary goods based on those particular primary goods can to that extent also be attained with present income constraints by a large number of consumers in our affluent society. It does not follow, of course, that the combined derived satiation limit (i.e., for all of the relevant primary reinforcers involved) will necessarily be reached simultaneously. Aside from any income constraints, "if a conditioned reinforcer has been paired with reinforcers appropriate to many conditions, at least one appropriate state of deprivation is more likely to prevail upon a later occasion" (Skinner, 1953, p. 77). In practice, therefore, the derived satiation limits (which depend upon reaching satiation for all of the relevant primary goods) are also not likely to be reached simultaneously.

In the case of a specialized secondary commodity that is based on a nonfunctional pairing with a primary reinforcer, the absence of a technological relation between the secondary commodity and the primary reinforcer means that there is no inherent relation between the satiation limit of the primary reinforcer and the consumption of the secondary reinforcer.[13] To this extent, the derived satiation limit for such commodities is indeterminate. As long as the individual is in a state of deprivation with respect to the primary reinforcer, the amount of the secondary reinforcer that might be consumed will depend on the chance occurrence of the appropriate discriminative stimulus for that particular secondary reinforcer. This inherent indeterminacy about the reinforcer-effectiveness limit of a nonfunctional secondary commodity is exacerbated by the fact that its renewal as a secondary commodity depends on an unknown schedule of pairing with the primary reinforcer—and the schedule of reinforcement is a powerful determinant of the strength of a secondary reinforcer. This uncertainty does not exist for a functional secondary commodity, because it is likely to be renewed on a crf schedule as part of a chain that leads to the primary reinforcer. By contrast, the strength of the nonfunctional secondary commodity could either veer towards extinction or towards strength, depending on the reinforcement schedule that chance presents.[14] If the secondary commodity is not renewed by association with the primary reinforcer, a reinforcer effectiveness limit will be reached by extinction. Since the schedule of renewal (or nonrenewal) depends on chance, it is impossible even in principle to determine at what point an extinction limit might come into effect. Hence, the extinction limit for a given secondary commodity that is based on a nonfunctional pairing is also indeterminate. Finally, this indeterminacy about the reinforcer-effectiveness limit makes it impossible to speculate about whether, or to what extent, income is a constraint in preventing large numbers of consumers from reaching an extinction limit for any given specialized nonfunctional secondary commodity.

A commodity can also become a generalized reinforcer when it is based on a nonfunctional pairing with more than one primary and/or conditioned reinforcer. As in the case of the specialized nonfunctional secondary good, the absence of a technological relation between the secondary commodity and the underlying primary reinforcer on which it is based means that the reinforcer-effectiveness limit for such commodities is indeterminate. Moreover, since the generalized secondary commodity is based on multiple primary reinforcers, there are likely to be a large number of positive discriminative stimuli to set the

[13] This is also true for indirect specialized secondary goods, i.e., those based on a functional pairing leading to a secondary reinforcer.

[14] It will be recalled that a schedule of intermittent reinforcement can build a secondary reinforcer of great strength.

stage for the emission of buy behavior with respect to that secondary commodity. This further increases the indeterminacy about the limit, because the presentation of the discriminative stimuli depends on chance, and hence the schedule of reinforcement that affects the potency and durability of the secondary reinforcer is also a matter of chance. In short, the reinforcer-effectiveness limit for nonfunctional generalized commodities is indeterminate both in principle and in fact. Since the limit is indeterminate, it is not possible to state whether large numbers of consumers are prevented by their present income levels from reaching an extinction limit for nonfunctional secondary commodiites. It is probably a mixed picture—income is probably a prior constraint in some cases but not in other cases.

Reinforcer-effectiveness limits for escape/avoidance commodities. Since escape/avoidance commodities are secondary reinforcers, they are not susceptible as such either to independent deprivation or to satiation. In addition, satiation is not a relevant concept for escape/avoidance commodities, because their reinforcing capacity depends on their ability to mitigate an aversive stimulus and not on any underlying deprivation. As shown earlier (p. 30), in the case of escape/avoidance commodities, the reinforcement-establishing operation that parallels deprivation is a change in the intensity of a negative reinforcer. The reinforcer-effectiveness limit for escape/avoidance commodities (i.e., the point where they cease to reinforce) can be reached in either of two ways: (1) when the consumption of the escape/avoidance commodity has reduced the level of aversive stimulation to zero or to (a point analogous to) the shock-tolerance level,[15] or (2) when the level of aversive stimulation exceeds the shock-tolerance level, but the escape/avoidance commodity ceases to reinforce due to extinction. The limit due to the first reason will be called the tolerance limit; the limit due to the second reason will be called the extinction limit.

The reinforcer-effectiveness limits are different for different kinds of escape/avoidance commodities. In the case of specialized escape/avoidance commodities that are based on a functional pairing of stimuli leading to escape from a particular primary negative reinforcer, a tolerance limit will be determined by the functional relation between the escape/avoidance commodity and the primary negative reinforcer, i.e., by the amount of the commodity that is (physically) necessary to reach a tolerance level with respect to the aversive stimulus. In principle, the tolerance limit is determinate for such functional commodities, given the level of aversive stimulation. The ability of consumers

---

[15] Cf. my earlier discussion of this concept (p. 57).

to reach the tolerance limit within existing income levels depends in part on the kind and intensity of aversive stimulation. It is a common observation that some functional escape/avoidance commodities (e.g., aspirin, raincoats, umbrellas, etc.) are regularly purchased to the tolerance limit by large numbers of consumers within their present income levels; and it is just as apparent that the purchase of other functional escape/avoidance commodities (e.g., air conditioning) is constrained by income limitations applicable to large numbers of people even in an affluent society.

An escape/avoidance commodity is generalized when it is paired with more than one kind of aversive stimulation. The analysis of tolerance limits for generalized escape/avoidance commodities is similar to the case of specialized escape/avoidance commodities. In the case of a generalized escape/avoidance commodity based on a functional pairing with more than one kind of aversive stimulation, the tolerance limit is the sum of the tolerance limits for each kind of aversive stimulation. As in the case of a specialized functional escape/avoidance commodity, the reinforcer-effectiveness limit for a generalized functional escape/avoidance commodity is determinate in principle. For any given constellation of aversive stimulus intensities, it depends on the role of the escape/avoidance commodity in the chain that leads to termination or reduction of the aversive stimuli. It seems likely that the tolerance limit for some generalized functional commodities is well within the income limits of many individuals, but just as obvious that only the wealthy have enough income to reach those limits in the case of other generalized functional escape/avoidance commodities.

When specialized escape/avoidance commodities are based on a nonfunctional pairing with a primary (or conditioned) negative reinforcer, a technological relation does not exist between the escape/avoidance commodity and the primary negative reinforcer. Hence, there is no inherent relation between consumption of the escape/avoidance commodity and attainment of the tolerance limit of the primary (or conditioned) negative reinforcer. For example, a placebo pill that is taken for relief from, say, allergy symptoms is nonfunctional (by definition); and no amount of consumption of the placebo can relieve the allergy symptoms.[16] The extinction limit is indeterminate for specialized nonfunctional escape/avoidance commodities because, like other nonfunctional commodities, their conditioning as reinforcers is due to adventitious reinforcement con-

---

[16] For this discussion, I ignore the evidence that placebos are sometimes effective.

tingencies.[17] Hence, there is no way to predict the schedule on which taking the placebo will happen to pair the placebo with symptomatic relief, i.e., whether relief will follow for other reasons when the placebo happens to be taken. The result is that we cannot predict whether the placebo will reach an extinction limit before the aversive stimulus is terminated for independent reasons. In practice, there is also a lot of uncertainty about the number of occasions on which the aversive stimulus will be present and at what intensity. Given this indeterminacy and uncertainty, it is impossible both in principle and in practice to state whether the extinction limit for nonfunctional specific escape/avoidance commodities is regularly reached by large numbers of people before income constraints are reached. A good guess is that both situations are likely to be encountered by different people with respect to different nonfunctional escape/avoidance commodities.

In the case of a nonfunctional generalized escape/avoidance commodity, the extinction limit is indeterminate for reasons already explained in connection with the specialized nonfunctional escape/avoidance commodities. In this case, there is also more uncertainty about whether the income constraint is binding for a particular commodity. Since more sources of aversive stimuli are involved, there is more uncertainty about the number and intensity of the negative discriminative stimuli that will be encountered in any given time period. Because of the indeterminacy and uncertainty, we cannot say whether the income constraint is likely to be binding in general. Again, a good guess is that the situation is mixed for different individuals with respect to different nonfunctional generalized escape/avoidance commodities.

This discussion of reinforcer-effectiveness limits for different kinds of commodities—primary, secondary, and escape/avoidance commodities—leads to a significantly different view about such limits than is found in traditional economics. In principle, the possibility of satiation is recognized in standard economic analysis; in practice, the possibility is ignored.[18] As Galbraith (1958, p. 143) has noted, "The

---

[17] The consumption of such commodities illustrates "superstitious behavior," viz., behavior that is conditioned when there is only an accidental connection between the response and appearance of a reinforcer (Skinner, 1953, p. 85). "Accidental" here refers to a connection that is not permanent.

[18] Walsh (1970, p. 139) has remarked that "not only introductory texts but also intermediate and advanced ones still habitually present consumption theory within the straitjacket of the Hicks-Allen effective region, so that no recognition of satiation appears anywhere in the picture." In formal analysis, the possibility of satiation is typically excluded under an axiom of nonsatiation. In Debreu's "Insatiability Assumption on Preferences," satiation is possible with respect to individual commodities, but not with respect to all commodities (Debreu, 1959, p. 55).

concept of satiation has very little standing in economics." The reason, of course, is the widely accepted presumption about the apparent "insatiability of human wants." In this view, income limits dominate satiation limits for most consumers, except perhaps for the super-rich. More recently, this traditional view has begun to be modified on the grounds that a series of scientific revolutions is making a reality of the possibility of being "physically in a position to pass the optimal region for significantly many things" (Walsh, 1970, pp. 56–57). In an operant view, by contrast, the same level of scientific revolutions would not be required. In affluent countries, it is a frequent and common occurrence for consumers to reach their reinforcer-effectiveness limits for a wide range of commodities before reaching their income limits. Accordingly, the constraints imposed by reinforcer-effectiveness limits can be an important determinant of the potential effective demand for a host of individual commodities. In the next chapter, the reinforcer-effectiveness limits will be formally incorporated into our model of buy behavior.

Reinforcer-effectiveness Limits for Two or More Commodities Considered Jointly

Interdependent and independent limits. The preceding section of this chapter examined the reinforcer-effectiveness limits for different categories of consumer goods and services when only one commodity was allowed to vary in each hypothetical experiment, i.e, when each commodity was considered separately. This section examines those limits under hypothetical experimental conditions for cases in which two commodities are allowed to vary. These experiments will test whether the limit for a particular commodity is different when it is the only commodity and when it is available along with some other commodity. Specifically, for a given level and kind of reinforcer-establishing operation, will the reinforcer-effectiveness limit for commodity X be affected, and if so by how much, by the quantity of commodity Y that the individual consumes? In order to determine whether the limits for X and Y when considered jointly are the same or different than when they are considered separately, we might conduct (hypothetical) experiments and classify all pairs of commodities according to the results obtained.[19] In these experiments, we would first put into effect a given reinforcer-effectiveness operation appropriate to the commodity in

---

[19] Here (and elsewhere in this study) we follow the convention employed in economics according to which "a choice involves a comparison between two or more objects which we can always consider as being taken two at a time, i.e, in binary form" (Shone, 1975, p. 19).

question (e.g., a given level of deprivation in the case of food) and then find the reinforcer-effectiveness limit—the satiation quantity in this example[20]—for each commodity separately in different experiments and under a crf schedule. Up to this point, we have just repeated for each commodity separately the satiation experiments of the preceding section when only one commodity was available. We now run the experiment again, but allow the subjects access (on a crf schedule) to both commodities simultaneously.[21]

Interdependent RELs. One possible outcome of this experiment is that the subject would consume all of Y and none of X. Since the satiation quantity of X when both commodities are available without any restriction on the total quantities that can be consumed on a crf schedule is less than the satiation quantity for X when X is considered separately, Y and X are shown to have interdependent reinforcer-effectiveness limits. In successive experiments, we could discover the pattern of this interdependent relationship at different levels of the reinforcers by progressively reducing the total quantity of Y available to be consumed on a crf schedule below the separate REL_y while continuing to make X available without restriction on a crf schedule. We would then observe the combined maximum quantities that are jointly consumed under these constrained circumstances. The locus of the combined maximum quantities for different given restrictions on the total quantity of Y is $REL_{x,y}$ (figure 9), the joint limit for X and Y together (or, in this case, the joint satiation curve). An $REL_{x,y}$ curve that is convex to the origin (panel A) would indicate strong interdependence of the reinforcer-effectiveness limits—the combined limits when both products are consumed together are less than a linear combination of the limits for each commodity when consumed separately. At the other extreme, an $REL_{x,y}$ curve that is concave to the origin (panel C) depicts the case of weak interdependence of the reinforcer-effectiveness limits—at the limit, the concave curve approaches the reinforcer-effectiveness limit curves for independent commodities (i.e., the satiation quantities for each considered separately). A linear curve (panel B) shows the case of intermediate interdependence of the reinforcer-effectiveness limits.

In the preceding examples of interdependent limits, the reinforcer-

---

[20] The satiation paradigm is employed for convenience. The same kind of hypothetical experiments could be run, mutatis mutandis, using aversive stimulation rather than deprivation as the reinforcer-effectiveness operation.

[21] In these experiments that allow two products to vary, reinforcer-effectiveness limits are determined for all practical purposes without reference to either income or prices, just as in the earlier experiments in which only one product was available.

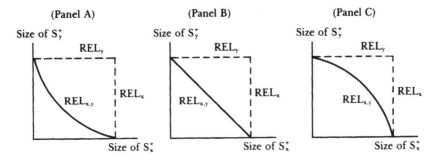

Figure 9. Interdependent Limit Quantities

effectiveness limit of, say, X goes up as the quantity of Y available to be consumed goes down. This pattern is most likely to occur when Y and X are controlled by a common reinforcer-establishing operation.[22] Although commodities with interdependent limits typically have a common reinforcer-effectiveness operation, two commodities that are controlled by different deprivations may nevertheless exhibit interdependent limits if the operation is at an extreme level for at least one commodity.[23] This latter possibility can be ignored for our purposes on the grounds that, in countries like the United States, we can normally exclude such extreme levels of deprivation. For our purposes, therefore, a common reinforcer-effectiveness operation is a necessary condition for two commodities to exhibit interdependent limits. However, a common reinforcer-effectiveness operation is not a sufficient condition for interdependent limits because the level of the operation can also be an important influence. Some commodities that are controlled by a common operation exhibit interdependent limits when the operation is at a high level, but not when it is at a low level. The reason is that "by increasing the deprivation we increase the range of effective stimuli or, to put it another way, reduce the importance of differences in stimuli" (Skinner, 1953, p. 218).

Other things being equal, two commodities that are otherwise eligible candidates to exhibit interdependent reinforcer-effectiveness

[22] The existence of a common deprivation for any two goods must be determined empirically. Skinner (1953, p. 149) has noted that "If the probabilities of eating two kinds of food always vary together, we assume a common hunger, but if at certain times an organism eats salt more readily than sugar and at other times sugar more readily than salt, we find it necessary to speak of separate salt-and-sugar hungers. Presumably separate operations of satiation and deprivation have accompanied these changes."

[23] For example, laboratory animals under extreme food deprivation have consumed less water than they would under the same conditions of liquid deprivation, but with a less severe level of food deprivation.

limits are more likely to do so for a given individual if the commodities have similar stimulus characteristics. The reason is stimulus induction—behavior (approach behavior) that has been strengthened by the reinforcement of a particular product generalizes to products with similar characteristics. Thus someone whose buy behavior has been reinforced by, say, a Red Delicious apple is likely to emit the same operant (buy) response when the reinforcement is a Golden Delicious apple. The presence of some stimulus similarity does not guarantee, however, that stimulus induction (and, therefore, interdependent limits) will occur between two otherwise eligible commodities. Two apples that differ in appearance only by color may also be different in terms of other stimulus characteristics, and these other characteristics can become the basis for discriminating behavior. In such cases, some particular discriminative stimulus comes to control an operant response.[24] Even when discrimination occurs, however, the interdependent limits of two eligible products with similar characteristics are unlikely to be eliminated. The reason is that the persistence of generalization is strong under such circumstances, and "it [is] impossible to discover a perfect case of discrimination in which only a single S^D controls a response" (Millenson and Leslie, 1979, p. 330). In such cases, therefore, the degree of interdependence in terms of joint reinforcer-effectiveness limits will depend in part on the relative strength of generalization and discrimination.

Although stimulus similarity is an important basis for interdependent limits, interdependence can also exist between two eligible commodities when the stimulus characteristics are dissimilar. For example, under appropriate conditions of food deprivation, such dissimilar commodities as, say, bread and apples could exhibit interdependent limits.[25] In the case of food, the dissimilar members can readily be transformed to reveal a common underlying relation—"we need merely ingest it and wait for the resulting transformed situation" (Millenson and Leslie, 1979, p. 333). In other cases, the dissimilar

[24] Skinner (1953, p. 134) has emphasized that:

Discrimination is also not a form of action by the organism. When we establish a discrimination between red and orange spots of light, we simply sharpen a natural gradient. By reinforcing red spots while extinguishing orange spots, the control of the property of redness is strengthened, while that of the property of orange is weakened. In such an experiment, other properties of the stimuli—e.g., size, shape and location—are both reinforced and extinguished.

[25] In this case, the commodities are called a "disjunctive concept" (Millenson and Leslie, 1979, pp. 331 ff). The term "disjunctive" has the same meaning as in set theory. The term "concept" has a special meaning. As Millenson and Leslie (p. 309) explain, "The word 'concept' denotes the behavioral fact that a given response is under the control of a class of related S^D's." "Related" can refer to spatially related, related in topological structure, related by size (bigger, smaller), etc.

members might have an underlying common relation—music may be such a case. In still other cases, any relation of the dissimilar members is arbitrary. When the hypothetical experiments involve simple commodities, it is easy to see how stimulus induction can lead to or enhance interdependent reinforcer-effectiveness limits. However, when complex commodities are involved (e.g., commodities that are used as part of a lengthy "production" process), the operant behavior of buyers may be brought under the control of subtle relationships that exist within a given situation (Millenson and Leslie, 1979, p. 325). In laboratory work, L-set procedures are used to bring the operant behavior of animals under the control of the relationships existing in the situation.[26]

In practice, the following are examples of the kinds of commodities for which the reinforcer-effectiveness limits could be both interdependent and determinate: (1) two primary commodities with a common deprivation (e.g., steak and hamburger, butter and margarine); (2) two specific functional secondary commodities that could, objectively speaking, replace a given member or link in the chain[27] that leads to the same primary reinforcer (e.g., taxi or bus as substitutes in a chain leading to a restaurant); (3) two specific functional escape/avoidance commodities that could, objectively speaking, fill the same members or links in a chain of escape or avoidance from the same aversive stimulation (e.g., raincoat and umbrella).[28] It will be noted that this list of commodities with determinate and interdependent reinforcer-effectiveness limits does not include nonfunctional reinforcers even when they have a common reinforcer-establishing operation. For example, it does not include (1) two specialized nonfunctional secondary commodities based on a common deprivation; (2) two generalized nonfunctional secondary commodities based on a common deprivation; (3) two specialized nonfunctional escape/avoidance commodities based on the same aversive stimulus; or (4)

---

[26] An L-set procedure is a "systematic way of ordering the reinforcement history that leads to concept behavior" (Millenson and Leslie, 1979, p. 329), e.g., how alternative commodities could be used to fill a particular chain in a long "production" process.

[27] As noted earlier (chapter 2, n. 13), "A chain of operant behavior is a sequence of operant responses and discriminative stimuli such that each R produces the S^D for the next R. The successive R's in a chain are its members; the successive S^D's are its links."

[28] Functional goods that are not fully effective in reducing aversive stimulation to the tolerance level would have determinate but not necessarily interdependent reinforcer-effectiveness limits. In some cases (e.g., raincoat and umbrella), the limits would be interdependent at lesser levels of aversive stimulation (e.g., light drizzle), but they would exhibit independence when the commodities are not effective in reducing the aversive stimulation to the aversive-stimulus tolerance levels.

two generalized nonfunctional escape/avoidance commodities based on the same aversive stimulus. Our earlier analysis showed that such commodities do not have determinate reinforcer-effectiveness limits when consumed separately; and, for the same reasons, they do not have determinate limits when consumed together. Since their reinforcer-effectiveness limits are indeterminate, the question of whether their limits are interdependent is moot.

A digression on positively sloped $REL_{x,y}$ *curves.* In the preceding section on interdependent reinforcer-effectiveness limits, the $REL_{x,y}$ curves had negative slopes; and the possibility that the outcome of the hypothetical experiments might be an $REL_{x,y}$ curve with a positive slope was (tacitly) ignored. The reasons for ignoring the possibility that joint consumption of two commodities can extend the limits beyond those that would be reached for each separately are inherent in the possible causes for positively sloped $REL_{x,y}$ curves. One possible explanation is that joint consumption of two commodities can in some cases change the level of the applicable reinforcer-effectiveness operation. This can occur in those cases in which consumption of one of the commodities is, per se, a reinforcer-effectiveness operation that leads to increased (probability of) consumption of the other commodity. For example, the consumption of salted peanuts is an operation that leads to greater consumption of liquids. The positively sloped $REL_{x,y}$ curve that appears to result in such cases is excluded, however, because it violates the condition of our hypothetical experiment that requires the reinforcer-effectiveness limit for the positive reinforcers to be determined for a given level of the reinforcer-effectiveness operation. In order to examine the $REL_{x,y}$ curve for, say, salted peanuts and beer, while holding the reinforcer operation constant, it would be necessary to hold constant the amount of salt used on the peanuts, while experimenting with different quantities of salted peanuts and beer.

A second possible explanation is that the incentive function[29] of two products is different when they are consumed together than when they are consumed separately.[30] In this case, we refer to the quality of the reinforcer rather than its quantity. The pertinent point is that a change in the stimulus properties that define quality can also lead to a change in the total quantity consumed.[31] In laboratory experiments

[29] The incentive function refers to the behavioral effects of varying the quality or quantity of primary reinforcement (Millenson, 1967, p. 391).

[30] This has also been noted by Lancaster (1966, p. 134) who has pointed out that goods in combination may possess characteristics different from those pertaining to the goods separately.

[31] For example, Millenson and Leslie (1979, p. 403) note that adulteration of reinforcer affects total quantity consumed.

with animals, the incentive function of quinine might be changed by the addition of a sweetener with the result that the reinforcer-effectiveness limit for quinine is greater for the combination than it is for each commodity when consumed separately. Among human consumers, the incentive function of coffee is altered when sugar or cream is added to the coffee with the result that the reinforcer-effectiveness limit for the enhanced coffee is greater for some consumers than it is when each component is consumed separately. In other cases, joint consumption of two products alters the incentive function in a "technological" way—e.g., when joint consumption leads to a chemical interaction that enhances the reinforcing value of the two goods, as in the case of certain drugs. These cases, too, violate the condition of the hypothetical experiments that requires the reinforcement-effectiveness limit to be determined for *given* products, which includes given stimulus characteristics. Since joint consumption changes the stimulus characteristics in these cases, it seems preferable to treat, say, two such products as a single product when they are consumed in combination and to treat them as two different products when they are consumed separately. In this way, we maintain given stimulus characteristics in the experiments.

A third explanation is that some products are not effective unless they are consumed together (e.g., flashlight and battery, or automobile and gasoline). Such cases violate the conditions of the hypothetical experiments based on separate consumption, because one or both of the products taken singly is not a reinforcer. The apparent complementarity of such products when they are consumed jointly is an artifact of our culture that produces and markets them as separate and distinct products. It seems preferable, therefore, to treat (and test) them as a single product; or, alternatively, if they are to be tested separately, to stipulate that "separately" includes a given amount of the required other product. If any of those products can also be effective (i.e., if it is a reinforcer) when used separately, it should be treated (and tested) as two different products when used jointly and separately—e.g., gasoline as part of the automobile-and-gasoline product, and gasoline for cleaning purposes.

A fourth explanation is that some products that have an innate or acquired capacity to reinforce when used separately will often be consumed jointly because joint consumption, per se, is an independent source of reinforcement. In such cases, therefore, the reinforcer-effectiveness limits would appear to be extended beyond those for separate consumption. The culture is an especially fertile source of joint consumption that is reinforced as a combination—e.g., in the social conventions about the joint consumption of certain food products, of particular clothing items, of house furnishings, etc. In such cases, where each item taken separately is also reinforcing for other reasons, it seems simpler to acknowledge the existence of the social reinforcement for joint consumption and to treat the jointly consumed commodities as different products from their individual components.

Independent reinforcer-effectiveness limits. Another possible outcome of the experiments to determine reinforcer-effectiveness limits under joint consumption is that the limits for each commodity are the same whether they are consumed together or consumed separately. It would appear, therefore, that such commodities have independent limits. As in the earlier example, this interpretation is based on a series of hypothetical experiments in which the quantity of Y available on a crf basis is progressively reduced (in different experiments) while X is available without restriction on a crf basis. If REL_x (i.e., the maximum amount of X that is actually consumed) remains unaffected by any quantity of Y that is made available and consumed, REL_x and REL_y are independent (figure 10).[32]

Size of S_y^+

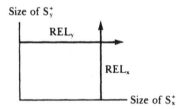

Figure 10. Independent Limit Quantities

The case of independent reinforcer-effectiveness limits[33] draws on the same kind of analysis already used for interdependent limits. Thus, in keeping with our earlier analysis, commodities with different reinforcer-effectiveness operations (e.g., different kinds of deprivation) could exhibit independent reinforcer limits as long as they are also either primary commodities (e.g., salt and sugar; bread and water), specialized functional secondary commodities leading to primary reinforcers (e.g., food plate and bed), or specialized functional

[32] As a double check, this experiment could also be run the other way around; and presumably the results would be the same, i.e., independent limit quantities.

[33] As already noted, there may not be any goods that exhibit independent limit quantities under sufficiently extreme reinforcer-establishing conditions. We can ignore such extreme cases for ordinary living; and, in any case, the notion of independent limit quantities is a useful concept of a kind of limiting case.

escape/avoidance commodities leading to different primary negative reinforcers (e.g., raincoat and sunshade). On the other hand, nonfunctional secondary goods or nonfunctional escape/avoidance goods do not have determinate reinforcer-effectiveness limits. Hence, it is moot whether they could exhibit independent limits even if they have different reinforcer operations. Although independent limits are usually found among commodities with different reinforcer-effectiveness operations, some commodities that are controlled by a common operation may nevertheless exhibit independent limits. As noted above, this is related to the level of the operation—other things being equal, independent limits for commodities with a common operation are more likely to be observed under a low, rather than a high, level of the operation. This applies to commodities that are controlled by a common deprivation (e.g., two food products) and to those that are controlled by a common aversive stimulation (e.g., raincoat and umbrella).

CHAPTER SIX

Equilibrium Outcome
of Buy Behavior

The Analysis by Successive Approximations

Chapter 4 showed how a buy behavior outcome was determined in a simplified model that included an income limit (IL) but not a reinforcer-effectiveness limit (REL), and in which the size of reinforcement was variable for only one commodity (in a one-commodity model). Chapter 5 examined the nature of the reinforcer-effectiveness limits. The present chapter develops the analysis for determining the buy behavior outcome when the dual constraints (income limit and reinforcer-effectiveness limit) are both included and the size of reinforcement is variable for both commodities in a two-commodity model. For exposition purposes, it is convenient to present the full model in three successive approximations. In all approximations, the hypothetical experiments permit size of reinforcement to be varied for both commodities. However, the first two approximations are incomplete models, because one of the constraints does not appear. In the first approximation, the income limit is the only effective constraint, and the reinforcer-effectiveness limit is ignored; in the second approximation, the reinforcer-effectiveness limit is the effective constraint, and the income limit is ignored. In the third approximation, both constraints are included; both are effective; and the response strength (RS) curves are consistent with the final equilibrium.

First approximation: IL constraint effective. In this approximation, we design a hypothetical experiment for a two-commodity world in which a consumer with given income can buy different quantities of the two commodities under the prices stipulated in the contingency of reinforcement. Figure 11 employs a four-panel diagram to analyze the equilibrium buy behavior for the case where the $IL_{x,y}$ curve lies below the REL curves.[1] Since the IL curve lies below all points on the REL curves (NE panel), the income limit is clearly the binding constraint. In this approximation, therefore, the existence of the REL curve is ignored.[2] The axes of the NE panel show size of S$^+$, measured in units of Y and units of X, respectively; and these are reproduced in the NW and SE panels as well. As explained earlier (p. 55), each size of S$^+$ is paired with a particular size of S$^-$, given the contingency of reinforcement. Hence, size of S$^-$ is implicitly measured along these axes as well as size of S$^+$. The contingencies of reinforcement in this hypothetical experiment are implicit in the slope of the $IL_{x,y}$ curve (NE panel) that shows the maximum size of S$^+$ combinations of (quantities of) X and Y that can be acquired when operant (buy) behavior is emitted under a given income limit.

The NW and SE panels show the response strengths for AB (and EB) for different size of positive (and paired size of negative) reinforcement of Y and X commodities, respectively. In this and all later two-commodity models, the AB curves for each commodity[3] (and also the EB curves) are derived from hypothetical experiments in the manner explained in chapter 4. It will be recalled that, in each hypothetical experiment, the product is given, i.e., a commodity with given stimulus characteristics (including the quality of the reinforcer), and the level of the reinforcer-effectiveness operation is also given. Since EB curves for each commodity are related to size of outlays, the strength of EB_x is equal to the strength of EB_y when the outlay on X is equal to the outlay on Y in a two-commodity model (experiment).

In accordance with the earlier analysis, the AB curves are positively sloped until the reinforcer-effectiveness limits are reached. At that

[1] This assumption is, of course, also implicit in the standard microeconomic presentation of this case.

[2] This is done for convenience of presentation at this stage. As shown in the next section, the REL curve plays an important role in the final equilibrium even when the IL curve is the binding constraint.

[3] The definition of a commodity must be determined empirically. For example, when an individual would not consume either or both of two commodities separately but would consume them together, the jointly consumed commodities are treated like any other single commodity, and a separate AB curve is determined for that composite commodity by appropriate hypothetical experiments. For a further discussion on a similar point, see pp. 78–80.

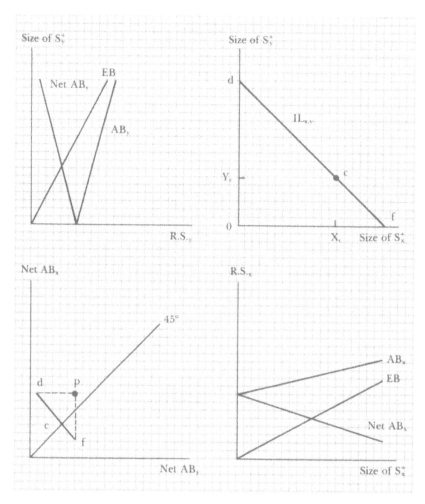

Figure 11. IL Constraint Effective

limit, the strength of approach behavior drops to zero because the commodity ceases to be a reinforcer beyond that point.[4] The EB curves are also positively sloped and, as explained earlier, we assume that the slope for EB curves is greater than for the AB curves.[5] At the point where the entire income is expended on one commodity, the EB curve for that commodity reaches a limit.[6] The NW and SE panels are drawn so that the size-of-S $^+$ axis is keyed to the corresponding axis in

[4] For convenience, the inelastic part of the AB curve is not shown.

[5] In chapter 7, we consider cases where the reverse holds.

[6] Again, for convenience, the inelastic range of the curve is not shown.

the NE panel. The curve in the SW panel is derived from the curves in the other three panels, viz., the Net AB curves and the effective boundary curve ($IL_{x,y}$ in this case). The axes of the SW panel show the net response strength (specifically, the Net AB strength) for different quantities of the two commodities. Thus the curve *df* (SW panel) shows all the combinations of Net AB_x and Net AB_y that lie along the effective boundary (i.e., the binding constraint) on buy behavior.

In the earlier analysis of buy behavior in a single-commodity model (i.e., a single commodity with different possible quantities) and with only an income constraint, buy behavior tended to be emitted until Net AB = 0 (i.e., until AB = EB), unless blocked before that point by the income limit. This tendency also operates in the two-commodity model. Depending on the strength of the Net AB curves, this equilibrium point may be reached before or at the income limit (or, in the full model, the reinforcer-effectiveness limit, whichever is encountered first). In a two-commodity model, however, the tendency for buy behavior to be emitted for any one commodity as long as Net AB is positive may be counteracted by the countervailing strength of conflicting behavior related to the other reinforcer. In figure 11, the individual is located at *p* (SW panel) before any buy behavior has been emitted (i.e., at the beginning of the hypothetical experiment, he has no X and no Y) which is the same as the zero point in the NE panel. If buy behavior is emitted along *pd*, Net AB_y will be minimized at point *d*; similarly, if buy behavior proceeds along *pf*, Net AB_x will be minimized at *f*. Given the income constraint, however, it is not possible to minimize Net AB (reach zero Net AB) for both commodities together. The *df* line (SW panel) shows all the combinations of Net AB_x and Net AB_y that are consistent with the IL boundary (i.e., that do not exceed the IL curve in NE panel). Accordingly, buy behavior can be emitted for any combination that lies within the triangular area *pdf*—this is the equivalent of the attainable set of combinations, O*df*, in the NE panel. When buy behavior reaches the *df* line (SW panel), any behavior that reduces Net AB for one commodity will raise it for the other. Hence, along this line, buy behavior is controlled by the relative strength of Net AB_x and Net AB_y—as demonstrated in the earlier discussion of two commodities with a single quantity for each (chapter 4). The 45° line (SW panel) shows the combinations of X and Y where Net AB_x = Net AB_y.[7] At any point to the left of the 45° line, Net AB_x > Net AB_y; hence, buy behavior will tend to be emitted towards X. Similarly, at any point to the right of the 45° line, Net AB_y > Net AB_x; hence, movement is towards Y. In other words, in both situations, the movement is back towards a point along the 45° line. Ac-

[7]The rationale for assuming a common scale on both axes is explained on p. 45.

cordingly, buy behavior will continue to adjust until it reaches c, the intersection of the df curve and the 45° line. In this first approximation model, this point is thus identified as the position of (short-run) equilibrium, and the equilibrium combination of commodities is Y_c and X_c (NE panel). To repeat, in this simplified two-commodity model, (short-run) equilibrium is achieved when the level of Net AB is at a minimum (greater than or equal to zero) for the two products together. In this example, (short-run) equilibrium occurs at the point that Net AB_x = Net AB_y and the $IL_{x,y}$ constraint is not exceeded.

Second approximation: REL constraint effective. A situation in which the REL curve lies wholly below the IL curve is the reverse of the case described in the preceding section.[8] In this approximation, we ignore the existence of the IL curve.[9] The AB curves in this example drop to zero[10] when the reinforcer-effectiveness limit for each commodity separately has been reached. Hence, the Net AB curve must always become negative beyond the REL point for each commodity taken separately. Figure 12A shows this example for commodities with independent reinforcer-effectiveness limits. As shown in the preceding section, buy behavior for each commodity will tend to be emitted until the Net AB reaches zero for each commodity taken separately—unless buy behavior is blocked before reaching that point. In this case of commodities with independent limits, buy behavior is blocked by a reinforcer-effectiveness limit[11] as shown by the REL_y and REL_x lines in the NE panel and by the boundary line *gec* in the SW panel. This means that buy behavior with respect to X-product cannot proceed to the point where Net AB_x is pushed below *ec* (SW panel) and that Y-product purchases cannot proceed to the point where Net AB_y is pushed below *ge*. However, some of the points in the rectangular area *pgec* would not be reached because they are combinations at which Net AB_y is negative, i.e., EB > AB for Y-product. Hence, buy behavior would not be emitted in the rectangular area *fged*. Given the available set of minimum values for Net AB_x and Net AB_y (i.e., along *fdc*), the lowest values for Net AB for the two products together are at d (SW

[8] This is different from the usual assumption in microeconomic analysis that the bliss point is not attainable with existing income.

[9] As in the case of the first approximation, this is done for convenience of presentation at this stage. As shown in the next section, the IL curve plays an important role in the final equilibrium even when the REL curve is the binding constraint.

[10] For simplicity, this is not shown in the diagrams.

[11] The reinforcer-effectiveness limit is not literally a constraint on the emission of the operant response, but it indirectly has that effect, and will be so described for convenience.

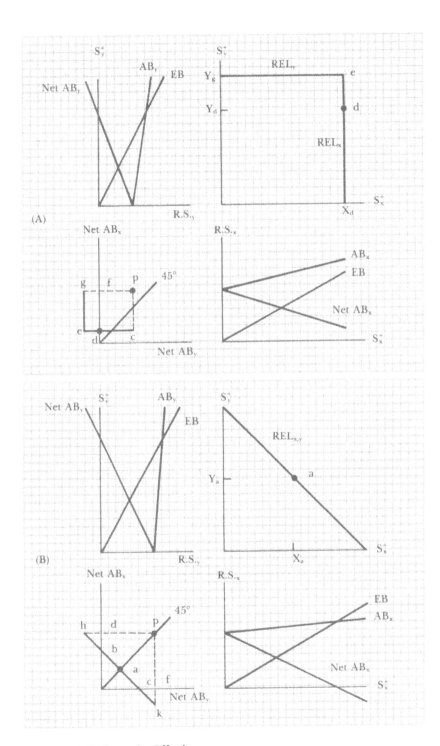

Figure 12. REL Constraint Effective

panel). Net AB_y is zero at that point, and Net AB_x has reached its lowest possible point. In the NE panel, this (short-run) equilibrium is reached at Y_d and X_d.

Figure 12B is another example of an REL curve that lies wholly below the IL curve (not shown). It differs from the case in figure 12A because X and Y have interdependent limits ($REL_{x,y}$ curve in the NE panel; *hk* curve in the SW panel); but it is similar because the IL curve is ignored in this example. The relevant part of the *hk* curve is the segment *bc*—combinations outside of this range have negative Net AB for at least one of the commodities. Hence, buy behavior will be contained within the area *pdbcf*. Since Y and X have interdependent reinforcer-effectiveness limits, buy behavior cannot simultaneously proceed to the points where Y-product and X-product Net AB's are each equal to zero (viz., *db* and *cf*, respectively). Under those conditions, (short-run) equilibrium will be reached at a point along the segment *bc* where Net AB_x = Net AB_y, viz., at *a* (SW panel) and at Y_a and X_a (NE panel).

A digression on free goods. Free goods are an interesting example of a case in which the reinforcer-effectiveness limit is the effective— indeed, the only—constraint. In operant terms, a free good refers to any commodity (reinforcer) that is available to an individual after an operant response that is not followed by the aversive consequence of a loss of dollar reinforcers. Many collective goods (libraries, museums, parks, beaches, freeways, bridges, child care, schools, etc.) are examples of free goods, but they do not exhaust the list. For this discussion, the significance of free goods is that the emission of buy behavior is not constrained by an EB curve. In an economic model, it is of course contradictory to speak of "buy" behavior in connection with free goods. In an operant approach, however, the case of free goods can be accommodated within the model of buy behavior by a small alteration in the arbitrary topography of the operant response (act of purchase) and by eliminating the aversive consequence of the response. In our preliminary model of buy behavior, we stipulated that the only acceptable form of payment was by bank card rather than by currency (p. 54). To maintain a parallel with this earlier model, we again stipulate that "payment" is by means of appropriate cards in the context of a two-commodity model—say, library books and bridge crossings. In our hypothetical experiments, library books can be obtained by presentation of a library card that is available without charge, and toll bridges can be crossed by presentation of a pass that is also available without charge to all local residents. In an appropriate set of hypothetical experiments, we could determine the strength of approach behavior for different quantities of each reinforcer separately (e.g., number of books that can be checked out at one time, and number of crossings that can be made in a given period). The information derived from the separate experiments about response strength and about reinforcer-effectiveness limits could then be assembled in a two-commodity model to determine the operant (buy) outcome when both commodities are available in variable quantities.

If X and Y have independent reinforcer-effectiveness limits, the operant outcome could be determined by means of a substantially modified figure 12A. First, since these are free commodities, escape behavior would not be reinforced. Diagrammatically, the EB curves in figure 12A would have to be removed and, therefore, also the Net AB curves, leaving only the AB curves (NW and SE panels). In the NE panel, the REL curves would remain. In the SW panel, the REL constraints would be shifted to accord with the AB curves. After these changes had been made, figure 12A would look like figure 13A. In the latter figure, AB does not conflict with EB—and AB gets stronger as size of reinforcement increases up to the reinforcer-effectiveness limit for each commodity taken separately. In this case, buy behavior will be contained within the rectangular area *pbed*, and it will continue to be emitted until the reinforcer-effectiveness limits are reached for both commodities, i.e., until maximum AB strength is reached for both commodities. This will occur at *c* (SW panel, which corresponds to *c* on the NE panel). The equilibrium quantities are Y_c and X_c (NE panel). It will be noted that even a weak reinforcer like Y-product will be consumed to the reinforcer-effectiveness limit when it is free, whereas even a wealthy individual might stop buying it before that limit is reached when the operant behavior has aversive consequences (loss of money surrendered in payment) as well as positive consequences (acquisition of commodity).[12]

The buy outcome for free commodities with interdependent reinforcer-effectiveness limits is shown in figure 13B, which has the same AB curves (NW and SE panels) and the same reinforcer-effectiveness limits for each commodity taken separately as in figure 13A. Buy behavior is contained within the triangular area *pbd*. Because of the interdependent reinforcer-effectiveness limits for X and Y products, however, it is not possible for buy behavior to be simultaneously at maximum net response strength for both X-product (viz., at *b*) and also for Y-product (viz., at *d*). Clearly the outcome will be determined at the point where Net AB is strongest for the two com-

---

[12] The important policy implications of this analysis are beyond the scope of this study.

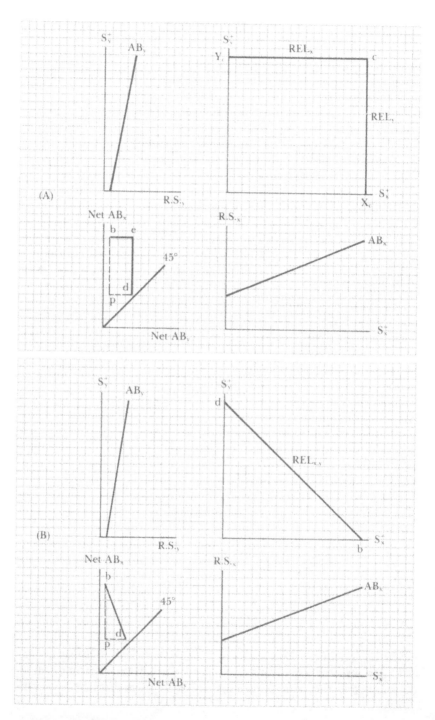

Figure 13. Free Goods

modities together. For example, at d, Net AB_x > Net AB_y—note that d lies to the left of a 45° line; hence, approach behavior to X will be stronger than approach behavior to Y, and buy behavior will be emitted in favor of X. This will move the individual along db until b is reached. At b, Net AB_x is still stronger than Net AB_y, but b is a constraint point. In this particular example, therefore, equilibrium is reached at b (SW panel)—which corresponds to b in NE panel—i.e., he "buys" all X and none of Y, even though both products are free. By contrast, in the case of free goods with independent reinforcer-effectiveness limits, each product was consumed to the reinforcer limit for each separately.[13]

Third approximation: IL and REL constraints effective. In this third approximation, the contingency of reinforcement and the parameter values have been selected in a way that makes both of the dual constraints effective in determining the equilibrium outcome of buy behavior. In addition, the response strength curves are consistent with the final equilibrium. Figure 14A shows such a situation for commodities with independent reinforcer-effectiveness limits.

The initial position is at p, and the available set lies in the rectangular area $pbca$ (SW panel). The effective boundary within which buy behavior must be contained (bc and ac, NE panel) consists of those segments of the dual constraint curves that are binding. The bca curve (SW panel) shows all the combinations of Net AB_x and Net AB_y that lie along the effective boundary on buy behavior. The 45° curve (SW panel) shows all the combinations of the commodities at which Net AB_x = Net AB_y, and the intersection of this 45° curve with the effective boundary determines the limits on the emission of buy behavior. The equilibrium outcome is at c (SW panel), and the equilibrium combination of commodities is Ob and Oa (NE panel).

Figure 14B shows the equilibrium outcome for an example of commodities with interdependent reinforcer-effectiveness limits. In this example, the budget constraint curve ($IL_{x,y}$) intersects the $REL_{x,y}$ constraint curve at a (NE panel), and the effective boundary on buy behavior, bae (NE panel), consists of part of the budget constraint and part of the REL constraint. In the SW panel, the initial position is at p, and buy behavior is constrained to lie in the irregular area $pbae$. The equilibrium occurs at a, the intersection of the budget constraint and $REL_{x,y}$ constraint curves and the outcome at which Net AB_x = Net AB_y. Therefore, both constraints are effective.

---

[13] For additional discussion of equilibrium outcomes when Net AB curves have positive slopes, see chapter 7.

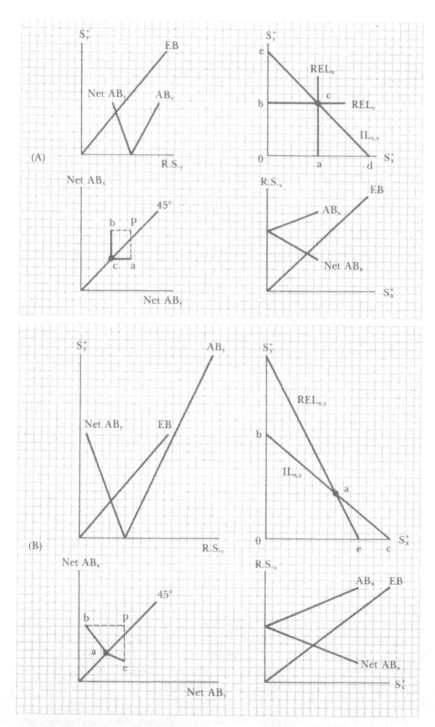

Figure 14. Dual Constraints Effective

As this discussion of the third approximation has shown, the equilibrium conditions are the same for goods with independent reinforcer-effectiveness limits and those with interdependent limits. In both cases, an equilibrium exists when the minimum levels that can be reached on the Net AB curves occur at the point where the dual constraints are equal. As shown below, however, this is a special case of equilibrium in which the response strength curves are consistent with the final equilibrium. We consider next some cases in which this consistency condition does not hold.

When the Response Strength Curves Are (Initially) Not Consistent with Final Equilibrium

In both examples above of the third approximation to the equilibrium outcome, the Net AB curves for both commodities were consistent with the level of the reinforcer-effectiveness operation (REO) at the outcome where Net AB was minimized for both together. When the Net AB curves are not consistent with a final equilibrium, the equilibrium adjustment occurs in two stages. The preliminary (or short-run) equilibrium occurs where Net AB is minimized (Net AB $\geq$ 0) for a given level of the reinforcer-effectiveness operation; the final (or long-run) equilibrium occurs where Net AB is minimized for a level of the reinforcer operation that allows for feedback effects from the short-run equilibrium outcome.[14] The nature of this two-stage equilibrium adjustment is discussed below and under two headings: (1) when the short-run equilibrium includes a deficit, and (2) when the short-run equilibrium includes a surplus. The hypothetical experiments discussed under both headings will be limited to primary commodities. The nature of the modifications that are necessary to apply the analysis to other than primary commodities will be briefly discussed at the end of this section.

1. When the Short-run Outcome Includes a "Deficit"

$IL_{x,y} = REL_{x,y}$ *at some combination.* Consider the case of primary commodities (say, food) with interdependent reinforcer-effectiveness limits, as depicted in figure 15A. The initial position (before either commodity is purchased) is at p, and the attainable set lies in the area *pagb* (SW panel). Although a point of intersection exists between the dual constraints—$REL_{x,y} = IL_{x,y}$ at g—buy behavior would proceed

---

[14] The distinction between the short-run and long-run periods hinges on the stability of the reinforcer-effectiveness operation level. In the short run, that level is given; in the long run, it can vary, as explained in the text.

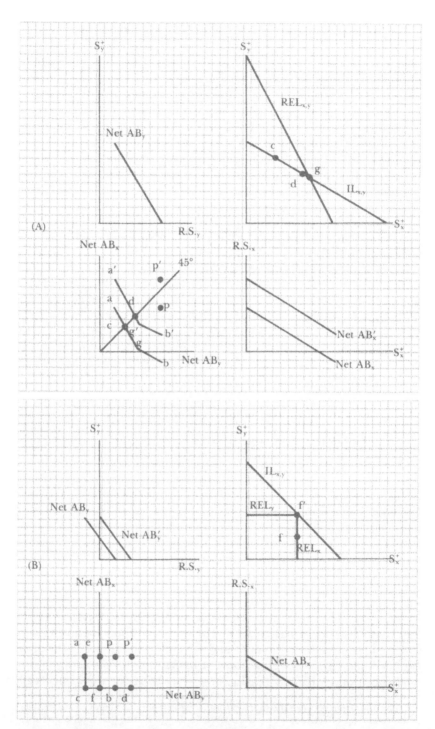

Figure 15. Short-run Buy Outcome with a Deficit

to c, and any further emission of buy behavior would be blocked by the income limit. As the NE panel shows, however, c does not lie along the $REL_{x,y}$ curve. Thus one consequence of the operant behavior which brings the consumer to c is that an unrelieved margin of deprivation remains at c. For brevity, we use the term "deficit" to describe the amount of a commodity(ies) that would be required to reach $REL_{x,y}$ from any given short-run buy outcome.

A deficit is an unrelieved margin of deprivation; and, as noted earlier (p. 23), deprivation is an important reinforcer-establishing operation which conditions approach behavior. The persistence of a deficit raises the level of that reinforcer operation,[15] and that can have two effects.[16] First, since AB curves depend on a given level of the reinforcer-effectiveness operation, a higher effective level will cause an upward shift of the AB curves for both commodities as the experiment is repeated. Although there are limits on the increase in reinforcing value as deprivation is increased, those limits can be ignored, as explained earlier (p. 25). Strictly speaking, the $REL_{x,y}$ curve would also be affected by the deficit (i.e., higher level of deprivation). As a practical matter, the reinforcer-effectiveness limit (for primary reinforcers) is probably asymptotic within the range of variation of deprivation that would be typically experienced by consumers in countries like the United States. For convenience, therefore, we also ignore the presumably minor changes in the reinforcer-effectiveness limit that might occur in response to the deficit (i.e., to a technically larger reinforcer operation). Second, in the case of commodities that are controlled by a common deprivation (and, therefore, also have interdependent reinforcer-effectiveness limits), there is a change in discrimination that is reflected in a relatively greater upward shift of the AB curve for the less expensive commodity. The reason for the change is that behavior that leads to a reduction of the deficit is thereby reinforced; and, in these circumstances, that clearly requires greater discrimination with respect to the less expensive commodity. In this context, the less expensive of two commodities with interdependent reinforcer-effectiveness limits is the one that, for any given outlay, brings the individual closer to the reinforcer limit.[17] Other

[15] In animal experiments, deprivation is commonly measured in terms of the animal's body weight—"a rat kept at 80 percent of its normal body weight is strongly deprived; a rat kept at 95 percent of its normal body weight is only mildly deprived"—or fixed duration of deprivation, e.g., twenty-three hours (Millenson and Leslie, 1979, p. 402).

[16] The first effect of a higher reinforcer-effectiveness operation is applicable to the case of goods with independent reinforcer-effectiveness limits as well as those with interdependent limits; the second effect, only to goods with interdependent limits.

[17] Greater discrimination with respect to the relative expensiveness of a commodity can, of course, be associated with reduced discrimination with respect to other attributes

things being equal, this relative shift of the AB curves would tend to move buy behavior towards the less expensive commodity. Since the deficit-induced shift of the Net AB curves would continue as long as the deficit persists, the deficit would eventually be either minimized or eliminated.

To illustrate the effects of a deficit, consider the examples shown in figure 15. In panel A, X is the less expensive commodity, and there is a deficit at c. As explained above, the deficit will cause the AB_x curve to rise proportionately more than the AB_y curve. For diagrammatic simplicity, the relatively greater upward shift of the AB_x curve has been shown by holding the AB_y curve constant while permitting the former to shift upwards. The attainable set now lies in the area $p'a'g'b'$, and the new outcome is at d. Since there is still a deficit at d, the Net AB curves continue their relative shifts. This process will come to a halt when the buy outcome reaches g (NE panel), the point at which $IL_{x,y} = REL_{x,y}$. Thereafter, the Net AB curves for the base level of deprivation in this experiment would be at their new adjusted level. If the Net AB curves ever drifted back towards their initial positions, the deficit would again raise the deprivation above the base level, and the Net AB curves would be restored to the level that is consistent with long-run equilibrium. This is the mechanism by which the Net AB curves become consistent with long-run equilibrium if they are not initially consistent with it.

In the preceding example of commodities with interdependent reinforcer-effectiveness limits, the initial position of the Net AB curves led to a buy behavior outcome along the IL curve. Given the relation between the IL and REL curves, any movement toward the $REL_{x,y}$ curve would then proceed along the IL curve. We next consider a case in which the initial position of the Net AB curves leads to a buy behavior outcome that is below the IL curve as well as below the REL curve. Since the preceding example dealt with interdependent reinforcer limits, this example uses a case with independent limits (figure 15B). As in figure 15A, here, too, there exists an outcome at which $IL_{x,y} = REL_x = REL_y$, but the Net AB curves are initially not consistent with this outcome. Suppose that the Net AB curves lead to a preliminary outcome at f—e.g., suppose that the available set is $pacb$ and that Net AB_x = Net AB_y = 0 at f. When buy behavior is at f, it has reached REL_x but not REL_y. As the hypothetical experiment is

of the commodity. A familiar example of reduced discrimination, cited by Millenson and Leslie (1979, p. 402), is that "When we are only slightly hungry, we are very selective about what we will eat. Eventually, as we grow increasingly hungry, our standards of what we will accept go down. If we are starving, we will eat almost anything."

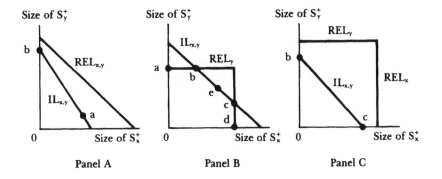

Figure 16. Dual Constraints Not Consistent with Equilibrium

repeated in successive trials, the persistence of the deficit with respect to Y raises the level of REO_y. According to our hypothesis about a deficit,[18] this will gradually shift the AB_y curve (and, therefore, also Net AB_y) upwards until the available set becomes $p'efd$ (SW panel) and buy behavior comes to a halt at f' (NE panel). As in the preceding case, that would be a final equilibrium position, because the Net AB curves will have adjusted to the level required to reach the joint intersection at f'.

$IL_{x,y} \neq REL_{x,y}$ *at any combination.* To illustrate the case in which the response strength curves are not consistent with final equilibrium and the dual constraints are not equal at any combination of the commodities, consider figure 16 (which shows only the NE quadrant of the four-quandrant diagram).[19] Panel A shows an example of primary commodities with interdependent reinforcer-effectiveness limits. It is not possible to reach the REL curve by any movement along the income curve. Our previous analysis suggests that, if the initial outcome were at, say, a, buy behavior would eventually move towards b. This outcome is stable, in spite of the deficit at b, because it is not possible for the AB curves to adjust in a manner that can eliminate the remaining deficit.

A different kind of outcome may be indicated when the dual constraints are not equal at any combination for commodities that have independent reinforcer-effectiveness limits (panel B). Suppose that the response strength curves are such that buy behavior initially moves to b, i.e., Net AB_x = Net AB_y at b. Since the buy outcome at b is equal to REL_y, the REO_y is constant each time the hypothetical experiment

[18] Since this case is about goods with independent satiation limits, the shift of AB_y is related only to the first of the two effects mentioned on p. 95.

[19] The NE quadrant is the only one shown in order to simplify the presentation.

is repeated; but, since the buy outcome at b lies below REL_x, the level of REO_x will rise due to the effects of a deficit. This relative increase in REO_x will cause in turn an upward shift in AB_x and, therefore, also in Net AB_x with the result that buy outcome starts to move towards c. It may not reach c, however. As the outcome moves towards c, the level of the reinforcer operation will increase for both commodities. During the course of this move, an intermediate point may be reached at which any further increases in the level of each reinforcer-effectiveness operation (due to any remaining deficit) will have an equal and proportionate effect on the Net AB curves for each commodity. At that point, the buy outcome would be in long-run equilibrium notwithstanding the continuing shift in both Net AB curves. Except for this possibility, a long-run equilibrium does not exist in this case. For example, suppose that the buy outcome reached c, a point that is equal to REL_x but is a deficit position with respect to Y. This would start the process working in the other direction. In that event, the buy outcome would oscillate between the extreme ends of the trade-off part of the effective boundary (viz., along the segment bc).

A variation on panel B is shown in panel C. As in panel B, the long-run equilibrium in panel C might occur at some intermediate point along bc, or the outcome might oscillate between b and c. In addition, it is also possible for the buy outcome to be in long-run equilibrium at a corner solution (b or c). Since a corner solution in this case involves a deficit for both commodities, a long-run equilibrium could occur at a corner only if the increases in both reinforcer-effectiveness operations had an equal and proportionate effect on the Net AB curves of both products such that Net AB_x = Net AB_y at, say, all Y (point b in the diagram).

In sum, when the dual constraints are not equal at any combination, the buy outcome for commodities with independent reinforcer-effectiveness limits will occur along the trade-off segment of the effective boundary. This much is guaranteed by the forces that bring about a short-run equilibrium outcome. In the long run, buy behavior might reach an equilibrium at some point along the trade-off segment of the effective boundary, or it might oscillate between the extreme points on that segment. Whether the outcome moves towards long-run equilibrium or oscillates depends on the particular relation of the dual constraints, the comparative strength of the reinforcer-effectiveness operations, and the impact of the relevant reinforcer operation levels on the Net AB curves of the two commodities. Finally, the reason for the different outcomes between commodities with independent reinforcer-effectiveness limits and those with interdependent limits is that the latter imply a common reinforcer-effectiveness operation. By contrast, commodities with independent reinforcer limits are controlled by different deprivations, and it is impossible in these examples to reach the reinforcer limits for both commodities simultaneously.

2. *When the Short-run Outcome Includes a "Surplus"*

In the above examples in which the response strength curves are not consistent with final equilibrium, the first-stage equilibrium adjustment led to a deficit and thus to a higher level of the reinforcer-effectiveness operation that controls the reinforcing value of the commodity reinforcers (level of the AB curves). It is also possible, however, for a first-stage equilibrium to lead to a "surplus" (explained below) and thus to a reduction of the aversive consequences of any given loss of dollars surrendered in payment. This is illustrated in figure 17 for one case in which $IL_{x,y}$ and $REL_{x,y}$ are equal at some combination and another case in which they are not equal at any combination.

Figure 17A illustrates a surplus for commodities with interdependent reinforcer-effectiveness limits and in a situation in which $IL_{x,y} = REL_{x,y}$ at one combination of the commodities. The effective constraint line, abc, is composed of segments of the IL and REL curves, respectively (NE panel). The first-stage equilibrium at g lies along the $REL_{x,y}$ curve, but below the $IL_{x,y}$ curve. Thus one consequence of the operant behavior that brings the consumer to g is that he is left with an unexpended margin of income at g. For brevity, we use the term surplus to describe the amount of dollars (outlay) that would be required to reach $IL_{x,y}$ from any given short-run buy outcome.

A surplus is an unexpended margin of income, and the persistence of a surplus reduces the intensity of the aversive stimulus from any given loss of money reinforcers surrendered in payment (e.g., in terms of blocked or impeded access to other reinforcers). As noted in chapter 3, the intensity of aversive stimulation is a reinforcer-effectiveness operation that conditions escape behavior. Hence, the existence of the surplus reduces the level of that reinforcer operation. Diagrammatically, this is shown as a downward shift of the EB curves and a corresponding upward shift of the Net AB curves for both commodities. The final outcome of these shifts depends on the relative prices and the relative strengths of the AB curves for the two commodities.[20] In general, any given, say, fall in EB strength would move the buy outcome towards the commodity with the higher Net

---

[20] To determine which AB curve is the lower, the comparative strength of AB_x and AB_y could be measured in terms of the same relation to the reinforcer-effectiveness limit for each, e.g., strength of AB_x at REL_x as compared with strength of AB_y at REL_y, or the weighted average AB strength for each AB curve over the entire range of size of S^+ from zero to the reinforcer-effectiveness limit.

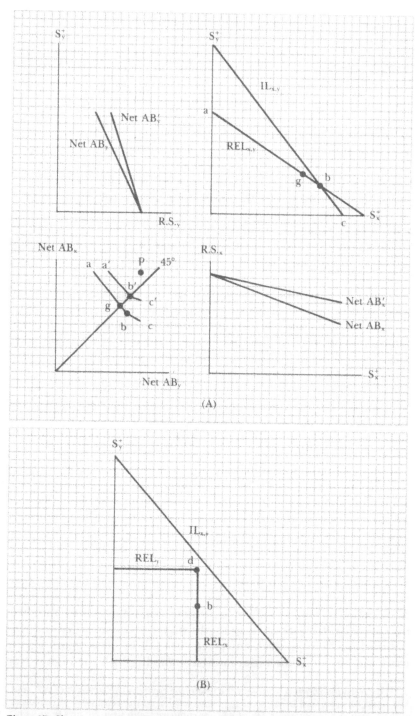

Figure 17. Short-run Buy Outcome with a Surplus

AB curves. For the case illustrated in figure 17A, the final equilibrium is at b (NE panel), a combination that lies along the effective boundary, but that does not include a surplus (or, for that matter, a deficit). However, a final equilibrium at a is an alternative outcome if the relative strength of the Net AB curves had been reversed. The outcome in this latter case is a long-run equilibrium, in spite of the surplus at a, because any further surplus-induced changes in the response strength curves do not lead to a further change in the buy outcome.

Figure 17B (which shows only the NE panel of the four-panel diagram) illustrates a surplus outcome for commodities with independent reinforcer-effectiveness limits, in a situation in which the dual constraint curves are not equal at any combination of the commodities. Suppose that the response strength curves lead to a first-stage equilibrium at b, a combination that lies along REL_x but considerably below REL_y. This deficit with respect to Y will tend to move the outcome towards Y. In addition, however, b also includes a surplus. The surplus will reduce the reinforcer-effectiveness operation for any given outlay of dollar reinforcers and will raise the Net AB curves for both commodities. This cannot lead to an increase in purchases of X (which are already at REL_x) but it would lead to a larger amount of Y purchased until an equilibrium is reached at d, the mutual reinforcer-effectiveness limit combination for the two commodities. This outcome is a long-run equilibrium in spite of the surplus at d, because (as in the case described above) any further surplus-induced changes in the response strength curves do not lead to a further change in the buy outcome.

The Composite Diagram: An Alternative Presentation of Buy Behavior Equilibrium

The first part of this chapter showed how equilibrium outcomes could be analyzed by means of a four-panel diagram that incorporated the dual constraints and the response strength (AB and EB) curves in a two-commodity model. In this study, the four-panel diagram is the basic model for analyzing buy behavior outcomes. However, it is often convenient to examine buy outcomes by means of an alternative presentation that compresses the information in the four-panel diagram into a two-panel composite diagram in which the Net AB curves for both products are juxtaposed (instead of being shown separately as in the four-panel diagram) and the SW panel is omitted. This diagram is also a convenient way to summarize alternative equilibrium possibilities and (as shown in the next chapter) to analyze the effects of changes in the parameters that control buy behavior equilibrium.

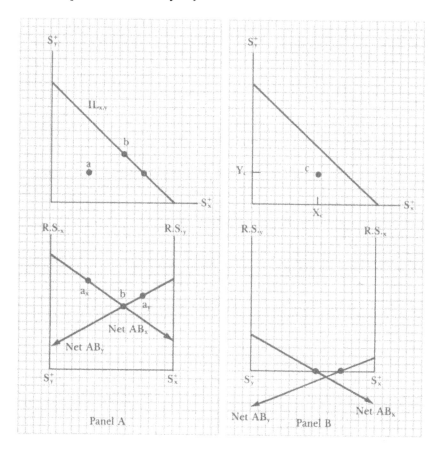

Figure 18. Equilibrium Outcomes—Composite Diagram

The present section shows how to analyze buy outcomes with the composite diagram. To convert the four-panel diagram into a composite diagram (in which, for convenience, the REL curve is temporarily ignored), the NW and SE panels are combined by reversing the abscissa for one of the panels, say, the NW panel, and superimposing one diagram on the other so that the combinations along the abscissa are the same as those along the IL curve in the NE panel. Second, the NW and SE panels are combined with the NE panel in the manner shown in figure 18. If the net response strength curves intersect (i.e., Net AB_x = Net AB_y) at a positive (or zero) level (panel A), the equilibrium buy behavior will be located along the IL line (unless it is blocked by the REL constraint). To illustrate, suppose that buy behavior is at an interior point, for example, at a.[21] (At interior point a, Net

---

[21] An interior point is a combination of X and Y that lies below the relevant constraint curve—in this case, the IL curve.

$AB_y = a_y$ and Net $AB_x = a_x$.) This is not an equilibrium position because the levels reached along the Net AB curves are not at a minimum for X and Y together (i.e., Net $AB_y \neq$ Net AB_x). Since Net AB at a is positive for both products, and since there is no constraint on buying more of both together, the consumption of both products will increase until the IL line is reached. When the IL curve has been reached, any further increase in one commodity must be accompanied by a reduction in the other. The final buy outcome along the IL curve will, of course, depend on which Net AB is the stronger. Hence, the adjustment process will continue until Net $AB_x =$ Net AB_y—and that point will lie on the IL curve, at point b in this example. Alternatively, if the Net AB curves intersect at a negative level (panel B), the equilibrium buy behavior will be located at an interior point. The reason, of course, is that a negative value for Net AB means that EB > AB. In this case, therefore, approach behavior would cease to be emitted when Net AB = 0 for both commodities; and the equilibrium outcome would occur at interior point c.

To illustrate the usefulness of the composite diagram for analyzing different situations, we present below the composite diagrams for the cases presented earlier in this chapter by means of four-panel diagrams. In doing so, we will also incorporate the REL constraints that were not included in figure 18.[22] To maintain consistency in drawing the composite diagrams (in this and later chapters), the abscissas of the response strength curves in the composite diagram will always be related to the IL curve (and not to the REL curve) even when the REL curve is the binding constraint. If the REL curve or any part of it lies beyond the IL curve, those combinations can be ignored because they are not attainable (i.e., dominated by the income constraint); if the REL curve or any part of it lies below the IL curve, those combinations can be treated like interior points from the IL curve; and if the REL curve or any part of it coincides with the IL curve, those combinations are automatically included along the IL scale.

In figure 19 (as in figure 14), the response strength curves are consistent with the final equilibrium. The REL curves in panel A intersect at c, a point along the IL curve. Since the Net AB curves are related to the scale along the IL curve, REL_x and REL_y can be shown by a single vertical line on the lower half of the composite diagram; and each Net AB curve stops at the REL constraint. Since Net AB_x and Net AB_y are minimized at the combination at which $IL_{x,y} = REL_x = REL_y$, the preliminary equilibrium at c is also the final equilibrium. In this particular case, Net AB reaches a minimum on both curves at a

---

[22] In formal (e.g., diagrammatic) terms, the REL constraint resembles a commodity rationing constraint in standard economic analysis. The interpretation is, of course, quite different, because a rationing constraint is not a reinforcer-effectiveness limit.

combination at which Net AB_x = Net AB_y. However, the same outcome (at c) could have been achieved in this situation if Net AB on both curves had not been equal, as long as the levels were positive (or equal to zero) at the combination that minimized Net AB for both together.

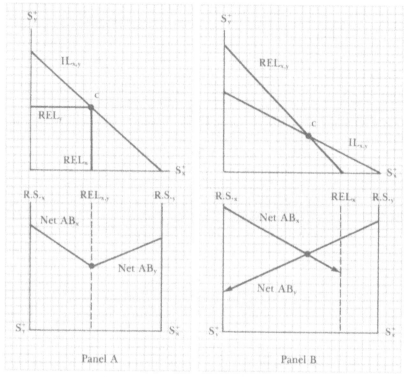

Figure 19. R.S. Curves Consistent with Final Equilibrium

Panel B depicts a similar situation, except that the commodities have interdependent reinforcer-effectiveness limits. In this case, REL_x is a vertical line on the lower part of the diagram, but REL_y is not shown because it lies beyond the IL curve. Here, too, there is no distinction between the preliminary and final equilibrium.

We turn next to cases in which the response strength curves are initially not consistent with the final equilibrium (figure 20).[23] In panel A, the $REL_{x,y}$ curve intersects the $IL_{x,y}$ curve just as in panel B of figure 19; unlike the latter, however, Net AB at that combination is not at the

[23] For convenience in presenting these cases, only the Net AB curves are shown on the composite diagrams. The reader can readily shift the AB or EB curves to make them consistent with the final equilibrium (in the manner explained earlier in this chapter).

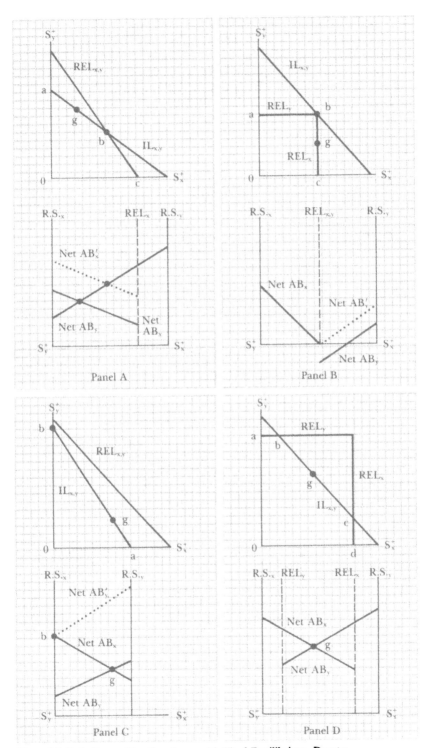

Figure 20. R.S. Curves Not Consistent with Final Equilibrium, Due to Deficit

minimum possible levels in terms of the initial Net AB curves. The effective constraint curve is abc, and the available set of buy combinations lies on or below the irregular area Oabc. Along the boundary segment Oa, an increase in the quantity of Y reduces Net AB_y and has no effect on Net AB_x; and the same holds (mutatis mutandis) for Net AB_x along the.segment Oc. Along the boundary segment abc, a reduction in the Net AB of one commodity (by increasing its quantity) is associated with an increase in the Net AB of the other commodity (which is being reduced in quantity). Therefore, short-run buy behavior comes to a halt at a point along abc at which Net AB_x = Net AB_y, viz., at g. After the relative shift in AB_x, however, final equilibrium is reached at b.

In panel B, there is also one combination at which $IL_{x,y}$ = REL_x = REL_y (just as in figure 19, panel A), but Net AB at that quantity is at a minimum for only one of the commodities. The Net AB for the other commodity reaches a minimum at g. Accordingly, the preliminary equilibrium is for the combination Oc of X and cg of Y. After the relative shift in AB_y, the final equilibrium is at b, at which point REL_x = REL_y = $IL_{x,y}$. In this case, Net AB_x is nonnegative throughout, whereas Net AB_y has a negative range. If both have a negative range, the preliminary outcome would be an interior point within the effective constraint boundary. If both curves had been nonnegative throughout, the preliminary outcome would be equal to the final outcome.

In panels C and D, unlike the situations depicted in panels A and B, $IL_{x,y}$ ≠ $REL_{x,y}$ at any combination of commodities. In panel C, the effective boundary (ba) consists entirely of the IL constraint; in panel D, the effective boundary ($abcd$) is composed of segments of both of the dual constraints. In both cases, the preliminary equilibrium (at g) involves a deficit. The final equilibrium is reached at b in panel C. In panel D, the buy outcome might oscillate in the segment bc in the long run; or it might reach a long-run equilibrium at some point along bc (as explained earlier in this chapter).

The two panels of figure 21 also show cases of Net AB curves that are not consistent with final equilibrium; but, unlike figure 20, the outcome in figure 21 leads to a surplus rather than a deficit. In panel A (figure 21), the available set lies in the irregular area, Oabc. As before, a movement along Oa reduces Net AB_y and has no effect on Net AB_x; the situation is reversed for a movement along Oc; and there is a trade-off along abc. Preliminary buy behavior comes to a halt at the point along abc at which Net AB_x = Net AB_y. In this case, however, that is not at k, the intersection of the Net AB curves, because that intersection implies the commodity combination at k', and the latter lies beyond the available set. The only point along *abc* at which Net AB_x = Net AB_y is point *r* (at which *m* = *n* in the lower half of the composite diagram). Since there is a surplus at *r*, the EB curves will shift downwards and Net AB curves will correspondingly shift upwards. In the final equilibrium, Net AB'_x = Net AB'_y at *b*, a point along the effective boundary and without any remaining surplus (or deficit) to disturb the buy outcome.[24]

In panel B, the effective constraint is the REL constraint, and it lies

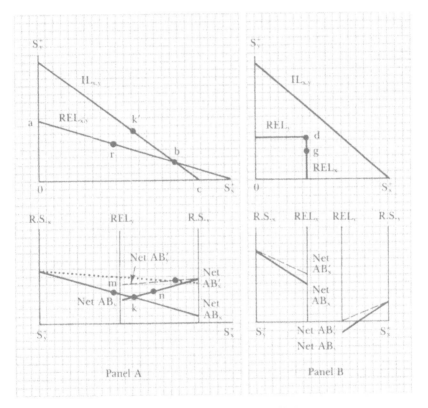

Figure 21. R.S. Curves Not Consistent with Final Equilibrium, Due to Surplus

[24] Panel A is drawn for an individual who exhibits greater Net AB strength for X, the more expensive commodity. Hence, the reduction in EB curves due to a surplus causes a shift in Net AB curves that will move the buy outcome towards X until the surplus is reduced or minimized. For an individual who exhibits greater Net AB strength for Y, the less expensive commodity, the reduction in EB curves due to a surplus would move the buy outcome towards Y until the surplus reaches a maximum. This, too, is compatible with a final equilibrium, as explained in the text.

wholly below the IL curve. Notwithstanding this fact, the preliminary equilibrium (at g) lies below REL_y (but it does reach REL_x). To this extent, there is a surplus which causes a downward shift of the EB curves and a corresponding upward shift of the Net AB curves. The latter shift cannot affect the buy outcome for X because it is already at REL_x; but it does lead to more purchases of Y until REL_y is also reached. In addition, buy behavior moves towards Y because the short-run outcome at g involves a deficit with respect to Y-commodity. If both Net AB curves had been nonnegative throughout, the reinforcer-effectiveness limit would have been reached for both commodities in the preliminary equilibrium; but, of course, a surplus would remain. In accord with our earlier analysis, this would lead to an upward shift of the Net AB curves. However, the final equilibrium and the preliminary equilibrium are necessarily the same in this case, notwithstanding the existence of the surplus.

Long-run Equilibrium Buy Outcome: Stability vs. Durability

Stability conditions of long-run equilibrium. On the basis of the model presented in this chapter, we may now summarize the conditions for both short-run and long-run equilibrium. In the short run, the response strength curves are given, and buy behavior is emitted until Net AB has reached a minimum for both commodities. If there is a deficit or surplus after short-run buy behavior has been emitted, the response strength curves will change and lead to a new buy outcome. Therefore, in order to be in long-run equilibrium, buy behavior must satisfy the following conditions: (A) Net AB will be at a minimum for both commodities (i.e., the short-run condition), and (B) either (1) a deficit or surplus will not exist after buy behavior has been emitted, or, (2) if a deficit or surplus does exist after buy behavior has been emitted, the resulting changes in the RS curves will not lead to a further change in the buy behavior outcome.

Condition A.   If the boundary constraint (SW panel of the four-panel diagram) is such that there is a trade-off between a reduction of Net AB_x and Net AB_y, this condition for short-run equilibrium will be satisfied at the point where Net AB_x = Net AB_y, i.e., at the intersection of the boundary curve and the 45° line in the SW panel (figure 22, panel A). On the other hand, if the boundary constraint (SW panel) has the shape shown in panel B, the two commodities are not in a trade-off relationship; and the short-run equilibrium condition is reached at the hook. The only exception is if the hooked-boundary constraint intersects one of the axes (panel C). In that event, the short-run equilibrium is reached at the intersection between the

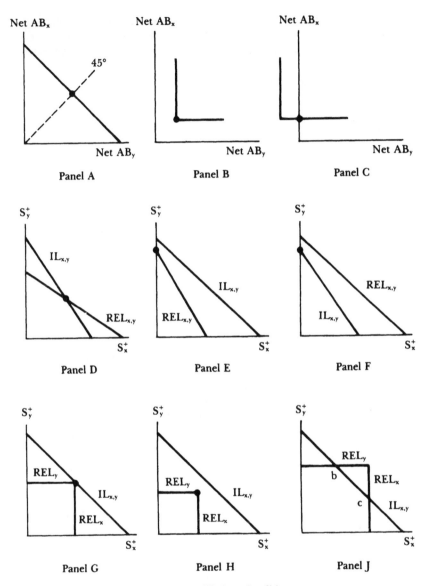

Figure 22. Short-run and Long-run Equilibrium Conditions

boundary curve and the Net AB axis—in panel C, this occurs where Net AB_y = 0 and Net AB_x > 0.

Condition B.   For goods with interdependent RELs, Condition B-1 can be met when $IL_{x,y}$ = $REL_{x,y}$ at some combination (panel D);

or Condition B-2 can be met when $IL_{x,y} \neq REL_{x,y}$ at any combination, but the short-run outcome is a corner solution (panel E or F). For goods with independent RELs, Condition B-1 can be met when $IL_{x,y} = REL_{x,y}$ at some combination (panel G); or, Condition B-2 can be met when $IL_{x,y}$ lies to the right of $REL_{x,y}$ (panel H); or, Condition B-2 can be met when $IL_{x,y}$ intersects (or lies below) REL_x and REL_y, and an oscillating outcome can be excluded—in panel J, this would be at some point along bc.

To summarize the equilibrium conditions:

(1) Condition A assures that, for any given set of response strength curves, the buy outcome is located along the effective boundary.

(2) Condition B assures that, for any given set of dual constraints, the buy outcome reaches a stable position along the effective boundary.

This analysis of equilibrium conditions was developed for the case of primary commodities, but it is substantially applicable also to the case of functional secondary commodities. The major difference is that any deficits or surpluses in the case of functional secondary commodities must be measured with respect to the primary reinforcers on which the particular secondary reinforcers are based. Since an independent operation of deprivation for a secondary commodity does not exist, the reinforcer-effectiveness limit for secondary commodities is a derived limit; and the strength of approach behavior for such commodities is controlled by the deprivation (reinforcer-effectiveness operation) that is applicable to the primary reinforcers on which they are based.

Nonfunctional secondary commodities are similar to functional secondary commodities because the strength of approach behavior depends on the reinforcer-effectiveness operation of the primary reinforcer on which the secondary commodities are based. They are different from functional secondary commodities because consumption of the nonfunctional commodity cannot bring the individual any closer to the reinforcer-effectiveness limit of the underlying primary reinforcer. Accordingly, as noted earlier (chapter 5), the reinforcer-effectiveness limit of nonfunctional secondary commodities is indeterminate. Like other commodities, the short-run buy outcome of nonfunctional secondary commodities is determined at the point where Net AB is at a minimum for both commodities; but there is no determinate long-run equilibrium buy outcome for nonfunctional secondary commodities. Diagrammatically, the short-run buy outcome of nonfunctional secondary commodities resembles our earlier discussion of buy behavior when an income constraint was included but a satiation constraint was ignored. (See first approximation case at the beginning of this chapter.) In the long-run, however, the Net AB curves of nonfunctional secondary commodities will drift upwards as long as the consumer has not reached either the derived reinforcer-effectiveness limit or the extinction limit, and the buy outcome could shift to a new position along the $IL_{x,y}$ boundary.

Escape/avoidance goods are a special category of secondary commodities that are controlled by aversive stimulation rather than by deprivation. For functional escape/avoidance goods, the reinforcer-effectiveness limit is the aversive-stimulus tolerance limit. As shown earlier, this limit can range from zero to some positive level, and it will be different for different kinds of aversive stimulation. The strength of approach behavior for the escape/avoidance commodities is controlled by the intensity of the aversive stimulation of the negative reinforcer. The analysis of buy behavior outcomes for escape/avoidance commodities is substantially similar to ordinary secondary reinforcers (discussed above).

Durability of a long-run equilibrium buy outcome. In real world applications, it is particularly important to distinguish between the stability conditions of a long-run equilibrium buy outcome (as described above) and the likelihood that any given outcome will be durable. The latter in turn depends on whether the parameters are long-lasting. In the real world (as distinct from a carefully controlled laboratory situation), there are a number of reasons why the givens in our hypothetical experiments (model) are unlikely to remain constant over time. First, the particular buy behavior outcome that is reached under any given set of controlling parameters depends partly on random events. In operant conditioning experiments, responses occur when an appropriate level of deprivation is combined with a positive discriminative stimulus (S^D). For example, a devotee of fast foods who is in a food-deprived condition may be equally likely to emit buy behavior leading to consumption of a hamburger or a pizza, depending on whether the S^D at the time that the food deprivation has become strong happens to be a hamburger outlet or a pizza outlet. Since it is impossible to predict the appearance of a particular S^D, it is also impossible to predict which commodity will be purchased in a given state of deprivation with respect to those commodities. In short, the allocation of income in a given income period to specific goods (given the level of deprivation or other reinforcer-establishing operation) is inevitably affected by inherently fortuitous and random events, viz., the appearance of appropriate discriminative stimuli for either positive or negative reinforcers. Moreover, it is not just the occurrence of the events but also the sequence in which they are encountered that is important to the final outcome. These considerations are particularly evident in the case of commodities with interdependent reinforcer-effectiveness limits; but, given the existence of income limitations, they are also likely to be important for goods with independent limits. In the equilibrium analysis of this chapter, it has been tacitly assumed that the appropriate discriminative stimuli were simultaneously in effect at the moment of allocation in the two-commodity model. That assumption is appropriate for analytical purposes, but it must be applied with caution in actual cases. In real world allocations, those conditions are likely to be met or approximated for only a limited number of the possible commodities that could be involved under given reinforcer-establishing operations. Under those circumstances, the sequential paradigm becomes an important part of the explanation for actual buy outcomes; and the path by which the equilibrium is reached will itself help to determine that equilibrium. For example, the particular combination of products that is bought during a given trip to a supermarket depends in part on the particular way in which the products are laid out in the store, i.e., on the location of important discriminative stimuli.

Second, the reinforcer-effectiveness limits for particular reinforcers as well as the strength of approach behavior associated with a given level of the reinforcer-effectiveness operation may not remain constant over time and the individual's experiences. One reason is the phenomenon called adaptation (also known as habituation), a process in which the magnitude of a response gradually declines as the organism is repeatedly introduced to the situation that produces the response. Although it is often discussed in relation to aversive stimuli, adaptation is equally applicable to positively reinforcing events. As Millenson (1967, pp. 462–63) has noted, "Even the good things in life can lose their appeal if we get 'used' to them." For positive reinforcers, the variability in the reinforcer-effectiveness limits and in the strength of approach behavior may also be related to the fact that variety (or novelty) is itself a reinforcer (Scitovsky, 1976).

Another reason why the strength of approach behavior may not be constant over time is particularly relevant in the case of functional escape/avoidance commodities, viz., the fact that the individual is insulated (by escape or avoidance) against the aversive stimulation insofar as the functional escape/avoidance commodities are effective. It will be recalled from the earlier discussion of the avoidance paradigm that a formerly neutral stimulus (S_1) acquires aversive properties when it is paired with an aversive stimulus (S^-). When the individual escapes from S_1 (by emitting a behavior that utilizes the escape/avoidance commodity), he avoids the S^- as a by-product. However, after the consumer has avoided the S^- for a long time (by a chain of escape behavior that incorporates the escape/avoidance commodity), the aversive properties of S_1 become attenuated or even disappear. As the bond between S_1 and S^- becomes weakened, approach behavior to the escape/avoidance commodity also becomes weakened. Diagrammatically, the AB curve for the escape/avoidance commodity shifts downward, and the buy outcome includes less of the escape/avoidance commodity. As a result, the next time that the aversive stimulation is present, the consumer experiences a greater intensity of the aversive stimulation. This renewed pairing of S_1 and S^- serves to recondition the S_1 and thus also to strengthen approach behavior to the escape/avoidance commodity that is incorporated into the chain of escape behavior from S_1. The upward shift in the AB curves thus tends to move buy outcome back towards the previous equilibrium position. In short, when one of the commodities in the two-commodity model is an escape/avoidance commodity, the buy outcome may exhibit a cyclical pattern around an equilibrium position (Skinner, 1953, pp. 218–19; Wertheim, 1968).

Third, the levels of the reinforcer-effectiveness operation that control approach behavior for different commodities are in a constant state of flux. This is partly a function of whatever consumption may have occurred, but also because many primary reinforcers exhibit cycles that are related to the passage of time. An obvious and important example is food deprivation. Moreover these time-related reinforcers have different cycles. As a practical matter, these different cycles are unlikely to be synchronized in such a way that the same buy outcome will emerge in each income period. In addition, of course, the lengths of the deprivation cycles are unrelated, except by chance, to the arbitrary time periods in which income flows are measured.

CHAPTER SEVEN

Buy Behavior After a Change in Income or Prices

Chapter 6 examined the equilibrium of buy behavior under given values for the conditioning parameters. This chapter shows how that equilibrium can be affected by changes in two important conditioning parameters: (1) a change in income, and (2) a change in the contingencies of reinforcement in the form of a change in relative prices. The first section deals with the effects of a change in income. The second section will examine the effects of a change in relative prices when reinforcer-effectiveness limits are ignored (for expository convenience) but income limits are taken into account. As it happens, this is also the framework for examining the buy outcome of nonfunctional secondary commodities (cf. p. 110). Hence, the second section can also be regarded as an analysis of the effects of relative price changes for nonfunctional secondary commodities.[1] The third section examines the effects of a change in relative prices when both of the dual constraints are taken into account and shows the buy outcome in terms of

---

[1] Unlike the case with other commodities, the $IL_{x,y}$ curve is the only effective constraint on buy behavior for this category until the consumer reaches the derived reinforcer-effectiveness limit or extinction limit. Since there is no determinate long-run equilibrium buy outcome for nonfunctional secondary commodities, this analysis of the effects of a relative price change describes only short-run effects for such commodities. However, it does not describe short-run effects for primary commodities and functional secondary commodities, because that analysis must include both of the dual constraints.

long-run as well as short-run equilibrium effects. This covers the cases of primary commodities and functional secondary commodities. The fourth section shows the relation between buy behavior and the Law of Demand. The fifth section looks at some determinants of response strength. The final section is a brief postscript on positively sloped Net AB curves.

Effects of a Change in Income

For the purposes of this study, the effects of an increase in income will be limited to the set of commodities that are included in a given individual's past history of conditioning, viz., those that were being purchased and consumed before the change in income. In this model, an increase in income has no direct effect on the total list of products consumed (i.e., included in a given life style), because a higher income per se does not constitute a change in the experiences of consumption that are embedded in a given past history of conditioning. After someone has experienced a (for him) new product and been reinforced by it, he may wonder how he ever got along without it; before that, however, it was not part of his past history of conditioning or life style. In short, a change in the list of commodities consumed means a change in life style; but, as noted, life style is not *directly* affected by a change in income.

These comments on the relation between a change in income and past history of conditioning are also applicable, mutatis mutandis, to the effect of the income change on reinforcer-effectiveness limits. An individual's life style is an important determinant of reinforcer limit quantities (under given levels of the reinforcer-establishing operation). The level of income has no direct effect on the limit quantities that are established under a given past history of conditioning and a given level of a reinforcer-establishing operation. Although a change in income has no direct effect on life styles or reinforcer-effectiveness limits, it can have an indirect effect on both. A higher income can indirectly affect life styles by its permissive effect on new conditioning experiences, if a stimulus for the change in the previous history of conditioning exists independently of the change in income. A change in life style can in turn affect the reinforcer-effectiveness limits, especially of secondary commodities; and, in this way, a change in income can also indirectly affect those limits. In this study, however, these effects are not included in the model.

A change in the level of income can affect the equilibrium buy outcome in two ways: (1) the "IL effect" shows how much of the change in buy outcomes is due to the shift in the IL curve, and (2) the

"EB effect" shows how much is due to the shift in the EB curves (i.e., a change in response strength for the same amount of outlay). Thus, for an individual with a given history of conditioning, the effects of a change (say, an increase) in income will depend in part on the size of the change in relation to the total income. When the new income is not much larger (e.g., 1 percent) than the former income, any change in the intensity of the aversive consequences of a loss of any given number of dollars surrendered in payment (e.g., in terms of impeded or blocked access to other reinforcers) is probably below a threshold level. Hence, the change in income has no effect on the slope of the EB curves. It does, however, affect their length, because those curves must be extended (presumably at the same slope) to cover a wider range of outlays to accord with the shift of the IL boundary—the IL effect. When the new income is sufficiently larger than the old income to bring about a measurable reduction in the intensity of the aversive consequences of a loss of any given number of dollars surrendered in payment, the reduction in intensity of the reinforcer-effectiveness operation for any given outlay will be reflected in a lower gradient for the EB curves—the EB effect. The question of how much the slope would be reduced can only be answered empirically. In the absence of sufficient experimental evidence on this matter, I will proceed on the working hypothesis (adopted primarily for convenience) that the terminal level of response strength of the EB curve would be the same as in the old income level. It should be stressed that, since the effects of a larger income are examined under the assumption that the past history of conditioning remains unchanged, this is a short-run analysis also in the sense that any income-related change in life styles would take place only gradually and over a longer period of time.

The case when the increase in income is too small to affect the level of the EB curves is depicted in figure 23A, in which REL constraints have been omitted for convenience. When the $IL_{x,y}$ boundary is IL_1 (NE panel), the EB and Net AB curves are the solid lines in the NW and SE panels; the available set of buy outcomes is bounded by *pab* (SW panel), and the equilibrium outcome is at *r*. When the $IL_{x,y}$ boundary shifts to IL_2, the EB and Net AB curves are extended (as shown by the dotted lines); the available set expands to *pcd*, and a new equilibrium is reached at *s*. The IL effect of an increase in income leads to an increase in the purchase of both commodities in this case, but this is not a necessary result when REL constraints are included in the model (as shown below).

The effects of a "large" change in income can be observed in figure 23B, which includes the dual constraints and all of the relevant response strength curves for both commodities. A large increase in

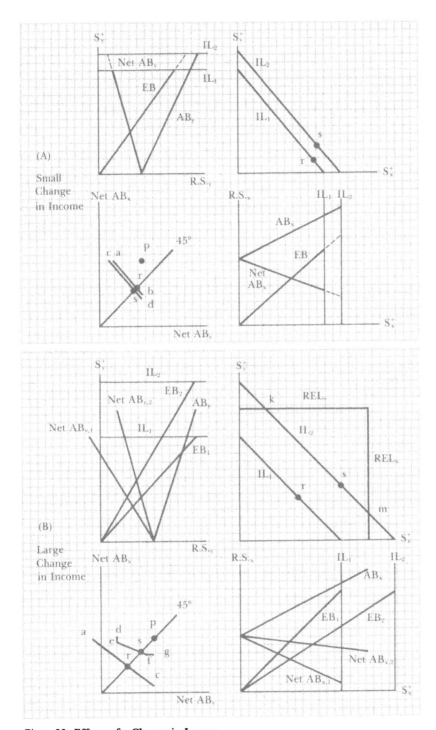

Figure 23. Effects of a Change in Income

117

income causes a fall in EB curves and an upward shift of the Net AB curves for both commodities. Before the increase in income, the available set of buy combinations is bounded in the area *pac* (SW panel), and the long-run equilibrium buy outcome is at *r*. After the increase in income, the boundary of the available set is *pdefg*, and the short-run equilibrium outcome is at *s*. In this example, the short-run effect of a higher income is to increase purchases of both commodities (NE panel).[2] Although the buy outcome at *s* is a deficit position, the consumer is closer to REL_x than to REL_y. According to our earlier analysis, this would gradually cause both AB curves to shift upwards with a greater relative shift in favor of Y product. These relative shifts would, at least temporarily, tend to increase the quantity of Y and to reduce the quantity of X. The final long-run outcome might oscillate in the *km* segment of IL_2 constraint (NE panel), or it might settle at a given point along that segment, as explained in chapter 6 (p. 98).

The possible short-run outcomes of a change in income are summarized in the composite diagrams of figure 24 (which for simplicity omit the REL constraints). These summary diagrams show the operant conditioning basis for the traditional economic classification of commodities according to the response to a change in income. Panel A shows the range of short-run outcomes for a large increase in income. The initial equilibrium is at point *r*. After the increase in income, the Net AB curves for both commodities shift upwards.[3] One possible set of Net AB curves is shown in the diagram. If the new intersection of Net $AB_{x,2}$ and Net $AB_{y,2}$ lies along the line DD, the quantity of X is unchanged and Y is a superior good. If the new intersection is to the left of line DD, X is an inferior good and Y is ultrasuperior; if it is along EE, Y is unchanged and X is superior; if it is to the right of EE, X is ultrasuperior and Y is inferior.[4] For any intersection between DD and EE, X and Y are both normal goods. For a given large increase in income, one good is likely to be ultrasuperior and the other inferior only if the former has a significantly stronger Net AB curve—e.g., the ordinate intercept is much higher and/or the

[2] However, a stronger AB_y curve than the one shown in panel B could give a quite different short-run outcome as a result of the increase in income, e.g., an increase in the quantity of Y and a reduction in the quantity of X.

[3] Given our working hypothesis that the terminal level of the EB curves is the same at different levels of income, it follows that the terminal points of *both* Net AB curves will be above the response strength level of the original Net AB curves.

[4] I have followed Hirshleifer (1980, p. 103) in describing the "partner" of an inferior good as "ultrasuperior." The term "superior" here describes a commodity that absorbs 100 percent of the increase in income, and "neutral" describes a commodity that exhibits no response to a change in income.

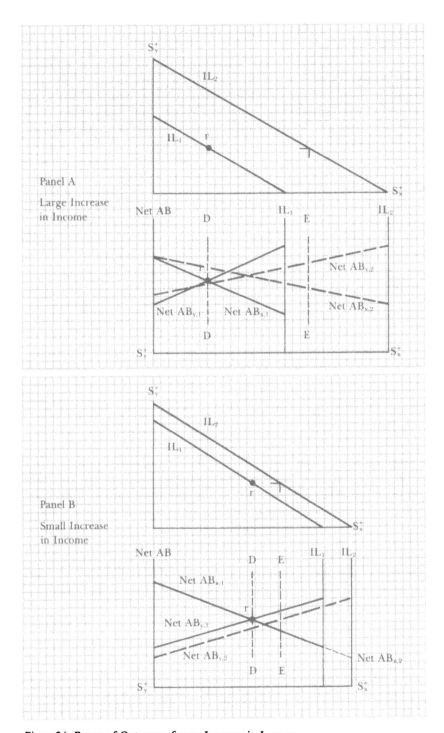

Figure 24. Range of Outcomes for an Increase in Income

entire curve lies well above the Net AB curve of the other commodity. Panel B shows the short-run outcomes for a small increase in income. The analysis of outcomes is similar to the above, except that the range of outcomes is bounded by DD and EE, i.e., both commodities are normal goods—or, at the limit, the quantity of one remains unchanged and the other is accordingly superior.

Although reinforcer-effectiveness limits have not been mentioned in connection with the above classification of commodities, it is apparent that the effects of a change in income will be determined in part by whether an individual's consumption of any given commodity is already at (or near) that limit. As noted earlier, large numbers of consumers in countries like the United States regularly attain reinforcer-effectiveness limits for many primary goods. To this extent, an increase in income per se would not lead to greater consumption of such commodities by such individuals. As mentioned above, however, if a higher level of income leads to a different life style, which incorporates not only new products but also new ways of using old products, the consumption of such commodities could be affected indirectly via the effect of higher incomes on reinforcer limits.[5]

Effects of a Change in Relative Prices When REL Is Ignored

Impact on AB and EB. According to the model of buy behavior developed in chapter 6, the equilibrium buy outcome is determined by a double conflict: (1) the inherent conflict between approach and escape behaviors for any given commodity, and (2) the inherent conflict in choosing combinations of commodities that may be incompatible in terms of the dual constraints (reinforcer-effectiveness limits and income limits), i.e., the conflict between minimizing Net AB_x and Net AB_y for any two commodities. Since equilibrium is analyzed in terms of approach behavior and escape behavior, our analysis of the effects of a change in relative prices must also work through its effects on these behaviors, i.e., on the determinants of the conflicts inherent in buy behavior.

The effects of a change in relative prices, like the effects of a change

---

[5] One form that a new life style might take is the use of old products in new ways. Thus an individual who formerly purchased a commodity to its reinforcer-effectiveness limit as a primary reinforcer may, after an increase in income, learn to use that commodity in different ways that are reinforcing because the commodity can also function as a secondary good (e.g., by its association with approval, prestige, etc.) or as an escape/avoidance good (e.g., to avoid the aversive consequence of running out of the commodity under circumstances in which it would be inconvenient or impossible to acquire additional supplies at the time and place of consumption).

in income, can be analyzed in terms of an IL effect and an EB effect. In the operant conditioning paradigm, a change in relative prices— suppose that price of X falls and price of Y remains unchanged—is a change in the contingencies of reinforcement. In the SE panel of the four-panel diagram, the contingency of reinforcement is reflected in the relation of the abscissa scale for size of positive reinforcement (shown explicitly) and the (implicit) scale for size of negative reinforcement. In order to show the new contingency, the (implicit) scale for size of S⁻ must be changed (while the scale for size of S⁺ is unchanged), and the EB curve must be redrawn to the new scale (figure 25). If X is a small item in the consumer's budget, a fall in the price

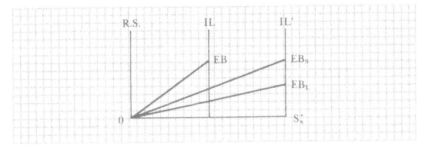

Figure 25. IL Effect and EB Effect

of X has no significant implications for the level of real income—the effect of a change in outlay is below a threshold level with respect to any change in the aversive consequences of any given outlay; and the full effect of the fall in price of X can be shown by the change in the contingency of reinforcement (and the associated shift from EB to EB$_S$)—the IL effect.[6] If X is a large item in the consumer's budget, a fall in the price of X implies a significant change in real income as well as a change in the contingency of reinforcement (matched pairs of size of S⁺ and size of S⁻). As shown earlier, the intensity of the aversive consequences of any given loss of dollar reinforcers is related in part to the level of income. If the fall in price of X raises the level of real income by a significant amount, the intensity of the reinforcer-effectiveness operation involved in any given loss of dollar reinforcers will be reduced. Diagrammatically, this is shown by a further shift of the EB curve from EB$_S$ to EB$_L$—the EB effect.

[6] The effects of a large increase in income and the effects of a relative fall in the price of a commodity that is a small part of the budget are both represented by a shift to the right of the EB curve. However, the EB curve shifts only in the SW panel (of a four-panel diagram) in the event of a fall in price of X, whereas it shifts in the NW panel as well in the event of an increase in income. In addition, the price change implies a change in the (implicit) scale of the S⁻ abscissa, but the income change has no effect on the scales of either the S⁺ or S⁻ abscissas.

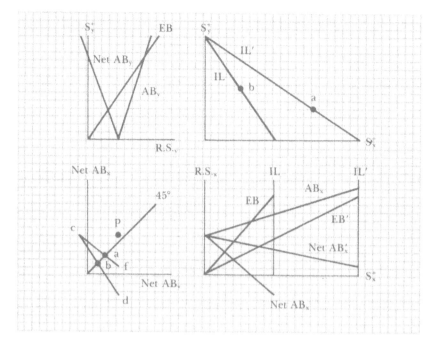

Figure 26. Short-run Effects of a Change in Relative Prices

We can now proceed to analyze the effects of a fall in price of X on the equilibrium position of buy behavior for an example in which the IL constraint is included but the REL constraint is ignored. For this preliminary presentation, the discussion will be limited to the case when X is a small part of the consumer's budget. The short-run equilibrium effects[7] can be observed in figure 26. In the NE panel, the fall in price of X causes the IL curve to shift to IL'; and this change is also included in the SE panel. In addition, the EB curve (SE panel) is redrawn to accord with the (implicit) new scale for size of S⁻, viz., from EB to EB'. The representation of the AB curve is, of course, unaffected by the change in the contingency of reinforcement. Although the level of the reinforcer-effectiveness operation for any given outlay is also unaffected by the change in the reinforcement contingency, the change which does occur in the (implicit) scale of the size of S⁻ abscissa (while size of S⁺ scale remains unchanged) implies that there will be an upward shift of the Net AB_x curve after the EB curve has been adjusted to the new scale. In the SW panel, the avail-

---

[7] The distinction between short-run and long-run effects of a relative price change will be discussed in the next section.

able set changes from *pcd* to *pcf*; and the equilibrium buy outcome moves correspondingly from *b* to *a* (SW and NE panels). Thus, in this example, the fall in the price of X shifts the buy outcome equilibrium to a new position with less Y and more X. In part, this is because the equilibrium lies along the 45° line in the SW panel, i.e., equilibrium occurs where Net AB_x = Net AB_y. It is quite possible, however, that the available set does not include any points along the 45° line (SW panel) either before or after the fall in price of X. In that event, the equilibrium outcome is a corner solution, and the price change would have no effect on the outcome.

Contrast effects and adaptation. One interesting effect of a change in relative prices is the possibility—ignored in traditional economic analysis—that the change qua change in the reinforcement contingency may affect the response. Behavioral contrast, a transitional rather than a steady-state effect, "represents an effect of a particular history of conditioning upon an animal's mode of adaptation to a new conditioning procedure" (Staddon, 1972, p. 240). For our purposes, it suggests that the consumer's buy behavior may temporarily overshoot the mark in moving towards a new equilibrium.

The evidence for the hypothesis that buy behavior may temporarily respond to a price change as such can be found in experiments that were designed to examine the effects of amount of reinforcement on learning and performance. Evidence was cited earlier (pp. 27–28) to show that operant response strength is positively related to the quantity of the reinforcer available to the organism upon each presentation of the reinforcer. In their review of the literature on this subject, Cofer and Appley (1967, p. 553) cited an experiment in which

Zeaman (1949) measured the latencies of the running responses of his rats for several amounts of food. The final level reached by the latencies at asymptote during the 19 acquisition trials was shortest for the animals rewarded with the largest amount of food (2.4 grams) and longest for the animals given the smallest reward (0.05 gram). Latencies for the other groups fell in between.

In these experiments, duration of latency is a measure of strength of response. After the nineteen acquisition trials, Zeaman shifted the 0.05-gram reward group to a reward of 2.4 grams and shifted the original 2.4-gram group to a reward of 0.05 gram with the following results: "Latencies of both groups changed at once, the group now receiving a larger incentive shortening its latencies and the other group increasing its latencies." This effect has also been found by

Wolfe and Kaplon (1941), Crespi (1942), Spence (1956), and (in a different design) by Metzger, Cotton, and Lewis (1975).

This much is familiar and well-established. The additional interesting evidence was found by both Crespi and Zeaman who reported that, in addition to the results described above, there were also "contrast" effects. As described by Cofer and Appley,

> These refer to the fact that after change in amount of reward, the group whose reward was increased performed even faster than the group originally trained on this reward ("elation" effect), and the group which had its reward reduced performed even more slowly than the group originally trained with the small reward ("depression" effect).

Although the evidence on the contrast effect is conflicting and uncertain,[8] its possible application to a change in relative prices is suggestive. The change in the amount of reinforcement in the above-cited experiments was a change in the contingencies of reinforcement to be found in the organism's environment, and it has a direct parallel in the change in relative prices in a consumer's market environment. As shown earlier, this change would typically lead to a change in the consumer's equilibrium buy behavior. If the contrast effect is borne out by further experimental inquiry, the consumer's response may at least initially overshoot the new equilibrium level. If the price of X falls relative to the price of Y, buy behavior with respect to X may temporarily exceed the new equilibrium (elation effect); and if the price of X rises relatively, purchases of X may temporarily fall below the new equilibrium (depression effect).[9]

Effects of a Change in Relative Prices under the Dual Constraints

When X is a small part of the consumer's budget. We are now ready to include both of the dual constraints in our analysis of the equilibrium

---

[8] "The elation effect was not found by Spence or by Metzger et al., although O'Connor and Claridge (1958), working with imbeciles who performed a repetitive task, did find it. Depression effects were found by Spence but not by Metzger et al., or by O'Connor and Claridge. . . . Ehrenfreund and Badia (1962) found both contrast effects in animals under high drive (85 percent body weight) but not under low drive (95 percent body weight). They measured running speed in a straight runway." (Cofer and Appley, 1964, p. 554).

[9] There is perhaps some experimental support for the contrast effect in connection with price changes. In an interesting study of consumer demand behavior, using laboratory animals, Kagel et al. (1975, p. 33) found that, following a 67 percent increase in the price of food, there was a change in consumption away from food and towards the cheaper water. Significantly, however, "This change in the composition of consumption was greatest in the period immediately following the price change and remained essen-

effects of a change in relative prices. In this discussion, we will examine the effects of a fall in price of X when X is a small part of the consumer's budget, and our discussion of equilibrium effects will be divided into short-run effects and long-run effects. We begin with an example of commodities with independent reinforcer-effectiveness limits and examine the effects of a relative price change by means of a composite diagram which (for simplicity) shows only the Net AB curves (figure 27). In the lower part of the composite diagram, Net AB_x shifts to Net AB'_x; and the Net AB_y curve is adjusted to the new abscissa scale for Y. In the latter adjustment, each point on the Net AB_y (adjusted) curve represents the same level of response strength for any given pair of size of S^+ and size of S^- as the corresponding point on the Net AB_y curve. In panel A, the effective boundary before the price change is $Ocdh$, consisting of the REL_y constraint and part of the IL constraint. The long-run equilibrium before the price change (at point b) was reached in the manner described in chapter 6. The fall in price of X (with price of Y unchanged) would change the effective boundary to $Ocefg$, consisting of both REL constraints and part of the new IL constraint. In this example, the short-run equilibrium moves from b to a, and there is an increase in purchases of X. If the REL_x constraint had passed through point b instead of point f, the short-run effect would have been zero. However, except for the latter case (i.e., where the initial long-run equilibrium is at the REL_x constraint), a fall in the price of X *must* lead to a new short-run equilibrium in which a larger quantity of X is included.

Since this discussion of price effects is limited to the case in which X is such a small part of the consumer's budget that there is no EB effect from the fall in price of X, the short-run effects would not ordinarily lead to an increase in purchases of Y. The short-run effect could lead to more Y, however, if the purchases of X are stopped by the REL_x constraint at a point before the IL constraint is also reached. In figure 27, panel B, the initial long-run equilibrium is at b. After the fall in price of X, the expansion in X is blocked at b'', because Net AB'_x has reached the REL_x constraint. However, b'' is an interior point with respect to the IL' constraint. Hence, neither of the dual constraints relevant for Y (viz., $IL_{x,y}$ and REL_y) will block an expansion in the purchases of Y until point a is reached on the upper half of panel B.

Unlike the short-run effects of a relative price change, the long-run effects depend in addition on either a deficit effect or a surplus effect. In panel B, the short-run equilibrium after the price change is at point

tially unchanged for about three weeks. However, following this, consumption patterns started to drift towards baseline values over the next two weeks."

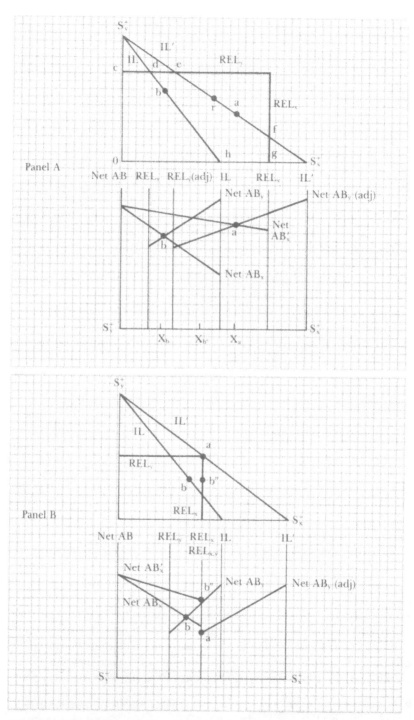

Figure 27. Relative Price Change—Independent RELs

a, the intersection of $IL_{x,y}$ and $REL_{x,y}$. Since there is neither a deficit nor a surplus at this outcome, the short-run equilibrium is also the long-run equilibrium; and the short-run effects of a relative price change are the same as the long-run effects. In panel A, by contrast, the new short-run equilibrium at *a* reduced the former deficit with respect to X, but it enlarged the deficit with respect to Y. In line with the analysis in chapter 6, that could raise Net AB_y relatively to Net AB_x, and the long-run outcome could move back along the boundary constraint to, say, point *r* (upper half). To that extent, the long-run effects could partially undo (and possibly even reverse) the short-run effects. Alternatively, the long-run outcome might oscillate along the *ef* segment of the effective boundary.

We turn next to an exposition of the effects of a relative price change for commodities with interdependent reinforcer-effectiveness limits (figure 28). The initial long-run equilibrium is at *b*, a combination in which further purchases are blocked by both of the dual constraints. A fall in the price of X moves the short-run equilibrium outcome from *b* to *e* (upper panel). It will be noted that *e* is not at the intersection of Net AB'_x and Net AB_y (adjusted), viz., at *t*. Since the intersection at *t* lies beyond the new effective boundary (*Ocfg*, upper panel) in this case, the new outcome is constrained by the segment *cf*. Because of the interdependent REL constraint, an increase in one commodity necessarily requires a reduction in the other along the $REL_{x,y}$ frontier. As shown earlier, short-run equilibrium is reached when Net AB is minimized for both commodities together. In this example, that condition is met at *e* (upper panel) where Net $AB'_x(= m)$ equals Net AB_y adjusted ($= n$) (lower panel). Point *e* does not, however, also satisfy the requirement for long-run equilibrium, because there is a surplus at *e*. This will lower the EB curves and raise Net AB curves for both commodities. In this example, the individual exhibits greater Net AB strength for the more expensive commodity, and the relative shift in Net AB curves moves the buy outcome towards X (the more expensive commodity in this case). For diagrammatic simplicity, the relative shift of the Net AB curves is shown by raising the Net AB'_x curve to Net AB''_x and leaving the Net AB_y curve unchanged. The result is a new long-run equilibrium buy outcome at *f*, a combination in which further purchases are blocked by both of the dual constraints.

In the preceding case, both the short-run and long-run effects of a fall in price of X led to larger purchases of X. Figure 29 illustrates a case in which this typical outcome does not occur. In contrast to figure 28, the price falls relatively for the commodity with the weaker Net AB curve, which is also the less expensive commodity in this case. The

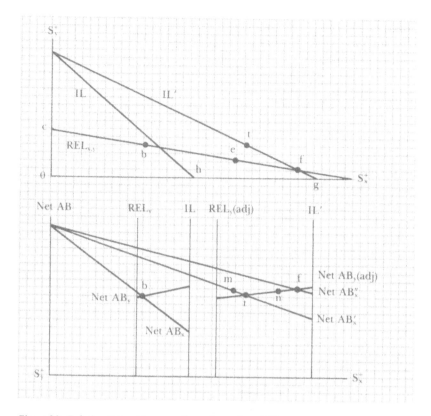

Figure 28. Relative Price Change—Interdependent RELs

short-run response is for buy outcome to move from b to e—Net $AB'_x(= m)$ equals Net AB_y adjusted ($= n$) at point e—i.e., towards more consumption of the commodity whose price has fallen relatively. Since e is a surplus position, this move will raise both Net AB curves. As in the previous case, the individual exhibits greater Net AB strength for the more expensive commodity (Y). Hence, the buy outcome moves towards Y—as shown by the shift of Net AB''_y—and to a long-run equilibrium at h. However, in contrast to the previous case, the long-run response of the fall in price of X is directly opposite to the short-run response with the result that the lower price of X leads in the long run to a reduction in quantity of X. In this example, X is a Giffen good over the long run but not in the short run.

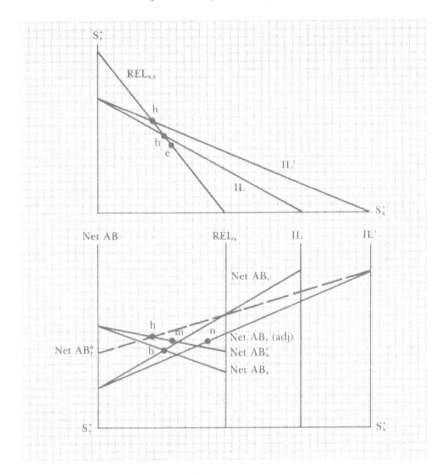

Figure 29. Atypical Outcome of a Relative Price Change

When X is a large part of the consumer's budget. In this discussion of the effects of a relative fall in price of X, we have thus far considered only those cases in which X is a small part of the consumer's budget. We now consider the modifications that are necessary when X is a large part of the consumer's budget.[10] When X is a small part of the budget, a fall in the price of X has an indirect effect on the Net AB_x curve via

[10] In traditional economics, this distinction is relevant in determining the relative importance of the income and substitution effects (see Hicks, 1946, p. 32).

its effect on the $IL_{x,y}$ boundary constraint—IL shifts to IL', and this implies a change in the matching pairs of size of S^+ and size of S^-. (This is the IL effect.) When X is a large part of the consumer's budget, a fall in the price of X will, in addition, reduce the level of the EB curves, and this has a direct effect on the Net AB curves of both commodities. (This is the EB effect.)

In the four-panel diagram of figure 30, the total effect of a fall in price of X is decomposed into an IL effect and an EB effect for the case when X is a large part of the budget.[11] The initial budget constraint is IL, and the initial equilibrium is at r (NE panel). After the fall in the price of X, the new boundary constraint is IL', and a new equilibrium is reached at t. The movement from r to t is the total effect of the fall in price of X. The IL effect is the movement from r to s. In the SE panel, the IL effect is reflected in the shift from EB to EB' and the corresponding shift from Net AB_x to Net AB'_x; and there is no change in the EB curve of the NW panel. Since X is a large part of the budget, a fall in the price of X also has an EB effect. This is reflected in the shift from EB' to EB'' in the SE panel and from EB to EB'' in the NW panel; and there is an associated shift to Net AB'' in both panels. As a result of these additional shifts, the quantity of X is (in this example) further increased by the amount st. In this case, the EB effect is positive for X; but it might have been zero or even negative.[12] Thus the total effect of a fall in price of X depends on the algebraic sum of the IL effect and the EB effect.

To summarize this discussion of the effects of a fall in price of X, buy behavior equilibrium is determined by (1) dual constraints—$IL_{x,y}$ and $REL_{x,y}$, and (2) strength of Net AB curves for both commodities. It follows that the effects of any change in the contingency of reinforcement, such as a relative fall in price of X, must be determined by the same variables. When a commodity whose price has fallen relatively is a small part of the consumer's budget, a fall in price of X (with price of Y unchanged) alters one of the dual constraints (viz., $IL_{x,y}$). The individual's buy outcome will then adjust to the new constraints but with existing Net AB curves. When X is a large part of the consumer's budget, the fall in the price of X will, in addition, alter the strength of the EB curves and thereby alter the strength of both of the Net AB curves. The individual's buy outcome will then adjust to the new constraints but with different Net AB curves.

[11] For simplicity, the REL constraints are not included; hence, this is a short-run analysis.

[12] For example, if AB_y had been stronger, the EB effect would have been negative for X. If the EB effect is sufficiently negative for X, X would be a Giffen good even in terms of a short-run analysis.

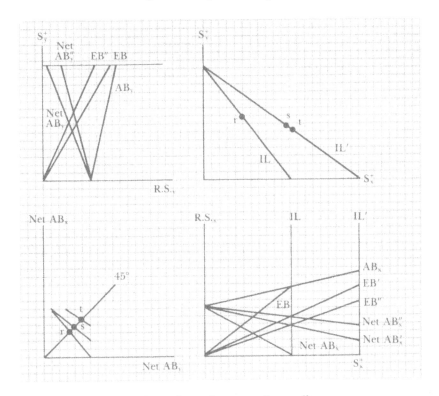

Figure 30. Relative Price Change for an Important Commodity

The effects of a fall in price of X also depend on the reinforcer-effectiveness limits, and the effects will be different for commodities with independent limits and those with interdependent limits. Consider first the case of commodities with independent limits. Other things being equal, a price change will have a lesser effect on quantity of X if buy behavior is constrained by the REL_x boundary than if it is not; and, in the extreme case of buy behavior which is at the REL_x boundary before the price fall, the price change will not affect X in the short run. The long-run effects may be quite different from the short-run effects. For example, when a fall in price of X moves buy behavior closer to REL_x but away from REL_y, the deficit in Y tends to raise AB_y relatively to AB_x. Other things equal, therefore, the subsequent response to a fall in the price of X could be to reduce the quantity of X from its newly reached short-run equilibrium position, and the net expansion in X might even become negative with respect to the quantity that was consumed (bought) before the price change. In this unstable situation, further shifts in the two AB curves are likely in response to further changes in the relative sizes of the deficits over time. The final outcome could be a stable equilibrium or it could be permanently unstable and oscillating, depending on the impact of the deficits on the Net AB curves for each commodity. (See also pp. 97–98.)

Both the short-run and the long-run effects can be quite different from the foregoing in the case of commodities with interdependent reinforcer-effectiveness limits. In the short run, a fall in the price of X would lead to an increase in quantity of X purchased even though X and Y taken together were already at $REL_{x,y}$. If the fall in the price of X is sufficiently large, the quantity of X could continue to increase until REL_x is reached. The long-run effects also can be different from the case of commodities with independent limits. For example, a fall in price of X which moves buy behavior along the $REL_{x,y}$ line so that it is closer to REL_x does not thereby create any deficit in Y which would raise AB_y relatively to AB_x. The move along the $REL_{x,y}$ line may instead bring about a surplus which would lead to a shift in both Net AB curves, and the final outcome would depend on the relative strength of the Net AB curves.

Buy Behavior and the Law of Demand

The operant analysis of the short-run effects of relative price changes[13] can also be related to the traditional analysis which divides the effects of a fall in the price of X (with price of Y unchanged) according to the effects due to a change in relative prices and a change in (real) income[14] (figure 31). The NE panel shows the standard Slutsky division between relative price changes and income changes— IL_a is the initial IL boundary constraint; IL_b is the new IL boundary after the fall in price of X (with price of Y remaining unchanged); and IL_c shows the change in relative prices and a lower level of income. The available set for curve IL_a is *pde* (SW panel) and the equilibrium is at *r*. The rotation of the IL curve about point *r* (NE panel) yields a

---

[13] As shown later in this section, traditional analysis ignores what are here called long-run effects.

[14] It is conventional to trace these effects using either the Hicks or Slutsky methods of division. The Slutsky approach is employed below, because it is more in keeping with the operational emphasis in this study.

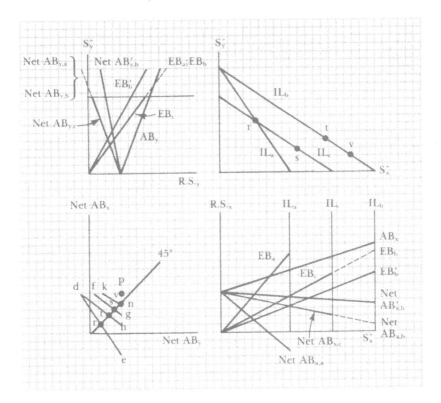

Figure 31. Substitution and Income Effects

new available set (*pfg*) and a new equilibrium at *s*. The increase in income from IL_c to IL_b can have two effects. The available set for the IL effect is *pdh*, and the equilibrium is at *t*; the available set for the EB effect is *pkn*, and the equilibrium is at *v*.

Figure 32 is a diagrammatic decomposition for tracing substitution and income effects by means of the composite diagram. In this figure, the lower part of the composite diagram has been subdivided into three different panels (B, C, and D). The left side of the figure shows the effects of a price change in terms of the EB curves.[15] Panel B shows how the EB curves for X (and Y) would shift when there is a change in relative prices but not in real income. The change in relative prices is shown by changing the implicit scale for size of S⁻ quantities (and

---

[15] Since the EB_x and EB_y curves are similar, mutatis mutandis, only EB_x curves are shown.

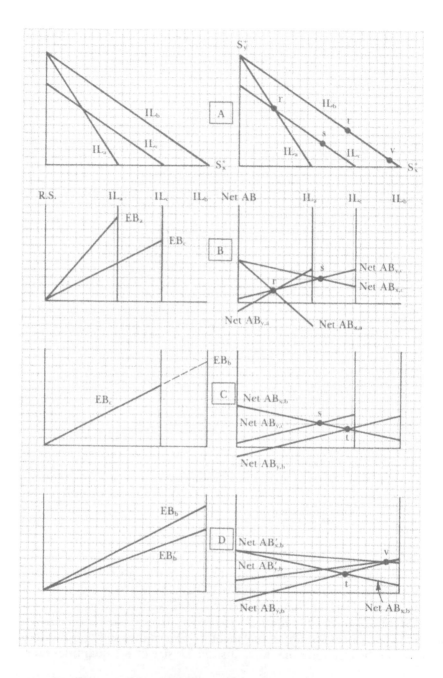

Figure 32. Diagrammatic Decomposition of Substitution and Income Effects

134

thus the matching pairs of the size of S^+ and size of S^- quantities along the abscissa scale for size of S^+) and then adjusting the EB curve to the new scale. The effect of the higher real income is removed by reducing the nominal income at the new commodity prices and then adjusting the EB curves for both commodities. Panel C shows how the EB curves for X (and Y) would be extended to the new IL boundary to conform with the change in nominal (as well as real) income when the only effect of a higher nominal (and real) income is an IL effect that pushes back the IL boundary constraint. Panel D shows how the EB curves for X (and Y) would be additionally shifted if the increase in nominal (and real) income also has an EB effect that reduces the strength of EB for any given size of outlay. The panels on the right side of the figure show how the changes on the left side would alter the Net AB curves for both commodities. The movement from r to s is the conventional substitution effect; the movement from s to t is the conventional income effect; and the movement from t to v is not discussed in the traditional analysis.[16] In this example, the movement from t to v happens to be positive, but it might have been negative or zero instead.

In the traditional analysis, the substitution effect is always positive; and the income effect is positive, negative, or zero. In most cases, the positive substitution effect overwhelms a possibly negative income effect. Hence, the Law of Demand.

A few points should be noted about the traditional analysis of the Law of Demand. First, neoclassical economics does not distinguish between an income effect that is due to a shift of the $IL_{x,y}$ boundary constraint and an income effect that is due to a change in the response strength of EB curves. This is a critical distinction for deriving the Law of Demand. In an operant approach, the IL effect is always positive (or zero) for the commodity whose price has fallen relatively. The EB effect may be positive, negative, or zero when that commodity is a large part of the budget; and it does not exist when that commodity is a small part of the budget. Thus, in an operant approach, the Law of Demand can only be guaranteed to hold when X is a small part of the budget, because that is the only way to be sure that a possibly countervailing EB effect will not exist. The law may also hold when X is a large part of the budget, but only if the EB effect is zero or positive; or it may hold if the EB effect is dominated by the IL effect in cases when the EB effect is negative.

---

[16] Since the traditional analysis does not distinguish between t and v, the actual (observed) buy equilibrium outcome is interpreted as (what I here call) t even in those cases when it would be more accurately described as (what I here call) v.

Second, the traditional analysis of the Law of Demand ignores the possibility that, due to contrast effects and adaptation, there may be a difference between the immediate and final impact of a change in relative prices. In addition, at least in terms of immediate impact, the effect may not be the same for one large price change or for a number of smaller price changes that are equal to the large change. Third, the traditional analysis ignores the possibility of a long-run effect based on the existence of either a deficit or surplus in the short-run outcome. These long-run effects can work in the same direction as the short-run effects (described above), or they could have an opposite effect. Thus the validity of the Law of Demand is also dependent on the possibility and importance of these long-run (deficit or surplus) effects. Fourth, the traditional analysis ignores the fact that the short-run effects of a price change can be different from long-run effects for commodities with different (independent or interdependent) reinforcer-effectiveness limits.

Fifth, the traditional analysis does not distinguish between the equilibrium quantity of a commodity (i.e., under given contingency of reinforcement, etc.) and the probability that the amount will actually be purchased under the stipulated conditions. The former depends upon the level of the reinforcer-effectiveness operation, quantity of reinforcement, delay in reinforcement, schedule of reinforcement, etc.; the latter depends in addition upon the presence of the appropriate discriminative stimulus. If all of the former are given but the discriminative stimulus (S^D) is absent, the behavior is less likely to be emitted. This is important not only when the choice is to buy or not to buy, but also when the commodities are controlled by a common reinforcer-effectiveness operation—e.g., when it is a hot day and the reinforcers are, say, ice cream or cold beer. In the real world (as distinct from the controlled conditions in a laboratory), the commodity that gets purchased may depend on which S^D (if either of them) happens to appear first.

Finally, neoclassical economics explains (or predicts) the Law of Demand from an analysis based on utility; but that explanation (or prediction) is empty, because utility is not an operational concept. Hirshleifer (1980, p. 112) has correctly noted that "this principle (Law of Demand), like convexity of indifference curves with respect to the origin, does *not* follow from the pure logic of choice. Its justification is empirical observation of the world." Neoclassical theory is consistent with the Law of Demand—but just as consistent with its converse. (See Mishan, 1961, pp. 335–36.) In a model based on an operant approach, the traditional conclusions about Law of Demand can be rooted in a framework that relies on experimental analysis and is therefore open to operational investigation.

Response Strength of Approach and Escape Behaviors

In the neoclassical model of consumer behavior, the substitution effect and the income effect are widely regarded as powerful instruments for analyzing the effects of a relative price change. The usefulness of the substitution effect–income effect dichotomy is linked in neoclassical theory to "the qualitatively different elements responsible for the income and the substitution effects" (Hirshleifer, 1980, p. 115).[17] In an operant analysis, the substitution and income effects are in turn explained by the impact of the price change upon the underlying conflicting behaviors, whose resultant determines the observed change in equilibrium buy behavior. In an operant model, buy behavior comes to a halt (reaches an equilibrium) because (1) it hits a boundary constraint (income limit or reinforcer-effectiveness limit), and (2) Net AB has reached the minimum point for both commodities along that boundary. A fall in the price of X (or an increase in income) alters buy outcome because (1) it alters the boundary constraint, and (2) it alters the Net AB curves. Accordingly, it is fitting to conclude this chapter with some additional comments on the response strength of the operational variables (approach behavior and escape behavior) that determine the equilibrium buy outcome.

The determinants of approach response strength can be conveniently, if somewhat arbitrarily, grouped under two characteristics of the AB curve—its level and its slope. Other things being equal, a given price change will have a greater effect on consumption (purchase) the higher the average level of the AB curve. In figure 33, panel A, the two AB curves are identical in slope but different in level. The fall in price of the commodity leads to a shift from IL to IL' and from EB to EB'.[18] For a given price change, equilibrium buy behavior responds more for AB_1, the higher AB curve (viz., from r to t), than for AB_2, the lower AB curve (viz., from R to T). In the case of commodity reinforcers, the most important determinant of the (average) level of the AB curve (and perhaps its slope as well) is the level or intensity of the operation that makes the reinforcer effective.

The slope of the AB curve is also an indicator of response strength. Specifically, the greater the slope, the larger the quantity purchased for any given fall in the price of X. In panel B, the given fall in the

[17] Mishan (1961, p. 337) has questioned the traditional view:

The distinction between substitution and wealth effects . . . runs right through price economics. It helps to organize our thinking on complex questions. I have sympathy with this view, but it cannot be decisive. For until we have tested the implications of those theorems which utilize this distinction, we cannot legitimately vouch for the advantages of having our thoughts organized in this particular way.

[18] The commodity is assumed to be a small part of the budget; hence, there is no EB effect.

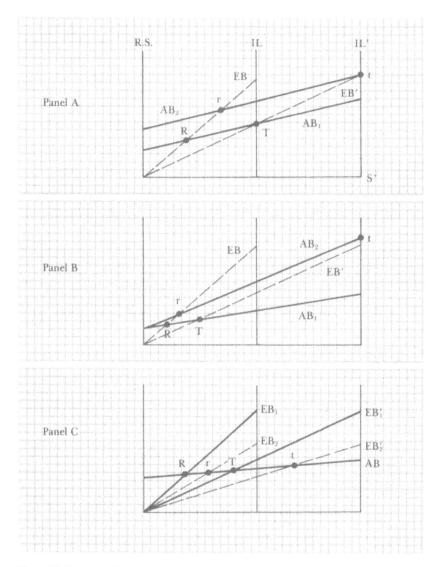

Figure 33. Response Strength for Approach and Escape Behaviors

price of X is shown by the shift from EB to EB'. This price change has a greater effect on equilibrium buy behavior along AB_2, the AB curve with the larger gradient (*r* to *t*) than along AB_1, the AB curve with the smaller gradient (*R* to *T*). The slope of the AB curve reflects the consumer's capacity to be reinforced by different quantities of the reinforcer after emitting the operant act. A capacity to be more reinforced by a larger quantity of the reinforcer than by a smaller quantity is (generally) a more efficient response; and an individual who is endowed with this capacity gains an evolutionary advantage (Skinner, 1953, p. 125). The laboratory experiments cited in chapter 3 suggest that a capacity to be more strongly reinforced by a larger quantity of the reinforcer is part of an individual's inherited characteristics.[19] This evolutionary bias in favor of efficient responses is also reflected in the Law of Least Effort, which states that "given two reinforced zones, the one that has the lesser work requirement will show the most strengthening" (Millenson, 1967, p. 168). Insofar as the strength of the AB response has a genetic basis, different individuals will presumably exhibit differences in their capacity to be reinforced by greater efficiency. This genetic diversity, which is reflected in the familiar variability of innate characteristics, appears to be part of the evolutionary mechanism.

The EB response strength is reflected in the slope of the EB curve.[20] The greater the slope, the greater the strength of escape behavior associated with any given loss of dollars surrendered in payment. In panel C, there is a single AB curve, but two EB curves with different slopes. For a given fall in price (as shown by the shift from IL to IL'), the equilibrium buy outcome is affected more when the EB curve has a smaller gradient (r to t) than for a larger gradient (R to T).[21] As shown in chapter 3, the gradient of any given EB curve depends on three variables, which can in turn be related to an individual's past history of conditioning and level of income.

A Postscript on Positively Sloped Net AB Curves

As explained earlier (p. 56), this study has proceeded on the working hypothesis that Net AB curves typically have a negative slope.[22] However, in analyzing the effects of a change in relative prices, it is

---

[19] In this connection, cf. Dawkins' view (1976, p. 71) that "natural selection favours genes which control their survival machines in such a way that they make the best use of their environment." The idea of a genetic basis for efficient responses has also been held by economists. For example, "Alfred Marshall believed that economic systems evolve in the same way as biological systems do, and maximizing behavior has been said to be prevalent essentially because of the selection and survival of maximizers" (Becker, 1976, p. 818, n. 6). In a similar view, Michael and Becker (1973, p. 392) have speculated that "genetical natural selection and rational behavior reinforce each other in producing speedier and more efficient responses to changes in the environment." For a further discussion of maximizing behavior and biology, see Samuelson (1978).

[20] Since I always draw the EB curve from the origin, there is no separate measure for the level of the EB curve.

[21] Again, it is assumed that the commodity is a small part of the consumer's budget.

[22] The only exception was in chapter 6 (pp. 88–91) in which the Net AB curves for free goods had positive slopes.

necessary to consider how the outcome of buy behavior might be affected if a change in relative prices brings about a positively sloped Net AB curve. Clearly, if the price of, say, X falls sufficiently (while the price of Y is unchanged), a point could ultimately be reached at which the gradient of approach is greater than the gradient of escape; and, the more similar are the gradients of AB and EB curves before the fall in price of X, the smaller is the fall in price of X required to change the sign of the slope of the Net AB curve. Although prices in the real world are probably typically at a level that makes for negatively inclined Net AB curves (except perhaps for the very wealthy), positively sloped Net AB curves cannot be ruled out in principle, and they may even occur in certain atypical situations—e.g., during the marketing promotion of a product.

When the Net AB curve has a negative slope, it becomes increasingly more difficult to overcome the resistance to further buy behavior that is associated with the loss of dollars surrendered in payment. However, when the price of a product falls sufficiently to bring about positively sloped Net AB curves, the steadily mounting resistance to buy behavior associated with the loss of a larger number of dollars surrendered in payment is easily overcome. When a commodity has a negatively sloped Net AB curve, the buy outcome is determined by a double conflict—the conflict between approach behavior and escape behavior for each commodity, and the conflict between the two Net ABs that is imposed by the dual constraints. A commodity with a positively sloped Net AB curve resembles a free good in that buy behavior is not brought to a halt until Net AB is *maximized* (instead of minimized, as with a typical commodity). It differs from a free good because the buy outcome is affected by the strength of Net AB of other commodities.

To illustrate some of the implications of a positively sloped Net AB curve, consider the effects of a fall in the price of X when X is a small part of the consumer's budget. Figure 34, panel A, shows such a case for commodities with independent RELs. The initial long-run equilibrium position is at w. After the fall in price of X (with price of Y unchanged), Net $AB_{x,b}$ has a positive slope, and the new short-run equilibrium is at t. The buy outcome at t is equal to REL_x, but it is farther from REL_y at t than it had been at w. This deficit position at t will cause an upward shift (not shown in the diagram) of Net $AB_{y,b}$ and will move buy outcome back towards Y along the IL_b constraint. The buy outcome under these circumstances could reach a long-run equilibrium at a point along the effective boundary segment of IL_b or it might oscillate along that segment. In panel B (in which, for simplicity, the REL curves are ignored), the initial equilibrium at r con-

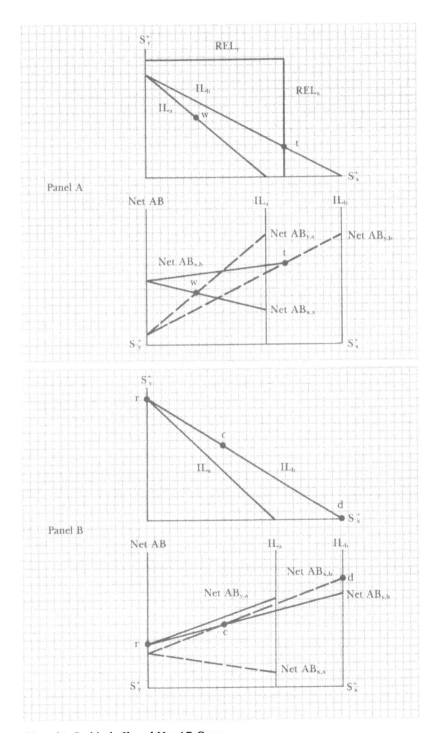

Figure 34. Positively Sloped Net AB Curves

tains all Y and none of X. After the fall in price of X, Net $AB_{x,b}$ has a positive slope; but, in contrast to the previous examples, it cuts Net $AB_{y,b}$ from below. In this curious case, a fall in price of X can have different effects for different consumers. The outcome at r could continue to be an equilibrium outcome for a consumer whose buy behavior had already been established at r before the price fall. The buy behavior of a "new" consumer (i.e., one who is not already established at r before the price fall) could reach an equilibrium at any of three possible points along IL_b—viz., at r, c, or d.[23] This is another illustration, therefore, of a point made earlier, viz., that the path by which an equilibrium is reached can help to determine that equilibrium.

[23] The combination at C is unstable, however, and in both directions.

CHAPTER EIGHT

An Operant Analysis
of Financial
Portfolio Composition

The basic model developed in this study to explain consumer buy behavior with respect to commodities can also be applied (mutatis mutandis) to explain the behavior of wealth-holders in composing their financial portfolios. In the analysis of wealth allocation, as in the earlier analysis of income allocation, the operant behavior is an "act of purchase" that is both positively reinforced (by commodities in the income allocation case, and by a stream of dollars from holding financial assets in the portfolio allocation case) and negatively reinforced (by the negatively reinforcing consequences associated with loss of dollar reinforcers surrendered in payment). In both cases, the behavioral outcome can be analyzed in terms of the relative strengths of the conflicting behaviors, viz., approach behavior and escape behavior. Moreover, the determinants of these conflicting behaviors are the same. Hence, the differences in the analysis are not due to a different list of independent variables but rather to the different importance (weight) of the variables in the two cases. Since it is possible to draw on the analytical framework already developed for consumer buy behavior, the model for portfolio behavior can be presented in a single chapter. The presentation will be as follows: (1) determinants of approach behavior for financial asset acquisition; (2) determinants of escape behavior; (3) the allocation of financial portfolios as the outcome of the conflict between approach and escape behavior; (4) effects of a change in an individual's wealth or a change in the contingency of reinforcement governing a security.

Determinants of Approach Behavior for Investors

Variables directly involved in the contingency of reinforcement. One of the most powerful determinants of the strength of approach behavior is the level of the reinforcement-establishing operation. As in the case of commodity reinforcers, a financial asset does not have the capacity to reinforce unless such an operation is in effect. As shown below, however, the schedule of reinforcement is also a powerful determinant of the strength of approach behavior—and a schedule can be effective even when the reinforcement-effectiveness operation is at a low level.[1] A second important variable that affects the strength of approach behavior for a financial asset is the size of the positive reinforcement upon each presentation of the reinforcer. The positive reinforcement for financial assets is the sum of payments (including the amount received at maturity or sale before maturity) that the holder of an asset receives during a given holding period. In a discussion of the determinants of approach behavior, the size of S^+ is measured in terms of gross number of dollars received during the holding period; and the number of dollars surrendered to acquire the asset is not deducted from that sum. In this model, the outlay (or cost) of the financial asset enters the analysis later, in connection with the determinants of escape behavior. The experimental evidence cited earlier in this study suggests that, when other things are equal, the strength of approach behavior will be greater for a larger size or amount of the reinforcer. Thus the strength of approach behavior is positively related to size of the stream of dollars received from a financial asset (just as it is positively related to size or amount of commodity reinforcers).

A third determinant of the strength of approach behavior is the delay between the operant response (act of purchase) and the receipt of the reinforcement. A delay is sometimes involved in commodity reinforcements—as when a purchased commodity is not presented

---

[1] Skinner (1969, p. 66) has described this effect as follows:

The greedy or lustful man is not suffering from deprivation (we do not call a starving man greedy); he is suffering from a particularly effective schedule of reinforcement. Don Giovanni is a classical example. Although an inherited or pathological condition may make a person "oversexed," a Don Giovanni is more likely to be the product of a particularly effective schedule. A moderate susceptibility to sexual reinforcement should be enough to make every attractive girl the occasion for attempted seduction if early successes are favorably programmed. An effective variable-ratio schedule should maintain the behavior at a high level even in a person who is sexually below normal.

(delivered) until a later time. Since a long-delayed reinforcement is not typical in most consumer purchases, this variable was mentioned but largely ignored in the discussion of commodity reinforcers. By contrast, delayed positive reinforcement is characteristic of financial asset reinforcers, e.g., bond coupons which can only be presented for payment on a preset schedule, or the inescapable delay of a holding period before the redemption or sale of a security. For purposes of our model of investor behavior, the delay can be measured by the percent of the total positive reinforcement received at different times during a given holding period for a security. Thus dollar returns that are concentrated in the early part of the holding period constitute a shorter delay than returns that are concentrated at, say, the end of the period. As shown earlier, approach behavior is weaker for a reinforcement with a long rather than a short, or no, delay. The importance of delayed reinforcement varies widely among different individuals with different past histories of conditioning. Other things being equal, it has less effect on the behavior of sophisticated investors who have had enough experience with financial assets so that the time interval between the operant response and the reinforcement has been bridged by a chain of conditioned stimuli whose members serve both as positive discriminative stimuli and positive reinforcers to link the response and the delayed reinforcement. By contrast, unsophisticated investors have had less experience with financial assets and their behavior has not been brought under strong control of conditioned stimuli that can serve to span the time gap.[2] For both kinds of investors, however, the strength of approach behavior is weakened more by long delays than by short delays—and very long delays reduce the strength of approach behavior towards the zero level. This is related to the experimental evidence that chains of conditioned responses become harder to maintain the longer the chain.

A fourth determinant of approach response strength is the schedule of positive reinforcement, which determines when the emission of an operant response is reinforced or not reinforced. The immediacy or delay of the reinforcement is not included in the description of the schedule, because it is an independent variable that influences response strength as described above. The schedule of reinforcement is an exceptionally important influence upon the strength of approach behavior.[3] In particular, as Skinner (1969, p. 118) has emphasized,

[2] In this model, the only relevant differences among investors are the differences in their past histories of conditioning rather than presumed differences in their preferences.

[3] Reynolds (1975, p. 66) has stated that:
Schedules of reinforcement have regular, orderly, and profound effects on the

"intermittent reinforcement raises the probability of responding above the value generated when all responses are reinforced."[4] In the case of commodities, the schedule in the reinforcement contingency for exchange is essentially uniform for all commodities, viz., crf. Since the reinforcement contingency is always "on," and any act of purchase is reinforced with the appropriate commodity reinforcer, the schedule is to this extent not responsible (in the typical case) for any *difference* in the strength of approach behavior with respect to different commodity reinforcers. By contrast, as shown below, different reinforcement schedules for different financial assets can lead to significantly different strengths of approach behavior for the operant purchase of those securities.

In the case of commodity reinforcers, the standard schedule is crf and the size of positive reinforcement upon each presentation is constant within a given experiment. By contrast, the overwhelming majority of financial assets would fall under the heading of crf schedules with variable-size positive reinforcement. The relevant schedule is crf because almost all financial assets generate some positive amount of dollar reinforcement in the form of dividends, interest, or redemption or sale value.[5] The only exceptions are the comparatively few financial assets that become worthless during a given holding period. Moreover, for most financial assets, the relevant size of reinforcement during a given holding period is variable over repeated emissions of the operant response.[6] The variable-interest T-plus account is an example of variable-size reinforcement. Stock market securities are an even

---

organism's rate of responding. The importance of schedules of reinforcement cannot be overestimated. . . . Schedules are the mainsprings of behavioral control . . . [and] the rate of responding can usually be more exactly controlled by manipulating the schedule of reinforcement than by any other method. Behavior that has been attributed to the supposed drives, needs, expectations, ruminations, or insights of the organism can often be related much more exactly to regularities produced by schedules of reinforcement. Many apparently erratic shifts in the rate of responding, which had formerly been ascribed to nebulous motivational variables or to "free will," have been traced by experiment to the influence of schedules of reinforcement.

[4] As Schoenfeld and Cole (1972a, p. 3) have noted, "That the occasional omission of reinforcements did not reduce probability of response occurrence but actually increased it . . . [was an] important discovery."

[5] The reader is reminded that size of reinforcement refers to gross number of dollars received during the holding period; it is not a rate of return on the financial asset investment. Hence, in the model employed in this chapter, positive reinforcement includes not only cases with a net return, but also those with a net loss, as long as there is some cash inflow at the end of the holding period.

[6] As in all instances of operant strengthening, it is assumed that, at least in principle, securities are purchased on repeated occasions. This analysis—and, indeed, any experimentally based analysis—is not applicable to unique events.

more striking example of variable-size reinforcement in which the sale price of the security can change from day to day even when the dividend payments are stable. Financial assets that combine crf and constant-size positive reinforcement are also possible, but they are not typical. That combination is most likely to occur when the interest rate is fixed by the government and remains unchanged for several years (as in U.S. savings bonds) or when the government establishes ceiling rates that do not change for several years (as in passbook savings accounts at commercial banks and savings and loan associations). In such cases, the reinforcement contingency is "on" every (business) day; and every emission of the operant response (act of buying a security) is followed, during the course of an appropriate holding period,[7] by a constant size of positive reinforcement for any given act of purchase.[8]

Unfortunately for our purposes, psychologists have not studied schedules with variable-size positive reinforcement in a form that is suitable for this discussion. This is a serious lacuna for this study, because one of the most striking differences among financial assets is in the sequence of size of positive reinforcement after a series of operant responses. In the absence of suitable experimental evidence on schedules with variable-size reinforcement, the application of the buy behavior model to the analysis of wealth allocation can only be suggestive. In order to show in principle how the model could be applied to financial assets if we had experimental evidence on the schedules involved, I will proceed on the plausible working hypothesis that the effect on approach behavior under a schedule with (essentially) continuous but variable-size positive reinforcement would be similar to that produced by intermittent but constant-size reinforcement.[9] To be specific, let us suppose—purely for purposes of

[7] In the earlier discussion of consumer behavior, the "act of purchase" was described as the buyer's behavior in entering into a purchase contract. For convenience in analyzing investor behavior, I will make the simplifying assumption that the purchase contract is negotiated with a broker and that the buyer's holding period is stipulated as part of the agreement. Thus the act of purchase covers the broker's authorization not only to buy a particular security, but also to sell or redeem it—or, if necessary, to reinvest—in keeping with the stated holding period.

[8] As explained on p. 55, the expression "given act of purchase" refers to the variant of the operant response that is followed by a particular pair of size of S^+ and size of S^-. Hence, the statement in the text that size of S^+ is constant presumes implicitly that size of S^- is also constant, i.e., a given outlay.

[9] The two basic kinds of intermittent schedules—more complicated schedules are combinations of these basic types—are ratio schedules and interval schedules. Under (fixed or variable) ratio schedules, reinforcement is determined by the behavior of the subject—e.g., the fixed ratio of reinforced to unreinforced responses in piecework pay; under (fixed or variable, including random) interval schedules, it is not—"nothing the animal does can speed up the delivery of the reinforcement" (Millenson, 1967, p. 151).

exposition—that a crf schedule with variable-size positive reinforcement would condition behavior in an essentially similar way as conventional variable or random interval[10] schedules with constant-size positive reinforcement.[11] This allows the experimental findings on conventional VI or RI schedules to be applied in a suggestive way to interpret investor behavior.

When an organism is reinforced on an interval schedule, its behavior is determined by the frequency of reinforcement.[12] If the reinforcement interval is short, the response is emitted at a higher rate; if the interval is longer, the response rate is also lower. Since the rate of response is taken as a measure of response strength in such experiments, the level of response strength under conventional interval schedules varies positively with the rate of reinforcement. Under conventional variable (including random) interval reinforcement, the reinforcement occurs after a variable interval of time has elapsed. For example, instead of reinforcement after, say, every five-minute interval on a conventional fixed-interval schedule, the reinforcement on a variable interval schedule may occur on an average of every five minutes. Response strength under variable (or random) interval schedules is not only stable and uniform but also very great. It has been reported that:

> Pigeons reinforced with food with a variable interval averaging five minutes between reinforcements have been observed to respond for as long as fifteen hours at a rate of from two to three responses per second without pausing longer than fifteen or twenty seconds during the whole period. It is usually very difficult to extinguish a response after such a schedule [Skinner, 1953, p. 102].

In addition, it has been shown experimentally that the lengths of the intervals in a random interval schedule can significantly affect the rate of response by virtue of their impact on the rate of reinforcement.

> For pigeons, as the rate of reinforcement increases from zero (extinction) to about fifty per hour, the rate of responding increases rapidly from nearly zero to about one response per second. Beyond fifty reinforcements per hour, the rate of responding increases very slowly [Reynolds, 1977, pp. 76–77].

[10] The standard abbreviation for variable interval is *VI*, and for random interval, *RI*.

[11] For brevity, the expression "conventional" schedule will be used hereafter to denote a schedule with constant size of positive reinforcement.

[12] Under conventional (i.e., with uniform size of reinforcement) fixed interval schedules, reinforcement occurs only for those responses that are emitted after a fixed interval of time has elapsed. The interval can be measured from any event. In laboratory work, it is usually measured from the end of the previous reinforcement (Reynolds, 1975, p. 66).

Thus, the strength of approach behavior will be different according to the length of the intervals in an interval schedule of reinforcement. In addition, the size or amount of the reinforcement under RI scheduling is another independent variable that affects the strength of approach behavior.

In order to apply the findings of conventional RI schedules to financial asset reinforcements, the mean interval must be approximated by a suitable proxy to accord with our working hypothesis about the role of variable-size positive reinforcement. Under a conventional RI schedule, the interval of reinforcement is the period between reinforced security purchases. Under the working hypothesis, the variability of the returns has an effect equivalent to length of interval. Accordingly, in applying the findings of conventional RI schedules to financial asset reinforcements, the effect of the interval length can be approximated by the size of an appropriate measure of variability.[13] Under the working hypothesis, a low value of the variability measure is the approximate equivalent of a short average interval under a conventional RI schedule; and a high value, the approximate equivalent of a long average interval. With this modification, the findings about conventional RI schedules can be applied to financial assets on crf schedules with variable-size reinforcement; and a change in variability will be treated like (and discussed as if it is the same as) a change in interval length.

The individual's particular history of conditioning with respect to financial asset acquisitions is always relevant in determining the strength of approach behavior, but it is particularly important under RI reinforcement. Each security that pays off on (the equivalent of) a conventional random interval basis can condition a particular strength of approach behavior—but only after it has been experienced by an individual. As Skinner (1969, p. 119) has observed, "a scheduling system has no effect until an organism is exposed to it." It is apparent, however, that an individual's own experience can never encompass more than a sample of the payoff schedule of any given security. In the case of RI schedules, the timing of the sample payoff schedule can be a crucial determinant of the strength of the maintenance level of approach behavior.[14] Figure 35 is an example of the payoff for a

---

[13] The "appropriate" measure of variability has not been specified, because it can only be suggestive in the absence of directly relevant experimental findings on the actual schedules that are applicable for financial assets. To further refine this method of approximating the effect of the average interval under conventional RI schedules would impart a sense of precision that is not warranted on the basis of the available empirical evidence.

[14] On the distinction between acquisition and maintenance, Reynolds (1975, pp. 67–68) has written that:

Dollars Received

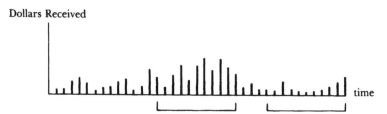

Figure 35. Payoff on (the equivalent of) an RI Schedule

particular security on (the equivalent of) an RI schedule. The average interval of reinforcement is approximated by an appropriate measure of variability; and the mean size of reinforcement is measured over the same section of the schedule. As the figure suggests, under an RI schedule, both the average interval (as approximated here) and also the average size of reinforcement may be different in different parts of the RI schedule. Accordingly, an individual's response strength can be quite different according to the part of this schedule that has been experienced in a past history of conditioning—e.g., compare the two periods shown in brackets. That such differences can condition strikingly different behavior has often been noted with respect to security purchases, especially common stock. The operant response of buying a particular stock will be strongly reinforced for someone who "hits it right" (i.e., samples a section of the RI schedule that exhibits a short mean interval and large average size of reinforcement); and, while that conditioning remains in effect, this conditioning experience will be reflected in a high-level strength of approach behavior for financial assets with such an RI schedule of reinforcement. By contrast, someone whose timing is badly "off" will not be strongly reinforced if at all by his sample of an RI schedule. Accordingly his approach behavior will be at a very low level of response strength and perhaps at a zero level.[15]

To summarize, this section has shown that the variables directly involved in the contingency of reinforcement for financial asset rein-

Each schedule of reinforcement produces a characteristic performance . . . . The appearance of this characteristic maintained performance is preceded by a period of *acquisition*, which occurs when the animal's responding is first reinforced according to the schedule. Although performance during acquisition is also regular and predictable, it differs from the maintained performance. During acquisition, the performance is always changing; but gradually, it comes closer and closer to the final maintained performance on the schedule.

[15] An individual's conditioning under a given RI schedule depends on the particular sample that he has experienced in his past history of conditioning; but, by definition, there is no possibility of sampling bias in the case of a conventional crf schedule.

forcers are the same as for commodity reinforcers—level of reinforcer-effectiveness operation, size of reinforcement, delay in reinforcement, and schedule of reinforcement. The impact of these four variables on the strength of approach behavior is summarized in figure 36, which shows the results of hypothetical experiments in which the level of the reinforcement-effectiveness operation and the length of any delay in receiving reinforcement after emission of the operant response are both held fixed. If the hypothetical experiments are conducted so that the delay, the holding period, and reinforcement-effectiveness operation are all constant, the relation between mean length of interval and mean size of reinforcement can be shown as in figure 36 for different acts of purchase involving a given security and for a given past history of conditioning. Each point in the figure represents a single average length of interval (as explained earlier) and a single average size of positive reinforcement. In other words, the individual's past history of conditioning, shown by a bracket in figure 35, is summarized as one point on the AB curve of figure 36. For a mean size of reinforcement of, say, 100, the (maintenance) response strength would be at *a* for a long mean interval, and at *b* for a short mean interval. Each point along a given AB curve shows how response strength would vary if, on the sample of the RI schedule, the average interval of reinforcement is held constant, but the mean size of the reinforcement is at different hypothetical levels. For a given individual, only one point on the AB curve is realized during a past history of conditioning, because the size of outlay is fixed in any given hypothetical experiment. The other points are based on extrapolation for different mean size of positive reinforcement and associated different size of outlay. The extrapolation rests on the empirically derived positive relation between size of positive reinforcement (or mean size in our case) and response strength. Along the

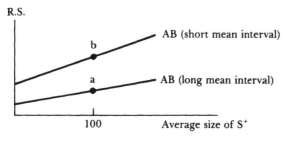

Figure 36. Approach Behavior for Different RI Schedules

abscissa, each point on the size of positive reinforcement scale is matched with an appropriate point on the size of negative reinforcement scale, as provided by the contingency of reinforcement. Although the diagram is drawn for a given past history of conditioning, and for given values of the delay, reinforcement-effectiveness operation, and length of holding period, the model can readily accommodate a change to a new set of values for any one or all of these parameters. For example, if the reinforcement operation is strengthened, but other things remain the same, the entire set of AB curves will shift upwards. The set of AB curves will also shift upwards if the delay is shortened and other things remain unchanged.

In the standard finance approach to portfolio allocation, the portfolio behavior of different individuals is explained by different attitudes towards risk—some investors are risk averse, and others are risk lovers. An operant analysis avoids the intervening variable of a risk attitude and explains the different behavior in terms of different past histories of conditioning under given schedules. Experiments with laboratory animals have shown that an organism's response strength is functionally related to the reinforcement schedule with which it is confronted. The different response to different schedules (and different securities) can in turn be explained as a phylogenic product of evolutionary selection. The hypothesis of this study is that phylogenic responses, selected for their survival value under primitive environmental conditions, continue to influence the response to reinforcement schedules that are often imbedded in contingencies of reinforcement that have little or nothing to do with survival in an evolutionary sense. If this hypothesis is correct, the response of individuals to the reinforcement schedules of particular securities is partly a phylogenic response but also partly ontogenic. Under the latter explanation, the differences in the strength of approach behavior by different individuals to a particular financial asset (with a given schedule of reinforcement) is not due to any innate differences in attitudes to risk bearing but rather to differences in operant conditioning based in turn upon different past histories of conditioning.

Stimuli which increase the probability of purchase. The probability that an act of purchase will be emitted by a consumer under conditions of a given contingency of reinforcement and given income depends not only upon the variables that affect the strength of approach behavior but also upon the presence of the appropriate positive discriminative stimulus (S^D) to set the occasion upon which the behavior is emitted. The probability that a given operant response (buy behavior) will be emitted can also be increased by the presence of substitute S^D's, i.e., discriminative stimuli other than the one that was initially conditioned as such during the reinforcement contingency experienced by the individual in a particular past history of conditioning. Three kinds of stimuli that can become conditioned as substitute S^D's are (1) similar stimuli; (2) stimuli provided by the environment in the form of rules, advice, or suggestions; and (3) stimuli provided by the behavior of others.

Similar stimuli can become effective substitutes for the original S^D by means of induction (generalization). As noted earlier in this study, stimulus induction occurs when a response that has been brought under the control of a given stimulus can also be controlled by a similar stimulus.[16] Stimulus induction can take a number of forms in contingencies leading to the acquisition of financial assets. For example, if a particular news item (e.g., an announcement about a particular change in Federal Reserve policy) has become a positive discriminative stimulus for the purchase of common stocks by a particular individual—i.e., the announcement is an S^D for behavior (operant response) that has been reinforced in the past—then a similar news item (e.g., an announcement about a similar change in government fiscal policy) may also increase the probability that the precurrent behavior leading to financial asset acquisition will occur. For any given AB curve, stimulus induction increases the probability that approach behavior will be emitted.

Stimuli provided by the environment in the form of rules, advice, or suggestions can become effective as substitutes for the original S^D if the individual has been reinforced in the past for acting on rules or advice. This source of operant strength can become particularly important in the behavior that leads to acquisition of financial assets. One reason is that (by contrast with consumers of commodities) only a comparatively small number of investors have direct experience with a wide range of financial assets. Hence, their behavior is more readily influenced (at least initially) by the advice of "experts." A second reason is that (again unlike commodity contingencies) the reinforcement for most financial assets occurs on (the equivalent of) an intermittent schedule. Hence, any individual's (necessarily) limited experience with a particular financial asset acquisition may turn out to be an unreliable indicator of the possible returns from holding that asset. This, too, makes it more likely that the behavior of acquiring financial

---

[16] By contrast, response induction occurs when the reinforcement of one operant brings about greater strength in some other operant.

assets will be influenced by the reports, analyses, and advice of experts. However, expert advice per se will not affect operant behavior unless the individual has a past history of being reinforced by following advice in this or other areas. It is unlikely, moreover, that the strengthening of the operant behavior of buying a particular kind of financial asset as a result of following expert advice will be maintained if the consequences of the operant response are not positively reinforced. In general, rule-governed behavior (e.g., investment behavior based on a study of stock market statistics, a course in finance, etc.) is less strong than behavior that is conditioned by direct experience. On the other hand, since the schedule of reinforcement from buying financial assets is, in effect, intermittent, the advice may nevertheless remain effective as an S^D, because intermittent schedules can be even more powerful than crf schedules in maintaining operant behavior. It follows that there will be a demand for expert advice even though that advice is often wrong.

Stimuli provided by the behavior of others can become effective as substitutes for the original S^D if the individual has been reinforced in the past for emitting imitative behavior, i.e., "behaving in a way which resembles the observed behavior of another organism." This is different from the imitative behavior that is emitted under phylogenic contingencies. In this case, the imitative behavior is reinforcing because it has been reinforced in the individual's past experience. As explained by Skinner (1969, p. 194),

> When other organisms are behaving in a given way, similar behavior is likely to be reinforced, since they would probably not be behaving in that way if it were not. . . . we learn to do what others are doing because we are then likely to receive the reinforcement they are receiving.

This is a common phenomenon in contingencies of consumer behavior (e.g., at bargain basement counters, or in panic buying of a commodity rumored to be in short supply) but also in financial asset contingencies (e.g., in the wide swings of stock market activity that take place in one day as investors scramble to buy a touted stock). In financial market contingencies, imitative behavior is often fairly promptly "corrected" by the presence or absence of positive reinforcement.

Reinforcer-effectiveness limits on approach behavior. A financial asset is a conditioned reinforcer based upon money, another conditioned reinforcer. The association with money occurs because a financial asset is a claim on a stream of money, including the money received upon sale or redemption of the financial asset. Thus the relevant reinforcer-effectiveness limits for financial assets and money are essentially similar. Money is not only an acquired reinforcer, but also an extraordinarily powerful generalized reinforcer, linked to virtually all other reinforcers, both primary and conditioned. Moreover, its potency and durability are maintained at a high level by its links to many primary reinforcers, because deprivation for one or more of them is likely to exist at any moment of time. In addition, it is constantly renewed by association with the primary reinforcers on which it is based.

A clue to the nature of the reinforcer-effectiveness limit for money can be found in our earlier discussion of generalized reinforcers. Insofar as money (a secondary good) is based on a functional pairing with more than one primary reinforcer, the reinforcer-effectiveness limit is determinate in principle. In practice, however, the combined derived satiation limit for all of the relevant primary reinforcers is not likely to be reached simultaneously. Moreover, money is also based on a functional pairing with other secondary goods that are non-functional commodities. Since the reinforcement-effectiveness limit for the latter is indeterminate (as explained in chapter 5), the reinforcement-effectiveness limit for money is also indeterminate. Although an extinction limit could bring a halt to the acquisition of money in this latter case, that limit might never be reached in practice. As noted, the reinforcing power of money is constantly renewed by association with primary reinforcers, and the reinforcement-effectiveness operations for at least some primary reinforcers are likely to be effective at any given time. In sum, the reinforcement-effectiveness limit for money is indeterminate both in principle and in practice. As a practical matter, the possibility of such a limit for money can be ignored; and the same conclusion holds for financial assets.

Determinants of Escape Behavior for Investors

In an analysis of financial portfolios, approach behavior is strengthened by the acquisition of a financial asset, one consequence of the act of purchase; and escape behavior is strengthened by the loss of dollar reinforcers, another consequence of the act of purchase. The preceding discussion of the determinants of approach behavior for investors went beyond that developed for consumers, because intermittent schedules of reinforcement play a more prominent part in the analysis of investor behavior than of consumer behavior. By contrast, the earlier discussion of escape behavior for consumers does not need to be expanded here, because the aversive consequences of the act of purchase are identical for consumers and investors, viz., the loss of dollar reinforcers surrendered in payment, blocked access to other reinforcers (including other financial assets), and disapproval. Accordingly, to adapt the earlier analysis of escape behavior under income allocation to escape behavior under portfolio allocation, the only modification required is to replace the Income Limit (IL) with a Wealth Limit (WL)—or perhaps a Financial Wealth Limit (FWL).

It is important to note that the response strengths of approach behavior and escape behavior are not likely to be the same even though the same object (money) is involved in both positive reinforcement (acquisition of dollar reinforcers) and negative reinforcement (loss of dollar reinforcers). One reason is that the aversive consequence of the act of purchase occurs on a conventional crf schedule whereas the positive reinforcement associated with the same operant response is likely to be presented on (the equivalent of) a conventional random interval schedule. As noted, these different schedules can condition sharply different response strengths. A second reason is that the two contingencies typically differ significantly with respect to delay. There is usually little if any delay in the negative reinforcement, but there is often a very considerable delay in the positive reinforcement. As noted earlier, the strength of approach or escape behavior is inversely related to the length of the delay.[17] For these and similar reasons, the strength of the approach and escape responses with respect to any given amounts of money are likely to be different, and this will be reflected in the differences in level and slope of the AB and EB curves for different amounts of money acquired as positive reinforcement or lost as negative reinforcement.

Allocation of Financial Portfolios:
The Outcome of Approach vs. Escape Behavior

The model for analyzing an investor's behavior in allocating wealth among financial asset alternatives is basically similar, mutatis mutandis, to the model for analyzing a consumer's behavior in allocating income among commodity alternatives, viz., the conflict between approach behavior and escape behavior. However, two differences are worth noting. First, the reinforcer-effectiveness limit for financial assets is indeterminate. Hence, the portfolio model can only incorporate a single constraint (the wealth limit) instead of the dual constraints. This further means that our analysis of equilibrium must be restricted

---

[17] In traditional economics, the effects of delays are explained in terms of time preference for present and future consumption; in an operant approach, in terms of an empirical description of the variables of which response strength is a function. It turns out that delay is one of the independent variables.

to the short run, because the long-run equilibrium buy outcome is not determinate. Second, (the effective equivalent of) intermittent schedules of reinforcement are far more prominent for the financial asset model than for the commodity model. Based on our analysis of different schedules relevant for financial assets, all financial assets can accordingly be ranked along a spectrum between conventional crf at one extreme (i.e., crf with constant-size positive reinforcement) and crf with maximum variation in size of positive reinforcement at the other extreme. This ranking also corresponds to the riskiness of the securities, i.e., to the probability that the financial asset will pay off—those scheduled on conventional crf have the lowest risk, and those scheduled on crf with maximum variation in size of positive reinforcement have the greatest risk.

Our procedure for analyzing the allocation of wealth portfolios is to proceed by successive approximations. We begin with the case of a minimum-risk security ("bond"). In this first hypothetical experiment, the individual wealth-holder has a portfolio consisting entirely of money—this is the standard case of an allocation between money and bonds. In this model, an AB curve shows the response strength associated with different quantities of the reinforcer, under the assumption of given values for the other parameters that influence response strength. For convenience, the AB curve is shown as a straight line with an ordinate intercept; and, as explained above, the existence of a reinforcement-effectiveness limit can be ignored in this diagrammatic analysis. An EB curve shows the response strength associated with loss of dollar reinforcers surrendered in payment, under the assumption of given values for the other parameters (past history of conditioning and level of income) that influence response strength. For expository convenience, the EB curve is shown as a straight line from the origin (as in the analysis of income allocation). For simplicity, the hypothetical experiments exclude the possibility of borrowing. In the absence of borrowing, the individual's wealth sets a limit on the size of the loss of dollars surrendered in payment; and this is reflected in the limit on the length of the EB curve—diagrammatically, the EB curve ends at the WL curve. Since the reinforcement-effectiveness limit for "dollars acquired" is indeterminate, the effective constraint on the buy outcome is the wealth limit. Finally, in the absence of any empirical evidence on the matter, I will continue with the working hypothesis that the EB curve has a steeper gradient than the AB curve.

Suppose that the individual's total (liquid) wealth in this first hypothetical experiment is, say, 100. Thus the EB curve will extend from zero to 100 (figure 37, panel A). If the interest rate is, say, 15 percent, the relevant part of the AB curve (i.e., the limit that can be reached by emitting operant responses that lie within his wealth limit) extends

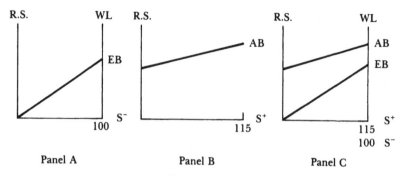

Figure 37. Portfolio Allocation: Bonds and Money

from zero to 115 (panel B). Given the interest rate, the abscissa scales in panels A and B can be matched as shown in panel C, i.e., for each act of purchase, there is a given pair of consequences measured in terms of size of S$^+$ and size of S$^-$. In this example, the wealth-holder puts the entire portfolio into the bond (instead of holding all or part of his wealth in the form of money) and is reinforced by 115 (the amount of principal and interest) after the bond matures.[18]

In a second hypothetical experiment, the contingency of reinforcement provides for a risky security ("equity"). The analysis in this case of an allocation between cash and equity is similar to the preceding case of conventional crf, except for the modifications required because equity pays off on (the equivalent of) an RI schedule of reinforcement. After a period of operant strengthening (acquisition), the RI schedule can maintain the strength of approach behavior over a considerable period even if the size and timing of the realized positive reinforcement should differ significantly from the average levels experienced during the conditioning period. As long as the conditioning from a given schedule remains effective (i.e., a maintenance performance), the individual's portfolio allocation behavior can be determined by the same kind of diagrammatic presentation that was used for the case of conventional crf scheduling.

In a third set of hypothetical experiments, the analysis can be expanded to include two or more financial assets (other than money) as part of the contingency of reinforcement. With an expanded menu of

---

[18] In this study, the EB curve is a straight line from the origin whereas the AB curve is a straight line with an ordinate intercept. The use of this expository convenience could lead to an outcome in which an individual would always buy some amount of a financial asset. That possibility can be ignored if the outcome is *exclusively* an artifact of a diagrammatic feature adopted for convenience. Under such circumstances, that outcome would not occur if both curves were drawn with ordinate intercepts.

financial assets, the experiment can include financial assets with different schedules of reinforcement. For example, suppose that one security (bond) is a low-yield instrument which pays off on a conventional crf basis, and that the other security (equity) is a high-yield instrument which pays off on (the equivalent of) a conventional randomized interval schedule with a very long average interval of reinforcement. The approach behavior curves for (the contingencies involving) these two securities are determinate given the individual's past history of conditioning, especially with respect to comparable schedules of reinforcement. Given the past conditioning relevant to escape behavior, the escape behavior curves for these two contingencies are also determinate—in fact, as shown below, they are identical. The loss of dollars surrendered in payment (i.e., the aversive consequence of the act of purchase) typically occurs at the time of the operant response or shortly thereafter. That loss will definitely be recouped when the contingencies provide for an appropriate amount of positive reinforcement on a conventional crf basis; but it may never be fully recouped within the individual's holding period when the contingencies provide for extremely low probability of reinforcement. In this model, the probability of payoff (i.e., schedule of positive reinforcement) affects exclusively the strength of the AB response; it does not have any effect on the strength of the EB response.

The four-panel diagram is a convenient way to examine the outcome in cases with two financial assets in addition to money. Each axis of the NE panel (and the corresponding axes on the NW and SE panels) shows the size of S^- measured in number of dollars (i.e., size of outlay). As in the case of contingencies of reinforcement involving commodity reinforcers, a particular size of S^+ is paired with any given size of S^- for a given act of purchase under any given reinforcement contingency involving financial assets.[19] Hence, the size of S^+ is implicitly also measured along these axes as well as size of S^-. In contrast to the cases of contingencies of reinforcement with commodity reinforcers, the explicit scale on these axes for financial asset contingencies measures size of S^- (rather than size of S^+). The reason is that, in analyzing financial asset contingencies, we will (later) be concerned with effects of changes in the contingency on the composition of the portfolio—and that is more easily determined from diagrams that are scaled as indicated instead of in terms of S^+ amounts.

[19] Although dollars are the common unit of measurement for size of S^+ and size of S^-, the dollar scales for each magnitude are not the same for both except by chance (i.e., unless the contingency of reinforcement happens to provide for an equal number of dollars in the positive and negative reinforcements that follow the operant response).

The $WL_{b,e}$ curve (figure 38, NE panel) shows the maximum sizes of both positively reinforcing and negatively reinforcing consequences that can be experienced when operant portfolio behavior is emitted under a given wealth limit. Any point along the S^- scale of either axis can be interpreted as the number of dollars invested in that financial asset. Alternatively, since wealth is fixed and the S^- scales are identical on both axes, any point along an S^- scale can also be interpreted as percent of total wealth invested in that financial asset. Thus, any point along the $WL_{b,e}$ curve shows the portfolio allocation either in dollar terms or in percentage terms for the two assets. Diagrammatically, the $WL_{b,e}$ curve must form an isosceles triangle with the axes of the NE panel, because the maximum size of S^- is identical on both axes.

The net response strength for each financial asset is depicted by a Net AB curve for each, as shown in the NW and SE panels. In each panel, one axis shows the size of the consequences of the operant response, and the other axis shows the response strength for consequences of different size. The level of response strength for approach behavior (not shown as such) is based on a given average interval of reinforcement and on a given average size of reinforcement that is associated with any given act of purchase.[20] The wealth limit imposes a constraint on the EB curve and, therefore, also on the length of the Net AB curve in both panels. The SW panel shows the "possibilities" curve, and at point a, the Net AB from holding equity is equal to Net AB from holding bonds. In figure 38, the allocation of wealth is partly into bonds (B_a) and partly into stocks (S_a).

If the possibilities curve (figure 38) had been entirely to the left of the 45° line, the outcome would have been a corner solution with all wealth in bonds. The reason, of course, is that the minimum Net AB from buying bonds would be greater than the largest Net AB from holding equity. This situation is depicted in panel A of the composite diagram, figure 39. Panel B illustrates an outcome with a three-way split in the allocation of wealth—equity, bond, and money. The equilibrium amount of equity is OE; the equilibrium amount of bonds is OB; and the equilibrium amount of money balances is the residual difference between allocable wealth (WL) and the combined amounts held in equity and bonds.[21] It is implicitly assumed in this case that idle money balances (currency and demand deposits) do not earn interest

[20] Recall that this expression implies a given size of outlay.

[21] Thus the model for wealth allocation explains hoarding (i.e., wealth held in money form) in the same way that the model for income allocation explains saving—and both models are simply different applications of the basic buy behavior model.

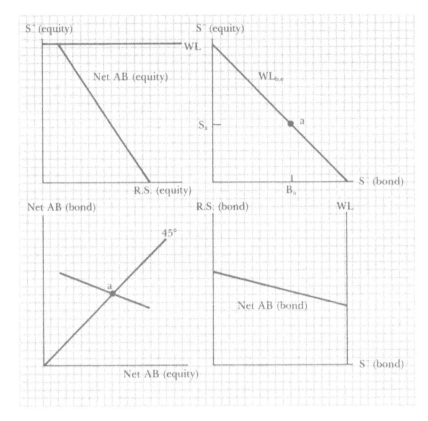

Figure 38. Portfolio Allocation: Money, Bonds, Equity

either explicitly (in cash) or implicitly (in services). However, if money does earn a return, the same basic analysis can explain the allocation of wealth portfolios by the addition of an AB curve for the stream of (delayed) returns from holding the financial earning asset, money. However, since all forms of money—those which earn interest and those which do not—are substitutes as generalized reinforcers, there is no EB curve associated with the operant response of "buying" an interest-bearing deposit account.[22] Under those circumstances, the

[22] In the case of a typical financial asset, the act of purchase has the following consequences: (1) an immediate loss (reduction) of dollar reinforcers, and (2) a delayed acquisition of dollar reinforcers. (In traditional economic language, there is a surrender of present dollars and a gain of future dollars.) But what happens if one form of

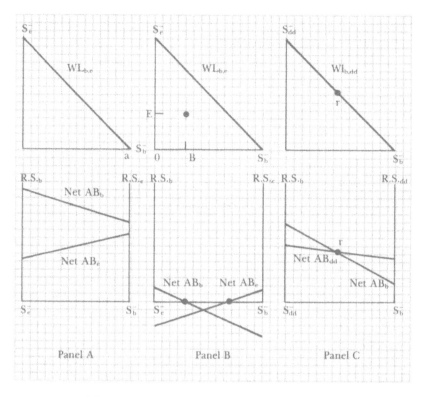

Figure 39. Portfolio Outcomes

Net AB curve for interest-bearing demand deposits would be equal to the AB curve for such deposits. Since the AB curve is positively sloped, the allocation would depend on the particular relation between the Net AB curve for interest-earning demand deposits and the Net AB curve for some alternative financial asset (e.g., bonds). In panel C, the equilibrium allocation is reached at point r. However, if the Net AB curve for demand deposits had cut the Net AB curve for bonds from below (instead of from above), the equilibrium at the intersection of

(present) money is simply exchanged for another form of (present) money? Recall that, in an operant view, money is a generalized reinforcer. (In traditional economic language, this is reflected in money's role as a medium of exchange.) When an individual surrenders one form of money (currency or non-interest-bearing demand deposits) and simultaneously acquires another form of money (interest-bearing demand deposits), his stock of generalized reinforcers remains unchanged, because all forms of money can serve as a medium of exchange. Since the exchange does not involve a loss of dollar reinforcers, there is no basis for escape behavior in such an operant response.

the curves would be unstable in both directions. Under those circumstances, corner solutions consisting of either bonds or demand deposits are alternative equilibrium possibilities.[23]

Effects of a Change in Wealth or Reinforcement Contingency

Change in wealth. The effects of a change in wealth on financial portfolio allocation can be analyzed in an essentially similar manner to the earlier analysis of the effect of a change in income on commodity composition. The effects of a change in wealth depend upon the size of the change in relation to total wealth. A small change (i.e., below a threshold effect in terms of the aversive consequences of a loss of dollars surrendered in payment) will have only a "WL effect" which pushes back the boundary constraint; a large change will in addition have an "EB effect" which alters the comparative strength of the Net AB of different securities. The diagrams for analyzing the effects of a change in income (figures 23 and 24) can be readily adapted to show the effects of a change in wealth on portfolio allocation. The required modifications are, first, to substitute securities (e.g., bonds and equity) for commodities X and Y; second, to substitute WL for IL; and, third, to substitute an explicit scale on size of S^- (i.e., size of outlay) for the explicit scale on size of S^+.

The WL effect of a small increase in wealth (like the earlier case of a small increase in income) is typically positive for both securities, and it will be zero for one of them only if that security is dominated by the greater Net AB of the other security. The EB effect of a large increase in wealth can be positive, zero, or negative. Since the EB effect can either reinforce or counteract the WL effect, the total effect depends upon the interaction of the EB and WL effects. As in the similar case of commodities, most financial assets are normal, i.e., an increase in wealth leads to a greater percentage of that financial asset in the wealth portfolio. For any given large increase in wealth, one financial asset is likely to be ultrasuperior and the other inferior only if the former has a significantly stronger Net AB curve. It will be noted that, in an operant analysis, an increase in wealth has no implications for "willingness to bear risk" or for any other intervening variable.

Change in reinforcement contingency. A change in any part of the contingency of reinforcement can lead to a change in portfolio allo-

---

[23] For a fuller discussion of equilibrium outcomes with positively sloped Net AB curves, see chapter 7.

cation. One possible change is, say, a shortening of the delay between the emission of the operant response and the receipt of positive reinforcement. As noted earlier, this change would be represented by an upward shift of the AB curve for that security. The result, as shown in figure 40, panel A, is a reallocation of the portfolio with a larger percent of the total in the security (say, bonds) with the reduced delay.

A second kind of change in the reinforcement contingency can take the form of a change in the average interval of reinforcement without any change in the average size of positive reinforcement. If the holding period and delay are held constant, a shorter interval (say, for equity) would cause an upward shift in the AB_e curve. Diagrammatically, these effects could also be shown as in panel A, adjusted for a shift of the equity curve rather than the bond curve. Other things being equal, the result would be a greater proportion of the portfolio held in equity.

A third possible change in the contingency is a change in the size of S^+ that is paired with any given size of S^- upon the emission of a given operant response. In its simplest form, this might take the form of a, say, increase in the interest rate on a bond. If there are no other changes in the reinforcement contingency, the effects of higher interest rates would depend on the implications for real wealth. If total wealth is too small and/or the rise in interest rates is too small for the incremental interest rate to have a significant impact on the level of real wealth (i.e., below a threshold level with respect to any change in the aversive consequences of any given outlay), the full effect of the higher interest rates will be limited to the WL effect on the boundary constraint of the AB curve. This takes the form of an upward rotation of the AB curve. Given the use of linear AB curves in this study, the maximum response strength reached under the new AB curve (i.e., due to the WL effect) would be equal to the level that could have been reached if the original AB curve had been extrapolated on the (implicit) original S^+ scale. In a two-asset model, the WL effect causes a shift of Net AB_b to Net AB'_b, and the equilibrium portfolio changes from r to k, a combination with more bonds and less equity (panel B). If the total level of wealth is large enough and/or the rise in interest rates is large enough for the incremental interest rates to have a significant impact on the level of real wealth, there would also be an EB effect. In panel B, the EB effect causes a shift from Net AB'_b to Net AB''_b and from Net AB_e to Net AB''_e. The EB effect is positive with respect to bonds and moves the portfolio towards a larger pecentage of bonds. As noted earlier, however, the EB effect can also be negative; and, if sufficiently negative, the total effect on bonds will also be negative, as shown in panel C. By contrast with panel B, the situation depicted in panel C shows a Net AB_e curve that is much stronger than

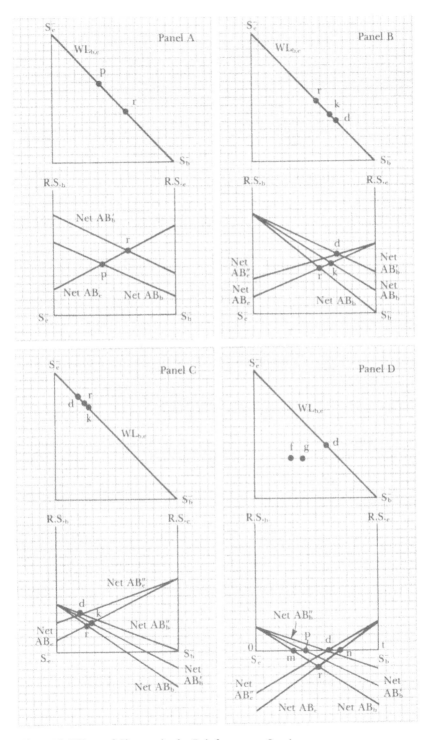

Figure 40. Effects of Changes in the Reinforcement Contingency

the Net AB_b curve. The different results in the two panels again emphasizes the importance of the individual investor's particular past history of conditioning.

As a footnote to this discussion of the effects of higher interest rates on portfolio composition, consider the implications for the demand for money. The two-asset models described above are actually three-asset models, because wealth is held in the form of money before the initial allocation occurs. Panel D (a modification of panel B in which the zero level of response strength is at point d) shows that the initial portfolio position would not be at r, because EB > AB for both equity and bonds at point r. Instead, the equilibrium is at interior point f. In the lower part of panel D, the percentage of the portfolio in bonds is Om; the amount in stock is nt; and the balance is held in the form of money. Thus a demand for money will exist when Net AB for other financial assets is not positive over a sufficient range to absorb the individual's entire financial wealth. Consider next the effects of an increase in bond interest rates. If the only effect of the higher interest rates is a WL effect, it would lead to a new equilibrium (g) with a purchase of more bonds (by the additional amount, mp) at the expense of a reduction in the amount of cash holdings. If the higher interest rates also had an EB effect, the EB effect would lead to a new equilibrium at d with more bonds and equity and a reduction in cash holdings to the zero level. According to this analysis, therefore, the demand for money is clearly interest elastic when a demand for money exists at all. The analysis also suggests, however, that a demand for money will not exist when the Net AB curves on alternative financial assets are sufficiently high.

A Final Comment on Financial Portfolios

This discussion of portfolio composition has underscored the fact that there is a scientific economy in an operant analysis of economic behavior that (like traditional microeconomic theory) is just as applicable to wealth allocation as to income allocation. The important differences between the reinforcement contingencies in these two cases are due to important empirical differences rather than to theoretical differences. One difference, as noted above, is that the schedule of reinforcement plays a larger role in an analysis of wealth allocation. Since commodities are typically scheduled on a conventional crf basis, the influence of the reinforcement schedule is to this extent uniform across all commodity contingencies. By contrast, this uniformity does not hold for financial assets; and the schedule of reinforcement accordingly plays a more prominent part in the analysis of wealth allocation.

A second difference concerns the role of the positive discriminative stimulus (S^D). In both cases, the operant response is more likely to be emitted in the presence of certain discriminative stimuli. Although the outcomes in both cases are determined by the conflict between approach and escape behaviors, that conflict remains "inoperative" until an appropriate discriminative stimulus sets the occasion on which the conflict of behaviors is then acted out. In the commodities case, an S^D is likely to be validly (i.e., "causally") related to the reinforcement (S^+). This is less likely for an S^D for financial asset acquisitions. If the random walk hypothesis is correct, the operant response that accompanies almost any S^D—say, a broker's buy recommendation—will inevitably fail to be positively reinforced on some occasions during repeated emissions of the behavior. One result is that the strength of S^D and, therefore, the probability of buy behavior, will vary according to the particular schedule of reinforcement experienced by the individual. The behavior of investors will also be variable, because the possible number of S^D's for financial asset acquisitions is large—and the strength of each will also vary for the reasons just given. In investing (as in any other form of operant behavior), we are always "fighting the last war"—but investors must do so in the context of an unusually large number of adventitious discriminative stimuli. It is no wonder that investor behavior—stock market behavior is a prime example—is notoriously erratic and volatile. In a literal sense, a lot of that behavior is "superstitious," i.e., under the control of discriminative stimuli that are not validly related to the reinforcement that follows the operant behavior. Under these circumstances, some individuals who do well on a particular investment will attribute the outcome to their skill in knowing what to buy and when to buy; others will attribute it to "dumb luck"—but probably all will find it difficult to remain immune to the sequence of events.

This discussion of portfolio composition has also underscored some interesting differences between the traditional and operant approaches to explain investor behavior. In a traditional analysis, the different portfolios of investors who are identically situated with respect to wealth and objective opportunities are explained in terms of differences in investor attitudes towards risk bearing. In an operant analysis, by contrast, an attitude towards risk[24] is not part of the model, because preference is not an operational variable. This difference leads in turn to different interpretations of observed investor behavior. For example, in the traditional analysis, risk aversion would lead the risk averse investor to shun (i.e., escape from, avoid) risky securities. In an operant view, however, there is no basis for escape or avoidance behavior from any security. All securities (including the most risky) are positive reinforcers because they are a claim on a stream of money returns. What may appear to be escape or avoidance behavior with respect to a risky security can be explained in operant terms by the fact that the schedule of reinforcement for risky securities has such a long average interval of reinforcement that strong AB responses may not have an opportunity to become conditioned. When the approach behavior reinforced by risky securities is very weak, Net AB will also be weak; and the result is that little or none of the risky security is incorporated into the financial portfolio of such an investor.

A second difference in interpretation concerns the traditional economic view that most investors are risk averse. In the traditional view, this is explained by utility. In an operant interpretation, the emphasis is on an investor's past history of conditioning rather than utility. All investors who buy risky financial assets (e.g., venture capital stock) experience the aversive consequence of the act of purchase, but only a few experience much positive reinforcement during their holding periods. This is inherent in the objective schedule of reinforcement applicable to venture capital undertakings (viz., a schedule with maximum variation in size of S^+). By contrast, almost everyone who buys a safe financial asset (e.g., an FDIC-insured certificate of deposit at a commercial bank) will be positively reinforced. This, too, is inherent in the objective schedule of reinforcement applicable to the safest securities (viz., a conventional crf schedule). The result is that approach behavior is reinforced for almost everyone who buys safe investments but only for a small number of those who buy high-risk securities. In an operant view, an individual's past history of conditioning could also explain the traditional view that an individual might exhibit risk-averse behavior in some situations and risk-prone behavior in other situations. For example, an individual who has been conditioned to gamble by a variable ratio schedule will exhibit risk-prone behavior in the presence of gambling equipment and gambling opportunities. But the same individual might exhibit strongly risk-averse behavior in the presence of other stimuli as a result of other kinds of past conditioning—e.g., he might buy medical insurance if he has had a prior history of conditioning with the aversive consequences of meeting medical bills without insurance.[25]

[24] Rubin and Paul (1979) have recently proposed the hypothesis that attitudes toward risk are the result of an evolutionary mechanism.

[25] In his Ely lecture, Simon (1978, p. 9) cited work by Kunreuther et al. which showed that the purchase of flood insurance by persons owning property in low-lying areas was related much more to personal experience with floods than to objective knowledge or subjective beliefs about risks and rates.

In contrast to the traditional approach, an operant approach also avoids resort to the intervening variable of rationality. In the traditional view, portfolio allocation is explained as the behavior of a rational investor who consciously and deliberately maximizes returns in the context of a given opportunity set and a given utility structure. In order to explain the behavior of a "pathological" gambler (i.e., one who gambles even though he continues to lose more than he wins), it is necessary to appeal to intervening variables—either he is "not behaving rationally" or he is a "risk lover." Neither explanation adds to the observation that he continues to gamble and to lose more than he wins. By contrast, an operant analysis avoids intervening variables in favor of the operational variables that determine the strengths of approach behavior and escape behavior.

CHAPTER NINE

Epilogue: An Overview
of the Conflict Model
# of Buy Behavior

This final chapter presents an overview of the model developed in this study. The first section draws on material from chapters 2–7 to recapitulate some of the model's major structural features. It does not include any material from chapter 8, which applies the buy behavior model to financial portfolio composition, because the structural features of the basic model did not have to be altered for that application. The second section reviews some special features of the model and compares them with the conventional model of consumer behavior. The concluding section points to areas for further research.

Recapitulation of Major Structural Features

Psychological footings. The core of the model developed in this study to explain buy behavior (the act of purchase) is the conflict (in the psychological sense) between the incompatible behaviors of approach and escape.[1] It is accordingly fitting to call this model a "conflict

---

[1] In the psychology literature, the term "conflict" is used to describe any of the following situations (Catania, 1968, p. 330):

a single response that produces both a reinforcer and a punisher (traditionally called *approach-avoidance conflict*); two or more incompatible responses each of which produces a different reinforcer (traditionally called *approach-approach conflict*); or two or more incompatible responses each of which terminates or avoids only one of two or more different aversive stimuli (traditionally called *avoidance-avoidance conflict*).

model." Since the model has been built on findings from the experimental analysis of behavior, it places great emphasis on the environmental control of behavior and, in particular, on the operant behavior paradigm. Operant (or instrumental) behavior is behavior that operates upon the environment and is instrumental in obtaining consequences.

The contingency of reinforcement, which lies at the heart of the operant conditioning paradigm, specifies the environmental stimulus consequences, both positively reinforcing (S $^+$) and aversive (S $^-$), after a given behavioral response (R) has occurred in the presence of a discriminative stimulus (S^D). Thus, a contingency of reinforcement is the interrelation among three components: (1) the occasion upon which a response occurs, (2) the response itself, and (3) the reinforcing consequences. In the operant conditioning model, the operant response is strengthened by its consequences. All of this is directly applicable to the microeconomic behavior of individuals. As this study has shown, the purchase strengthening paradigm can be interpreted as a particular instance of the operant conditioning paradigm. In the conflict model of buy behavior, the operant behavior is the act of purchase, defined as the buyer's behavior in entering into a purchase contract; the acquiring of the product and the loss of dollars surrendered in payment are the two consequences of the operant response; and the occasion upon which a buy response occurs is the discriminative stimulus.

In the contingency of reinforcement for economic exchange, an economic good is made contingent upon the emission of the buy response by the consumer. Since the buy response can be powerfully conditioned under this contingency of reinforcement, economic goods qualify as reinforcers as that term is used in the operant conditioning paradigm. Accordingly, it is useful to classify economic goods and services according to the ways in which they reinforce behavior. Consumer goods and services that are positively reinforcing can be divided into two categories according to the source of their capacity to strengthen consumer behavior—positive primary (i.e., unconditioned) reinforcers and positive secondary (i.e., conditioned) reinforcers. A secondary reinforcer has no inherent capacity to reinforce the behavior upon which it is (made) contingent, but it can acquire this capacity by an (appropriate kind of) association with other reinforcers. Primary reinforcers have (potentially) a universal appeal, but secondary reinforcers are highly culture dependent. In addition, the stimuli that become acquired or conditioned reinforcers for a particular consumer are determined by that individual's prior history of conditioning.

In the conflict model, primary reinforcers are designated as primary commodities. Secondary reinforcers are divided into secondary commodities and escape/avoidance (or, simply, escape) commodities. The former are positive conditioned reinforcers, based directly or indirectly on positive primary reinforcers; the latter are a special form of positive conditioned reinforcer that is based directly or indirectly on escape or avoidance of an aversive reinforcer. All secondary reinforcers are further classified according to whether they are based on one positive reinforcer (specialized) or more than one (generalized), and whether they are based on a functional or nonfunctional pairing of stimuli. This classification, which in no sense represents a hierarchy of economic goods, is essential in analyzing reinforcer-effectiveness limits and the nature and possibility of equilibrium outcomes for buy behavior.

Conflict between approach and escape. As already noted, the environmental consequences of operant buy behavior are both positively reinforcing and aversive. The positively reinforcing consequence of acquiring an economic commodity strengthens approach behavior (i.e., any behavior that makes the emission of the operant buy response *more* likely); the aversive consequences associated with the loss of dollars surrendered in payment strengthen escape behavior (i.e., any behavior that makes the emission of the operant buy response *less* likely). Buy behavior is the outcome (resultant) of these two incompatible behaviors. For the theoretical purposes of the conflict model, the list of operational variables that determine the strengths of these conflicting behaviors is essentially similar for both cases, as shown below.

The strength of approach behavior depends, first, on the level of the reinforcer-effectiveness operation. In general, the reinforcing value of a primary reinforcer (commodity) whose presentation is made contingent on a particular operant response increases as the level of the operation (e.g., deprivation) increases. Although there are limits on the height of the reinforcing value of a primary reinforcer, the level of deprivation necessary to reach those limits can probably be ignored in affluent countries like the United States. Significantly, a change in the level of deprivation can affect not only the reinforcing value of the withheld reinforcer but also of related reinforcers (by its effect on the strength of generalization).

A second independent variable, a delay between response (R) and reinforcement (S^+), reduces the effectiveness of the reinforcement. This variable can be ignored for most cases of consumer buying, because most are conducted without significant delays; but it can be important in other applications of the conflict model (e.g., the purchase of financial assets). A third determinant, the quantity of the reinforcer upon each presentation, strengthens the operant response. A substantial experimental literature has established that operant response strength is positively related to quantity of reinforcement upon each presentation. A fourth determinant is the quality of the reinforcer. Reinforcing value is closely positively related to reinforcer quality. In the conflict model, as in the experimental approach on which it is based, quality is not something that exists in the eye of the beholder—it is an operational variable that is defined in terms of a particular set of stimulus characteristics.

A fifth independent variable is the schedule of reinforcement. Each kind of schedule (continuous or intermittent) can condition a particular strength of operant response. Since the schedule of reinforcement can strongly affect the potency of conditioned reinforcers, it can indirectly influence the strength of approach behavior. Its direct influence is normally not large in consumer buy behavior, because that contingency of reinforcement typically provides for continuous reinforcement; but it can be very important in analyzing financial asset purchase behavior.

Although the above list of independent variables was described in terms of primary commodities, it also applies to secondary commodities (with appropriate modifications for the differences between primary and conditioned reinforcers). In particular, as noted above, the potency of a secondary commodity is affected by the schedule of reinforcement with the primary (or conditioned) reinforcer on which it is based. The above list also applies to escape/avoidance commodities, with modifications to allow for the differences between primary and escape/avoidance commodities. For example, the level of the reinforcer-effectiveness operation is determined by aversive stimulus intensity rather than by level of deprivation. Similarly, stimulus-off time for escape goods corresponds to amount of reinforcement for other positive reinforcers.

The strength of escape behavior depends on essentially the same variables that determine the strength of approach behavior. Again, the first is the level of the reinforcer-effectiveness operation. This refers to the intensity of the aversive stimuli associated with the three aversive consequences of an outlay (viz., disapproval, blocked or impeded access to other reinforcers, loss of dollar-reinforcers surrendered in payment). Aversive stimulus intensity is in turn related to two factors: (1) strength of the conditioning that makes any outlay a conditioned aversive stimulus, i.e., on the factors that affect the potency of the conditioned aversive stimuli associated with money outlays; and

(2) level of income, because the objective consequences of a given outlay, in terms of blocked or impeded access to other reinforcers, are more pronounced as the average level and stability of income are decreased.

A second independent variable is the delay between response (R) and punishment (S $^-$). The loss of dollars surrendered in payment is both punishment and negative discriminative stimulus from which escape is reinforcing. Credit transactions involve an operant delay; cash transactions do not. Hence, cash transactions strengthen escape behavior more than credit transactions. In addition, punishment in the forms of disapproval or of blocked or impeded access to other reinforcers can occur either simultaneously with the outlay or with a delay, and the strength of escape behavior is conditioned accordingly.

A third determinant is the quantity of the dollar-reinforcers surrendered in payment. The intensity of the aversive consequences of the loss of dollars surrendered in the course of operant buy behavior varies positively with the number of dollars involved. This applies to all three of the aversive consequences associated with loss of dollars surrendered in payment. For example, for any given level of income, the (objective) consequences in terms of blocked or impeded access to other reinforcers become more pronounced as the loss of dollars surrendered in payment is increased.

A fourth determinant, the quality of the dollar-reinforcers surrendered in payment, usually is not important in determining the strength of escape behavior, but it could become more important in the future. An obvious example is the qualitative (i.e., stimulus) differences when dollars surrendered in payment take the form of cash or of an electronic entry under EFTS. Finally, a fifth determinant is the schedule of reinforcement between response (R) and punishment (S $^-$). The relevant schedule of reinforcement between R (act of purchase) and S $^-$ in the form of a loss of dollar reinforcers is continuous reinforcement, but the relevant schedules for the other aversive consequences of a loss of dollars surrendered in payment can also include intermittent reinforcement. Thus, the punishment for loss of dollars surrendered in payment combines multiple aversive stimuli with a combination of crf and intermittent schedules that can build great strength and durability into escape behavior.

Equilibrium under an IL constraint. The approach and escape behaviors described above can be incorporated into a simplified version of the conflict model of buy behavior in which there is only one commodity and one constraint (income); and all determinants of approach behavior are held constant except size of positive reinforcement. In a diagrammatic presentation of this model, size of positive reinforcement is plotted along the abscissa; and level of response strength, along the ordinate. As already noted, the strength of approach behavior varies positively with size of S $^+$ on each presentation; and, in the absence of more specific experimental evidence, a linear relation is assumed for graphical convenience. A change in any of the other determinants of response strength is depicted by a shift of the AB curve.

An EB curve is derived in similar manner, mutatis mutandis. Specifically, all determinants of escape behavior are held constant except for the amount of loss of dollars surrendered in payment, i.e., size of S $^-$. The size of S $^-$ is plotted along the abscissa; and level of response strength, along the ordinate. Escape behavior strength varies positively with size of S $^-$ on each presentation; and, in the absence of more specific experimental evidence, a linear relation is assumed for graphical convenience. It will be noted that, although income is the only constraint, it plays a special kind of role in the conflict model. In particular, the (average size and stability of the) consumer's income has a dual influence on the EB response: (1) It sets a limit on the *possibility* of emitting escape behavior; and this is reflected in a limit on the length of the EB curve. (2) It influences the *intensity* of the aversive consequences of any given loss of dollars surrendered in payment (i.e., the level of the reinforcer-effectiveness operation that controls escape behavior); and this is reflected in the slope and level of the EB curve (i.e., the strength of the EB response for any given outlay).

The AB and EB curves can be plotted on a common diagram, because they have the same ordinate and each point on the abscissa scale of one can be matched to a corresponding point on the abscissa scale of the other for any given act of purchase (operant response). For expository convenience, the explicit scale is size of S $^+$, and the associated implicit scale is size of S $^-$. The income limit, represented graphically by an IL curve, blocks movement along the AB and EB curves. In the absence of more experimental evidence on the matter, I have adopted the working hypothesis (for most of the study) that the EB gradient is steeper than the AB gradient.

The equilibrium outcome of buy behavior in such a model occurs at the intersection of the AB and EB curves. This is where the AB response strength is exactly matched by the EB response strength. A change in any of the other determinants of response strength would be represented by an appropriate shift of the AB or EB curves, and the equilibrium outcome would change accordingly.

Reinforcer-effectiveness limits. The preceding simplified version of the conflict model ignores the possibility of a constraint other than the income limit, especially the reinforcer-effectiveness limit. This limit is the point at which any given commodity ceases to be a reinforcer, i.e., the rate of (operant) response approaches or reaches zero under given conditions of all the relevant parameters. In the conflict model, the IL curve defines a limit for the length of the EB curve—and it also limits the point on the AB curve that can be reached (experienced) as a consequence of the operant response. By contrast, the reinforcer-effectiveness limit (REL) curve sets a limit on the length of the AB curve, i.e., on the maximum size of positive reinforcement that could be reinforcing in the operant conditioning paradigm—and it also limits the point on the EB curve that can be reached (experienced) as a consequence of the operant response.

The nature of the relevant reinforcer-effectiveness limit can be different according to the type of commodity involved. Satiation is a powerful reinforcer-effectiveness limit for primary reinforcers, because they are controlled by deprivation. Satiation is not the relevant reinforcer-effectiveness limit for a secondary commodity, because an independent operation of deprivation is not possible. Therefore, the functional equivalent of a satiation limit for secondary commodities is the derived satiation limit at which the secondary commodity ceases to reinforce because satiation has been reached on the relevant primary reinforcer. Alternatively, the reinforcer-effectiveness limit for a secondary commodity can be an extinction limit, e.g., when the secondary commodity fails to be renewed at least occasionally by association with the primary reinforcer on which it is based. Finally, escape/avoidance commodities, like other secondary reinforcers, are also not susceptible as such either to independent deprivation or to satiation. In addition, satiation is not a relevant concept, because the reinforcing capacity of escape/avoidance commodities depends on their ability to mitigate an aversive consequence and not on any underlying deprivation. The reinforcer-effectiveness limit for escape/avoidance commodities can be reached either at an extinction limit or at a tolerance limit (at which consumption of the escape/avoidance commodity has reduced the level of aversive stimulation to zero or to a tolerance level).

This analysis suggests that reinforcer-effectiveness limits are quite different not only for primary and secondary commodities but also for different kinds of secondary commodities, depending on whether a particular secondary reinforcer is functionally related to a primary reinforcer. These differences, in turn, affect the likelihood that the reinforcer-effectiveness limit will be reached in practice. The reinforcer-effectiveness limit for expensive primary commodities is reached presumably only by the affluent; but the satiation limits of many other primary commodities are routinely reached by large numbers of nonwealthy people in affluent countries like the United States, and satiation rather than income is the effective constraint on consumption in such cases. This is also true for functional secondary commodities. By contrast, there is an inherent indeterminacy about the reinforcer-effectiveness limits of a nonfunctional secondary commodity; and, for many such commodities (e.g., jewelry), income rather than a reinforcer-effectiveness limit is the binding constraint. In the case of escape/avoidance commodities, the reinforcer-effectiveness limits are also different, especially for functional and nonfunctional commodities. The reinforcer-effectiveness limit is clearly the binding constraint for comparatively inexpensive functional escape/avoidance commodities (aspirin, raincoats, umbrellas), but an income limit is just as clearly the binding constraint on the consumption of many expensive escape/avoidance commodities (like air-conditioning). It seems likely that this is also true for nonfunctional escape/avoidance goods, except that the relevant limit is an extinction limit rather than a tolerance limit.

The analysis of reinforcer-effectiveness limits acquires an additional dimension when the scope is expanded from a single-commodity to a two-commodity model. One possibility is the case of interdependent limits, which can in turn be classified along a scale from strong to weak interdependence. In general, interdependent reinforcer-effectiveness limits occur when commodities are controlled by a common reinforcer-effectiveness operation (e.g., a common deprivation). The likelihood of interdependence is further increased when commodities have similar stimulus characteristics (which facilitates stimulus induction); but in more complex cases, interdependence can exist even when stimulus similarity is absent. Another possibility is the case of independent reinforcer-effectiveness limits. These are usually found among commodities with different reinforcer-effectiveness operations, but some commodities that are controlled by a common reinforcer operation may nevertheless exhibit independent limits at low levels of the reinforcer-effectiveness operations (e.g., under mild deprivation).

Equilibrium in the full model. The full model includes both (income limit and reinforcer-effectiveness limit) constraints in a two-commodity framework. In such a model, the income limit determines the length of the EB curve; the reinforcer-effectiveness limit determines the length of the AB curve; and the effective boundary is either of the limits or some combination. In a single-commodity model under the dual constraints, consumption would proceed until Net AB $= 0$, unless it is blocked by either the IL curve or the REL curve. Similarly, in a two-commodity model under the dual constraints, consumption would proceed until Net AB_x = 0 and Net AB_y = 0, unless they are blocked by the $IL_{x,y}$ curve or $REL_{x,y}$ curve. In the two-commodity model, however, buy behavior is determined by a double conflict, viz., the inherent conflict between approach behavior and escape behavior for each commodity, and the inherent conflict between Net AB_x and Net AB_y when the allocation is constrained by either or both of the dual constraints.

When buy behavior is determined under the full conflict model, the analysis of equilibrium outcomes (when they exist) can be divided into the preliminary (or "short-run") equilibrium that is determined for given levels of the reinforcer-effectiveness operations and the final (or "long-run") equilibrium that allows for changes in the reinforcer-effectiveness operations due to feedback effects from the short-run equilibrium outcome. The preliminary equilibrium of buy behavior is determined by the relative strength of Net AB_x and Net AB_y, and it occurs along the effective boundary at a point where the Net AB forces are in balance (i.e., at a minimum for both commodities) for any given set of Net AB curves. In order to be in final equilibrium, the preliminary equilibrium point must also be a point at which the balance of the Net AB forces is stable. In some cases, both a short-run and a long-run equilibrium are objectively possible; in other cases, only a short-run equilibrium is possible.

A short-run equilibrium will simultaneously be a long-run equilibrium if the consumer is in neither a deficit nor a surplus condition when Net AB is at a minimum for both commodities. This will occur if the combination at the equilibrium outcome simultaneously satisfies both of the dual constraints. Otherwise, either a deficit or a surplus condition will exist.

A deficit condition is said to exist when buy behavior in the short-run outcome has come to a halt before reaching the reinforcer-effectiveness limit for *both* commodities. This will occur if the income limit is reached before the reinforcer-effectiveness limit, or if the Net AB strength for one product or both reaches zero before both reinforcer-effectiveness limits are reached. In either case, the existence of a deficit raises the level of the relevant reinforcer-effectiveness operation and typically moves behavior towards a new equilibrium outcome. The new outcome is brought about in part by a shift of the Net AB curves, in accordance with the dynamic properties of the conflict model. In addition, for commodities that are controlled by a common reinforcer-effectiveness operation, an increase in the level of the reinforcer operation is associated with an increase in discrimination, which raises the Net AB curve proportionately more for the less expensive commodity. Other things being equal, this tends to shift buy behavior towards the less expensive commodity. This adjustment process, which continues as long as a deficit condition persists, will eventually move the buy outcome to a combination that simultaneously satisfies both constraints, if such a combination exists. If it does not exist (e.g., when any combination along $IL_{x,y}$ lies wholly below any combination along the $REL_{x,y}$ curve), a long-run equilibrium is nevertheless sometimes possible because the deficit-induced shifts in the response strength (Net AB) curves do not lead to a further change in the buy behavior outcome. As explained in chapter 6, this can occur in a corner solution and in certain noncorner outcomes in which an oscillating outcome can be excluded.

The short-run outcome can also be undermined by a surplus, a condition in which preliminary buy behavior has been brought to a halt by a reinforcer-effectiveness limit before the income limit has been reached. The resulting unexpended margin of income alters the intensity of the aversive stimulus of any given outlay (loss of money reinforcers surrendered in payment), e.g., in terms of blocked or impaired access to other reinforcers. The existence of a surplus reduces the level of the reinforcer operation and leads to a downward shift of the EB curves (and a corresponding upward shift of the Net AB curves) for both commodities. The final outcome of these shifts depends on the relative prices and relative strengths of the AB curves for the two commodities. In general, any given, say, fall in EB strength would move the buy outcome towards the commodity with the higher Net AB curve. This process, which continues as long as a surplus condition exists, eventually moves the buy outcome to a combination that simultaneously satisfies both constraints, if such a combination exists. As in the deficit case, a long-run equilibrium is sometimes possible under surplus conditions even if such a combination does not exist.

To summarize, the short-run equilibrium condition assures that, for any given set of response strength curves, the buy outcome is located along the effective boundary (constraint). The long-run equilibrium condition assures that, for any given set of dual constraints, the buy outcome reaches a *stable* position along the effective boundary. In certain cases, however, a stable equilibrium cannot be achieved, and the model predicts an oscillating outcome.

Income and price changes. A particularly convenient feature of the conflict model is that the same analytical framework can be used to show the effects of a change in income or a change in relative prices. In the conflict model, buy behavior comes to a halt (reaches an equilibrium) when (1) it has reached a boundary constraint and (2) Net AB has reached a minimum for both commodities along that boundary. Accordingly, the effects of a change in relative prices or a change in income can be analyzed in terms of their impacts on the boundary constraints and the Net AB curves. In both cases, the impacts can be divided into preliminary and final effects.

In keeping with the dual role of income in the conflict model, the short-run effects of a change in income or relative prices are reflected in an *IL effect* (a change in the length of the EB curve due to a shift in the IL curve) and an *EB effect* (a change in the level of the EB curve due to an income-related change in aversive stimulus intensity associated with any given outlay). The IL effect always occurs; the EB effect occurs only when the actual or effective change in income is above a threshold level (in terms of the impact on the intensity of aversive stimulation for any given outlay). Hence, it occurs only for a "large" change in income or for relative price changes for commodities that are an important part of the consumer's budget.[2]

In the case of a relative change in commodity prices (e.g., a fall in price of X with price of Y unchanged), the IL effect causes a change in the balance between Net AB_x and Net AB_y because of a change in the Net AB_x curve alone. Hence, the IL effect is predictably positive (or, in an extreme case, zero) with respect to consumption of X. Since most commodities are not individually important in the consumer's budget, the total short-run effects of a relative price change typically conform to the Law of Demand. By contrast, the outcome is less predictable when there is an EB effect, because the change in the balance of the Net AB curves is due to a change in Net AB_y as well as in Net AB_x. Hence, the outcome is also affected by the comparative base levels (i.e., before the relative price change) of the Net AB curves for the two commodities. In the usual case, the quantity of X increases. However, the EB effect for X could be negative if the base level of Net AB_y is exceptionally strong; and, in extreme cases, the net (algebraic) effect of a positive IL effect and a negative EB effect might also be negative—the case of a Giffen good.

The short-run effects of a fall in price of X also depend on reinforcer-effectiveness limits. For commodities with independent limits, a relative price change will have a lesser effect on quantity of X if buy behavior is constrained by the REL_x boundary than if it is not; and it will have no effect in the extreme case of buy behavior already reaching the REL_x boundary before the price fall. For commodities with interdependent limits, the quantity of X would increase even

---

[2] Since the analysis of the effects of a change in income or relative prices is basically similar, the balance of this summary presentation will for convenience be expressed entirely in terms of the effects of a change in relative prices.

though X and Y taken together had already reached $REL_{x,y}$; and, for a sufficiently large price fall, the increase would continue until REL_x had been reached and none of Y was being consumed.

The long-run effects depend on the indirect impacts of price or income changes on the levels of the reinforcing-effectiveness oper-ation(s) that control the strength of approach behavior or escape be-havior responses. These long-run effects on buy outcomes can be divided into a *deficit effect* (the effect on the strength of the approach behavior response due to a change in the reinforcer-effectiveness operation that controls approach behavior) and a *surplus effect* (the effect on strength of escape behavior response due to a change in the reinforcer-effectiveness operation that controls escape behavior). The deficit effect is reflected in a change in the level of the AB curves; and the surplus effect, in the level of the EB curves.

The long-run effects, like the short-run effects, are also influenced by reinforcer-effectiveness limits. For example, for commodities with independent limits, a fall in the price of X that moves buy behavior closer to REL_x but leads to (or increases the size of) a deficit in Y tends to raise AB_y relatively to AB_x. Other things being equal, therefore, the subsequent response to the price change could move the quantity of X below its newly reached short-run equilibrium position; and the *net* change in X might even become negative. In this unstable situation, further shifts in the two AB curves are likely in response to further changes in the relative sizes of the deficits over time. The final out-come could be stable or permanently unstable and oscillating, de-pending on the impact of the deficits on the Net AB curves for each commodity.

The long-run effects of a relative price change also depend on the relative strengths of the Net AB curves in the two-commodity model. For example, in the case of commodities with interdependent reinforcer-effectiveness limits, suppose that a fall in price of X moves the buy outcome from a previous long-run equilibrium position to a new short-run outcome that lies along the $REL_{x,y}$ curve but includes a surplus. The persistence of a surplus will lead to a fall in the EB curves and a corresponding increase in the Net AB curves for both com-modities. If the individual exhibits greater Net AB strength for, say, X (the commodity whose price has fallen relatively), the surplus will eventually be eliminated by a new buy outcome that includes more X. Thus, the long-run outcome as well as the short-run outcome will lead to larger purchases of X. If Net AB_x is generally weaker than Net AB_y, the long-run response would be directly opposite to the short-run response; and the lower price of X could even lead to a long-run reduction in its quantity.

In sum, the long-run effects of a change in relative prices depend on (1) whether the price changes indirectly lead to a deficit or a surplus; (2) whether the individual exhibits generally greater Net AB strength for the commodity whose price has fallen relatively; and (3) whether the reinforcer-effectiveness limits are independent or inter-dependent.

Some Special Features of the Model

Before bringing this study to a close, it may be useful to review some special features of the conflict model, which are contained (implicitly or explicitly) in the foregoing summary of its major structural features. In this recapitulation, they are put in perspective by means of a comparison with the rationality-utility model of traditional economics. For discussion purposes, I have listed (below) a half dozen features, even though there is overlap in some cases.

An interdisciplinary model. One distinctive feature of the conflict model of buy behavior is that it incorporates the findings of experimental psychology into a formal economic model. By contrast, the rationality-utility model deduces consumer behavior from the pure logic of choice, in keeping with a traditional division of labor in which economists deal with economic matters and psychology is left to psychologists. The traditional view that economic science should be completely independent of psychological assumptions (see p. 4) has probably always been an unattainable objective, because economics deals with (a particular aspect of) the behavior of human beings—and behavior is the very province of psychology. As a result, although psychology has been barred at the front door of microeconomic theory, it has crept back into standard economic models through the back door in the form of (often tacit) behavioral assumptions. Moreover, there is a systematic bias in that these behavioral assumptions have not been defined in operational terms, but tend rather to be inherently subjective and nonoperational (such as rationality, tastes, risk aversion, expectations, etc.).

The potentially fruitful role of intervening variables can readily be documented from the annals of the physical sciences, but such variables must be used with caution in a nonexperimental science like economics. It is one of the strengths of the conflict model that it not only incorporates psychology explicitly, but draws exclusively from the *experimental* analysis of behavior. This emphasis on experimental findings permits the conflict model to sidestep the troublesome questions in which traditional economics can get mired when it tries to figure out what goes on in the minds (and hearts?) of consumers, investors, or other buyers. As this study has shown, the conflict model can explain consumer buy behavior without appealing to the intervening variable of preference; and it can explain financial portfolio composition with risky assets and uncertain returns without reference to the intervening variables of risk aversion or expectations.

These are nonnegligible advantages. In traditional economics, some potentially troublesome aspects of consumer utility are routinely neutralized by the assumption that tastes do not change, or at least not often and not much. This assumption is not available for the equally troublesome questions that plague expectations, because it is generally agreed that expectations can change frequently and much. Under the circumstances, it is a convenient feature of the conflict model that it can deal with future events (e.g., in chapter 8) without calling upon expectations. Moreover, this is not an accidental omission. In an operant analysis, behavior (response) is conditioned by its *past* consequences; and the future is accordingly predicted by studying the past. This makes it possible for the conflict model to ignore expectations as a redundant intervening variable. In chapter 8, for example, the analysis of wealth allocation among financial assets with "different expected returns" eschews expectations in favor of the conditioning effect of the reinforcement schedules for different financial assets, as experienced in the past history of conditioning of any given individual. In sum, both in theory and in practice, the conflict model points to the *consequences* of past behavior to explain *present* behavior—and it is precisely *present* behavior that we seek to explain by means of expectations.

As a by-product of its interdisciplinary approach, the conflict model expands the explanatory power of the analysis of buy behavior. Traditional economics asks *what* we buy, but *why* we buy is left to the sister science of psychology. This study has attempted to demonstrate that our understanding of the traditional economic questions can be enhanced by a model that draws upon both disciplines. The interdisciplinary model of buy behavior developed in this study looks behind the rationality-utility model to discover why individuals (consumers, investors) behave as they do when they "decide" how to allocate income, wealth, etc. Significantly, however, the conflict model does not answer the *why* of buy behavior by probing the psyches of consumers (or investors). It looks instead to the independent and operational variables of which that behavior is a function. In the conflict model, causation is interpreted as a functional relation.

Lawful relations instead of rationality hypothesis. The traditional approach to consumer theory focuses on the choices made by an individual consumer. As noted above, the assumption that individuals behave rationally is an integral part of the traditional utility-maximization model, a wholly deductive theory based on the pure logic of choice. In that view, an individual surveys the elements of a choice set and selects the combination that maximizes utility.[3] In spite of the impressive explanatory power of this model, critics have pointed to serious limitations on the rationality assumption (Simon, 1965, pp. 80–84).

Many difficult questions that are inherent in the traditional approach can be avoided in the conflict model of buy behavior. In the traditional view, the problems associated with choice arise because of the implicit assumption that individuals act upon the world—indeed, that is the meaning of choice. The implicit premise of the conflict model is that, as noted earlier, "the direction of the controlling relation is reversed; a person does not act upon the world, the world acts upon him" (cited on p. 2). This permits attention to shift away from nonoperational questions involving rationality and choice and to focus instead on the environmental elements that have been discovered (by the experimental analysis of behavior) to have a lawful relation to behavior. A number of discoveries have been important in that schema—respondent conditioning, satiation, discrimination, extinction, etc.—but especially the findings related to the operant conditioning paradigm. Even when taken collectively, these do not, of course, constitute a complete description of human behavior; but that is not necessary for model building, because models are designed as simplified descriptions of complex phenomena. As this study has shown, a model based on lawful relations can provide a remarkably insightful and heuristic explanation for microeconomic behavior. Moreover, a theory based on lawful relations is wholly operational qua theory, and this makes it possible to end the present dichotomy in economics whereby our theoretical constructs can be useful in organizing our logical thinking about economic problems, but cannot always be applied directly to the empirical investigation of those problems (p. 3).

Testability of the model. The appropriate test of a model's reliability depends in part upon the model's purpose. According to one view, "the purpose of scientific theories is to obtain coherent explanations of phenomena and events" (Leibenstein, p. 13). Given this purpose, one important test of a model's reliability is the extent to which it faithfully

---

[3] However, cf. Leibenstein's objection that to "interpret utility in such a way that *all* behavior is subsumed under some version of utility maximization . . . would rob the concepts of utility and maximization of real meaning . . . . In other words, the idea of utility maximization must contain the possibility of choice under which utility is not maximized" (Leibenstein, 1976, p. 8).

reproduces the essential features of the more complex reality it purports to represent. In a model of human behavior, an obviously critical component is the realism of its behavioral assumptions;[4] but this raises the question of how to *test* for realism of assumptions. In conventional economic models, the behavioral assumptions do not lend themselves easily, if at all, to unambiguous empirical verification. The conflict model, by contrast, is built on variables that are defined in operational terms, and the realism of its behavioral assumptions can readily be demonstrated by the most powerful methodology known to science—replicability under controlled conditions.

According to another view, the purpose of scientific theories is prediction, and the test of a model's reliability is its success in passing the prediction test.[5] As explained more fully in the next section, the testable implications (predictions) of the conflict model (especially in chapters 6–8) emerged as a by-product in developing the model's structural features. It should be stressed, however, that these testable implications, plus others that could be generated with the model, can be put to the same prediction test as the testable implications from conventional microtheory. Indeed, as noted by an anonymous prepublication reviewer of this volume, one of the merits of the conflict model is precisely that it "has *testable* implications. The monograph's analysis of a buyer's response to price and income changes, and an investor's response to wealth changes, suggests that one could confront the model with the *same* price-income-expenditure observations to which conventional models have been fitted, so as to compare the explanatory power of the two approaches" (italics in original).

A learning model. Another noteworthy characteristic of the conflict model is that it is a learning model.[6] This is implicit in what has already been said above, but it is sufficiently important to warrant separate mention. In the conflict model, the relation of the $IL_{x,y}$ curve and the $REL_{x,y}$ curve determine whether a long-run equilibrium is objectively possible in any given situation. In the short-run, the equilibrium out-

---

[4] See Leibenstein's view that "great importance is attached to the realism of assumptions from a relative standpoint. In other words, theory A is superior to theory B if theory A's assumptions are more realistic than B's, other things equal" (Leibenstein, 1976, p. 21).

[5] In Leibenstein's view, "The importance of prediction as a scientific test is open to debate . . . [and] the majority view in economics . . . that the purpose and test of scientific propositions is prediction . . . is simply a matter of faith or of taste. . . . Predictive capacity without explanatory capacity is worthless" (Leibenstein, 1976, p. 13).

[6] In the psychology literature, learning (the acquisition of behavior) is contrasted with performance (the probability of behavior). (See Millenson and Leslie, 1979, p. 358.)

come is determined by the interaction of the response strength curves that may happen to exist when the consumer finds himself in a particular buy contingency. It is possible, however, that the initial positions of those curves are not compatible with a long-run equilibrium, even if such an equilibrium is objectively possible. In that event, the preliminary buy outcome would be different from the final buy outcome. The presence of either a deficit or surplus in the short-run buy outcome is evidence of a long-run disequilibrium.

As shown earlier, either a deficit or surplus will lead to a change in the strength of the relevant (approach or escape) behaviors, and this will be reflected in appropriate changes in the Net AB curves for both commodities in a two-commodity model. The consequences of a short-run outcome that is not consistent with a long-run equilibrium will automatically lead to an alteration of behavior strengths through a feedback mechanism that ultimately moves the buy outcome to a long-run equilibrium position, if such a position exists. If such behavior adjustments were included in conventional theory, they would probably be characterized as purposive behavior, guided to its goal by means of rationality. In the conflict model, as we have seen, such intervening variables can be ignored; and we can interpret observed changes in an individual's behavior in terms of a feedback mechanism that operates within the context of the operant conditioning paradigm.

The fact that the conflict model is a learning model also makes it unnecessary to appeal to, say, a change in tastes to explain a change in behavior. Similarly, it is not necessary to posit an experienced consumer, i.e., one who knows his tastes and who could proceed directly to a long-run equilibrium position (if one exists). In the conflict model, the behavior of an inexperienced consumer (e.g., a child who has not yet learned that he will experience blocked access to other reinforcers if he spends all of his money on any one reinforcer) can be explained as readily as the behavior of an experienced consumer—because the behavior of both falls within the purview of the operant conditioning paradigm.

Reinforcer-effectiveness constraints. There are two important constraints in the conflict model—the income limit and the reinforcer-effectiveness limit. The sole effect of an income limit in conventional models is to act as a budget constraint on buy behavior, but the income limit plays a double role in the conflict model (p. 176). The two models also differ with respect to reinforcer-effectiveness limits, owing to the different conceptual status of economic commodities in each model. In traditional economics, *all* kinds of consumer goods and services, however they may differ in other regards (e.g., normal or inferior, substitutes or complements) share an ability to "satisfy a consumer's needs and wants." In the conflict model, those nonoperational variables are avoided in favor of the operational differences among commodities that determine their basic capacity to reinforce and, hence, to become economic commodities. This leads to a three-way division of economic commodities: primary commodities, secondary commodities, and escape/avoidance commodities. As noted, primary commodities are unconditioned reinforcers; secondary commodities and escape/avoidance commodities are both conditioned reinforcers.

These basic differences among commodities are reflected in significant differences in the nature of their reinforcer-effectiveness limits—and in the different views about these limits in the conventional model and the conflict model. In traditional economics, satiation is the only form of (what I have termed in this study) a reinforcer-effectiveness limit, whereas it is only one possible form of such constraint in the conflict model. As shown earlier, satiation is applicable only to primary commodities. For secondary commodities, the relevant reinforcer-effectiveness limit is either a derived satiation limit or an extinction limit. For escape/avoidance commodities, the relevant limit is either a tolerance limit or an extinction limit. The greater richness of the conflict model classification schema for reinforcer-effectiveness limits is a significant advantage in assessing the potential effective demand for different kinds of products, because those limits can differ greatly not only among the three basic commodity categories but also among subcategories, classified according to whether they are specialized or generalized, functional or nonfunctional, and (if functional) direct or indirect. In addition, the reinforcer-effectiveness limits can differ according to whether the commodities exhibit independent or interdependent limits.

This discussion of reinforcer-effectiveness limits for different kinds of commodities can lead to significantly different views about such limits than are found in traditional economics. In the conventional model, satiation plays a minor role or none at all. As noted earlier, the possibility of satiation is recognized in principle but ignored in practice. In conventional economic analysis, an individual has needs and wants, and it is assumed that at least the latter extend beyond the income constraint for the overwhelming majority of individuals. In practice, therefore, the standard economic models are constrained only by income limitations. By contrast, satiation plays an important role in the conflict model, because an operant approach suggests that most consumers in countries like the United States regularly reach the reinforcer-effectiveness limits of numerous primary commodities in the ordinary course of consuming a wide range of commodities. In an operant view, therefore, the constraints imposed by reinforcer-effectiveness limits are an important determinant of the potential effective demand for a host of individual commodities.

The conflict model also differs significantly from the conventional economic model with respect to the role of satiation (or other reinforcer-effectiveness limits) in attaining an equilibrium buy outcome. In the conventional model, equilibrium is reached when the buy outcome has reached the budget curve. In the conflict model, that may be a position of short-run equilibrium, but it will not also be a long-run equilibrium unless the reinforcer-effectiveness limits have also been reached. In the conventional view, the equilibrium of the consumer is predicated upon the consumer's *inability* to reach satiation. In the conflict model, various reinforcer-effectiveness limits are routinely reached for the set of goods included in the consumer's prior history of conditioning; and the *failure* to reach such a limit leads to a disequilibrium condition. Under those circumstances, a long-run equilibrium might not exist, notwithstanding a budget-curve tangency in the conventional model.

In conventional analysis, satiation (and deprivation) is a nebulous psychological variable which, like the other psychological variables that have crept into conventional economic models, has not been defined in operational terms. As a result, although conventional analysis tends to ignore satiation, the concept of satiation (and deprivation, too) is applied equally to *all* consumer goods and services, including those that are here called secondary goods and escape/avoidance goods as well as those that are here called primary goods. This cannot occur in the conflict model, which is based on operational variables and the operant conditioning paradigm. In an operant approach, as explained earlier, a secondary commodity is based (directly or indirectly) on a primary reinforcer; hence, it is not possible to have an independent operation of deprivation for a secondary commodity. By definition, deprivation is possible only with respect to the primary reinforcer upon which the secondary commodity is based. Since escape/avoidance commodities are secondary reinforcers, they are also not susceptible as such either to independent deprivation or to satiation. In addition, satiation is not a relevant concept for escape/avoidance commodities, because their reinforcing capacity depends on their ability to mitigate an aversive stimulus and not on any underlying deprivation.

Equilibrium analysis. An equilibrium analysis has been employed to develop the conflict model because it is a convenient way to organize thinking about complex matters; but an equilibrium framework cannot be regarded as more than a first approximation in the study of human behavior. Some reasons have already been noted—e.g., in connection with short-run and long-run equilibrium outcomes, or in the possibility of an oscillating outcome. In addition, even a long-run equilibrium may not be durable in practice if the given values for some of the variables do not remain invariant. In the situations listed below, the conflict model makes explicit some limitations of equilibrium analysis that are ignored in conventional microtheory.

One reason for questioning the durability of a long-run equilibrium outcome is related to the fact that the probability of any given buy behavior is increased in the presence of an appropriate discriminative stimulus. In the equilibrium analysis of the two-commodity model (chapter 6), it was tacitly assumed that the appropriate discriminative stimuli were simultaneously in effect at the moment of income allocation. Under real-world conditions, however, the appearance of a particular discriminative stimulus is a stochastic element. Hence, there is an inherent randomness in many observed "choice" decisions. Although this is likely to be particularly important in the case of goods with interdependent reinforcer-effectiveness limits, it is also likely to be important (given income limitations) for goods with independent limits as well. As a result, the sequential paradigm becomes an important part of the explanation for observed buy outcomes in any period; and the path by which an outcome is reached will itself help to determine that outcome.

Consumer equilibrium outcomes may also not be durable because they are subject to an inherent decay over a sufficient period of time. In part this is related to the phenomenon of adaptation, a process in which the magnitude of the response gradually declines as the organism is repeatedly introduced to the situation that produces the response. For positive reinforcers, the variability in the reinforcer-effectiveness limit and in the strength of approach behavior may also be related to the fact that variety (or novelty) is itself a reinforcer. For functional escape/avoidance goods, the decay element inheres in the nature of the avoidance paradigm. When a formerly neutral stimulus (S_1) acquires aversive properties by being paired with an aversive stimulus (S^-), an individual who escapes from S_1 (by emitting a behavior that utilizes the escape/avoidance commodity) will avoid the S^- as a by-product. This success, however, will lead to an attenuation or even disappearance of the aversive properties of S_1. As the bond weakens between S_1 and S^-, approach behavior to the escape/avoidance commodity will also become weaker, and the buy outcome may oscillate around an equilibrium position. Finally, there is an inherent decay element in any long-run equilibrium outcome, because the levels of the reinforcer-effectiveness operations, which control approach behavior for different commodities, are in a time-related state of flux. For these and similar reasons, an equilibrium analysis must be employed with caution in real-world applications.

A Look Ahead

In concluding this volume, I would like to indicate some areas for further research along the lines suggested by the conflict model. First, there is room for further development of the basic model. My major objective in this study has been to develop a psychologically based economic model as an alternative to the traditional model based on utility and rationality. In order to do so, I have had to draw upon the findings from research in experimental psychology, but those experiments were not designed to meet the special interests of economists. Accordingly, at various points in this study, I have made use of working hypotheses to overcome lacunae in the experimental evidence. In these and other ways, there is an opportunity for fruitful cooperation between economists and experimental psychologists for jointly conceived research to complete the missing evidence and to orient future experimental work towards an integrated approach in the areas of common concern for the two disciplines.

Second, there is room for extending the basic analysis of the conflict model to make it applicable to areas other than consumer buy behavior. Although the basic model has been developed in terms of consumer behavior, it is not limited to that application. The use of the conflict model to explain financial wealth allocation (chapter 8) serves to illustrate the possibilities for model adaptation at the theoretical level of conceptualizing economic problems so that they are susceptible to analysis in terms of the basic conflict model. That application also demonstrated that the same variables are involved in the allocation of financial assets and the allocation of income; the only difference is in the weights assigned to the variables in the two applications. This scientific economy of the conflict model derives in turn from its roots in the operant conditioning paradigm and the wide range of behavioral responses that can be explained in terms of that model.

Third, there is room to expand the list of the model's testable implications. Since the conflict model represents a significant departure from conventional economic models, the major objective of this study has been to provide a convincing demonstration that economics *can* be built on an alternative foundation (viz., the lawful relations that have been discovered in the experimental analysis of behavior), and that the traditional foundation, which abstracts from human behavior and concentrates on utility and rationality, is not the only viable approach. Given this objective, the study has concentrated on the conceptualization problems in adapting the findings of experimental psychology to the construction of a formal interdisciplinary model of buy behavior. Inevitably, however, a number of testable implications were generated as a by-product of developing the structure of the conflict model. The stage is now set to use the conflict model in a more systematic attempt to harvest other generalizations and insights, not only with respect to consumer buy behavior, but also in other possible applications of the model.

Finally, and this is in some ways the most exciting possibility, there is room to develop applications of the conflict model to analyze policy options in both the private and public domains. As noted in the Introduction, the operational emphasis of the conflict model is one of its great advantages in practical applications. In this sense, the conflict model holds the promise of a significantly more effective formulation of economic policy problems than we have heretofore experienced.

My final comment concerns the nature of the relationship of further research on the conflict model and the conventional model of microeconomic behavior. In my view, these alternative approaches—the conventional model based on pure logical deduction and the conflict model based on experimental psychology—can be mutually reinforcing, just as, in the natural sciences, a purely deductive approach and an experimental approach are complementary rather than mutually exclusive. Ideally, a similar symbiosis is possible in economics.

References

Baumol, W. *Economic Theory and Operations Analysis.* Englewood Cliffs, N.J.: Prentice-Hall, 1977.

Becker, Gary S. "Altruism, Egoism, and Genetic Fitness: Economics and Sociobiology." *Journal of Economic Literature,* September 1976, pp. 817–26.

Bower, G. H.; Fowler, H.; and Trapold, M.A. "Escape Learning as a Function of Amount of Shock Reduction." *Journal of Experimental Psychology,* December 1959, pp. 482–84.

Brown, J. S. "Gradients of Approach and Avoidance Responses and Their Relation to Level of Motivation." *Journal of Comparative and Physiological Psychology,* December 1948, pp. 450–65.

Castro, B., and Weingarten, K. "Towards Experimental Economics." *Journal of Political Economy,* May/June 1970, pp. 598–607.

Catania, Charles A., ed. *Contemporary Research in Operant Behavior.* Glenview, Ill.: Scott, Foresman, 1968.

Cheyne, J. A., and Walters, R. H. "Punishment and Prohibition: Some Origins of Self-Control." In *New Directions in Psychology* 4. New York: Holt, Rinehart and Winston, 1970, pp. 281–354.

Cofer, C. N., and Appley, M. H. *Motivation: Theory and Research.* New York: Wiley, 1964.

Crespi, L. P. "Quantitative Variation of Incentive and Performance in the White Rat." *American Journal of Psychology,* October 1942, pp. 467–517.

193

Daly, Margaret. "How to Teach Your Youngsters the Value of a Dollar." *Better Homes and Gardens,* August 1976.

Dawkins, R. *The Selfish Gene.* New York and Oxford: Oxford University Press, 1976.

Debreu, G. *Theory of Value.* New York: Wiley, 1959.

Dinsmoor, J. A., and Hughes, L. H. "Training Rats to Press a Bar to Turn Off Shock." *Journal of Comparative and Physiological Psychology,* June 1956, pp. 235–38.

Dinsmoor, J. A., and Winograd, E. "Shock Intensity in Variable Interval Escape Schedules." *Journal of the Experimental Analysis of Behavior,* April 1958, pp. 145–48.

Due, J. F., and Clower, R. W. *Intermediate Economic Analysis.* 5th ed. Homewood, Ill.: Richard D. Irwin, 1966.

Ehrenfreund, D., and Badia, P. "Response Strength as a Function of Drive Level and Pre- and Postshift Incentive Magnitude." *Journal of Experimental Psychology,* May 1962, pp. 468–71.

Ferster, C. B., and Skinner, B. F. *Schedules of Reinforcement.* New York: Appleton-Century-Crofts, 1957.

Galbraith, J. K. *The Affluent Society.* Boston: Houghton Mifflin, 1958.

Glaser, R. "The Contributions of B. F. Skinner to Education and Some Counter Influences." In *Impact of Research on Education: Some Case Studies,* edited ited by P. Suppes. Washington, D.C.: National Academy of Education, 1978.

Greeno, J. G. *Elementary Theoretical Psychology.* Reading, Mass.: Addison-Wesley, 1968.

Guzzardi, W., Jr. "The New Down-to-Earth Economics." *Fortune,* December 31, 1978, pp. 72–79.

Heron, W. T., and Skinner, B. F. "Changes in Hunger During Starvation." *Psychological Record,* April 1937, pp. 51–60.

Herrnstein, R. J. "On the Law of Effect." In *Festschrift for B. F. Skinner,* edited by P. B. Dews. New York: Appleton-Century-Crofts, 1970, pp. 377–400.

Hicks, J. R. *Value and Capital.* Oxford: Clarendon Press, 1946.

Hirshleifer, J. *Price Theory and Applications.* 2nd ed. Englewood Cliffs, N.J.: Prentice-Hall, 1980.

———. "Economics from a Biological Viewpoint." *Journal of Law and Economics,* April 1977, pp. 1–52.

Hutt, P. J. "Rate of Bar Pressing as a Function of Quality and Quantity of Food Reward." *Journal of Comparative and Physiological Psychology,* June 1954, pp. 235–39.

Kagel, J. H.; Battalio, R. C.; Rachlin, H.; Green, L.; Basmann, R. L.; and Klemm, W. R. "Experimental Studies of Consumer Demand Behavior Using Laboratory Animals." *Economic Inquiry,* March 1975, pp. 22–38.

Kelleher, R. "Schedules of Conditioned Reinforcement During Experimental

Extinction." *Journal of the Experimental Analysis of Behavior*, January 1961, pp. 1–5.

Koenker, R. "Was Bread Giffen? The Demand for Food in England circa 1970." *Review of Economics and Statistics*, May 1977, pp. 225–29.

Lancaster, K. "A New Approach to Consumer Theory." *Journal of Political Economy*, April 1966, pp. 132–57.

Leibenstein, H. *Beyond Economic Man*. Cambridge: Harvard University Press, 1976.

———. "A Branch of Economics is Missing: Micro-Micro Theory." *Journal of Economic Literature*, June 1979, pp. 477–502.

Linder, S. B. *The Harried Leisure Class*. New York: Columbia University Press, 1970.

Metzger, R.; Cotton, J. W.; and Lewis, D. J. "Effect of Reinforcement Magnitude and of Order of Presentation of Different Magnitudes on Runway Behavior." *Journal of Comparative and Physiological Psychology*, April 1957, pp. 184–88.

Michael, R., and Becker, G. "On the New Theory of Consumer Behavior." *Swedish Journal of Economics*, December 1973, pp. 378–96.

Millenson, J. R. *Principles of Behavioral Analysis*. New York: Macmillan Co., 1967.

Millenson, J. R., and Leslie, J. C. *Principles of Behavioral Analysis*. 2nd ed. New York: Macmillan Co., 1979.

Miller, N. E. *Selected Papers on Conflict, Displacement, Learned Drives and Theory*. Chicago: Aldine-Atherton, 1971.

Mishan, E. "Theories of Consumer's Behavior: A Cynical View. *Economica*, February 1961, pp. 1–11.

Notterman, J. M. "A Study of Some Relations Among Aperiodic Reinforcement, Discrimination Training, and Secondary Reinforcement." *Journal of Experimental Psychology*, March 1951, pp. 161–69.

O'Connor, N., and Claridge, G. S. "A Crespi Effect in Male Imbeciles." *British Journal of Psychology*, February 1958, pp. 42–48.

Phelps Brown, C. H. "Underdevelopment of Economics." *Economic Journal*, March 1972, pp. 1–10.

Pubols, B. H., Jr. "Incentive Magnitude, Learning, and Performance in Animals." *Psychological Bulletin*, March 1960, pp. 89–115.

Reynolds, G. S. *A Primer of Operant Conditioning*. Glenview, Ill.: Scott, Foresman, 1975.

Rubin, P., and Paul, C. W., II. "An Evolutionary Model of Taste for Risk." *Economic Inquiry*, October 1979, pp. 585–96.

Samuelson, P. cited in *The Brookings Papers on Economic Activity*, vol. 1, edited by A. M. Okun and G. L. Perry. Washington, D.C.: Brookings Institution, 1973.

———. "Maximizing and Biology." *Economic Inquiry*, April 1978, pp. 171–84.

Schelling, T. C.; Baumol, W. J.; Hirschman, A. O.; McKean, R. N.; Phelps, E. S.; Roberts, M. J.; Spence, A. M.; Wolf, C., Jr.; and Zeckhauser, R. "Symposium: Time in Economic Life." *Quarterly Journal of Economics,* November 1973, pp. 627–75.

Schoenfeld, W. N. "Some Old Work for Modern Conditioning Theory." *Conditional Reflex,* October-December 1966, pp. 219–23.

Schoenfeld, W. N., and Cole, B. K. *Stimulus Schedules: the t–τ Systems.* New York: Harper and Row, 1972a.

————. "Behavioral Control by Intermittent Stimulation." In *Reinforcement: Behavioral Analysis,* edited by R. M. Gilbert and J. R. Millenson, pp. 147–64. New York: Academic Press, 1972b.

Scitovsky, T. *The Joyless Economy.* Oxford: Oxford University Press, 1976.

Seward, J. "Experimental Evidence for the Motivating Function of Reward." *Psychological Bulletin,* March 1951, pp. 131–49.

Shone, R. *Microeconomics: A Modern Treatment.* New York: Academic Press, 1976.

Simon, H. *Administrative Behavior.* 2nd ed. New York: Free Press, 1957.

————. "Rationality as Process and as Product of Thought." Richard T. Ely Lecture. *American Economic Review,* May 1978, pp. 1–16.

————. "Rational Decision Making in Business Organizations." *American Economic Review,* September 1979, pp. 493–513.

Skinner, B. F. *Science and Human Behavior.* New York: Free Press, 1953.

————. *Contingencies of Reinforcement.* New York: Appleton-Century-Crofts, 1969.

————. *Beyond Freedom and Dignity.* New York: Alfred A. Knopf, 1971.

————. *About Behaviorism.* New York: Alfred A. Knopf, 1974.

————. *Shaping of a Behaviorist.* New York: Alfred A. Knopf, 1979.

Slutsky, E. "On the Theory of the Budget of the Consumer." In *Readings in Price Theory,* edited by K. E. Boulding and G. J. Stigler. Chicago: Richard D. Irwin, 1952.

Spence, K. W. *Behavior Theory and Conditioning.* New Haven, Conn.: Yale University Press, 1956.

Staddon, J. E. R. "Temporal Control and the Theory of Reinforcement Schedules." In *Reinforcement: Behavioral Analyses,* edited by R. M. Gilbert and J. R. Millenson. New York and London: Academic Press, 1972.

Stigler, G. "The Intellectual and His Society." In *Capitalism and Freedom: Problems and Prospects,* edited by R. Selden. Charlottesville: University Press of Virginia, 1975.

Stigler, G., and Becker, G. "De Gustibus Non Est Disputandum." *Journal of Political Economy,* March 1977, pp. 76–90.

Tombaugh, T. N., and Marx, M. J. "Effects of Ordered and Constant Sucrose Concentration on Nonreinforced Performance." *Journal of Experimental Psychology,* June 1965, pp. 630–36.

Walker, E. L. *Conditioning and Instrumental Learning.* Belmont, Cal.: Brooks/Cole, 1967.

Wallis, W. A., and Friedman, M. "The Empirical Derivation of Indifference Functions." In *Studies in Mathematical Economics and Econometrics,* edited by O. Lange, F. McIntyre, and T. O. Yntema. Chicago: University of Chicago Press, 1942.

Walsh, V. C., ed. *Introduction to Contemporary Microeconomics.* New York: McGraw-Hill, 1970.

Warden, C. J. *Animal Motivation Studies.* New York: Columbia University Press, Press, 1931.

Wertheim, G. A. "Some Sequential Aspects of IRT Emitted During Sidman-Avoidance Behavior in the White Rat." *Journal of the Experimental Analysis of Behavior,* January 1968, pp. 9–15.

Wilson, E. O. *Sociobiology.* Cambridge, Mass.: Belknap Press of Harvard University Press, 1975.

Wolfe, J. B., and Kaplon, M. D. "Effects of Amount of Reward and Consummative Activity on Learning in Chickens." *Journal of Comparative and Physiological Psychology,* June 1941, pp. 353–61.

Young, P. "The Role of Hedonic Processes in the Organization of Behavior." *Psychological Review,* July 1952, pp. 249–62.

Zeaman, D. "Response Latency as a Function of the Amount of Reinforcement." *Journal of Experimental Psychology,* August 1949, pp. 466–83.

Zimmerman, D. W. "Durable Secondary Reinforcement: Method and Theory." *Psychological Review,* November 1957, pp. 373–83.

———. "Sustained Performance in Rats Based on Secondary Reinforcement." *Journal of Comparative and Physiological Psychology,* June 1959, pp. 353–58.

Index

Designer: Al Burkhart
Compositor: Interactive Composition Corporation

Text: 10/12 L202 Baskerville
Display: Baskerville

Lightning Source UK Ltd.
Milton Keynes UK
UKHW022219211022
410881UK00005B/251